For Red Sox Fans Only

By Rich Wolfe

with Rhonda Sonnenberg

Published by Lone Wolfe Press

ISBN: 0-9729249-1-4

Cover Photos: Courtesy of *The Sporting News*
Cover Design: Dick Fox and Don Marquess
Photo Editor: Dick Fox
Cover Copywriter: Dick Fox
Interior Design: The Printed Page, Phoenix, AZ

Most interior color photos are by Tim Samway, who donates all proceeds to the Jimmy Fund and the Boys and Girls Clubs of Greater Boston.

The photos from the Red Sox Fantasy Camp are courtesy of Greg Wagner.

www.fandemonium.net
www.marquessgallery.com
www.baseballfineart.com

Cover Design: The Flag of the Red Sox Nation designed by Dick Fox and Don Marquess

Ladies and Gentlemen, Boys and Girls, Welcome to this Book. Here's Today's Starting Line-up

Chapter 1. Leading Off **9**
THE FUTURE IS HISTORY 10
IF THERE WAS A SPONGE THAT CLEANED UP SOX FANS' BROKEN
    DREAMS, WOOLWORTH'S WOULD STILL BE IN BUSINESS 22
WIT HAPPENS 29

Chapter 2. Father's Day **39**
IF YOUTH KNEW, IF AGE COULD DO 40
I DO AND I DO FOR YOU KIDS AND THIS IS THE THANKS I GET 46

Chapter 3. There's No Expiration Date on Dreams **55**
DUQUETTE FINALLY SAID SOMETHING GOOD WHEN HE SAID GOODBYE . . 56
YAZ WAS JUST A REGULAR GUY WHO SOMETIMES WORE A CAPE . . 61
SHORT STORIES FROM LONG MEMORIES: GROWIN' UP 66

Chapter 4. Sweet Home Fenway **71**
THE ODDS WERE GOOD BUT THE GOODS WERE ODD!. 72
DRINK UP…IT'S LAUGH CALL 81
BAND IN BOSTON 88
FOR FEAR IT WOULD GO ON HIS PERMANENT RECORD 95
JUST A TEENAGE CRUSH ON FENWAY PARK. 97
FENWAY PARK—THE LAST REFUGE OF SCOUNDRELS. 99
A LOT OF OLD PEOPLE LIVE IN FLORIDA…WITH THEIR PARENTS . . 103
THEY TOOK THE "UGH" OUT OF DOUGHNUTS 105
BITS AND BITES, BEGGED AND BORROWED: FENWAY PARK 107

Chapter 5. Playin' Favorites **121**
THEY MIGHT BE SLOW, BUT THEY HAVE BAD HANDS. 122
YASTRZEMSKI—GREAT NAME IF YOU'RE PLAYING SCRABBLE. . . . 129
QUICK HITS AND INTERESTING BITS: HEROES 131

Chapter 6. I Saw It On the Radio. **145**
TURN YOUR RADIO ON 146
HEAR ME NOW, LISTEN TO ME LATER 152

Chapter 7. The ERA of the E.R.A. and the ERA **163**
ED JURAK CARDS ARE SELLIN' LIKE HOT CAKES—$2 A STACK . . . 165
THESE TEN THINGS ARE THE SEVEN SIGNS THAT YOU ARE
    HOOKED ON THE RED SOX. 169
CY YOUNG, CY OLD, CYBEX, CYANARA 178
I ALMOST WENT ON A CRUISE IN COLLEGE. THE DEAN SAID
    I WAS #1 ON HIS SHIP LIST.. 183
EQUAL RITES 186

Chapter 8. Heartbreak Pill— The Real Boston Marathon of 1986 . . . . . **187**
  LARRY BARNETT WAS ONE OF THE BEST UMPIRES IN THE COUNTRY.
      THE COUNTRY WAS MONGOLIA 188
  THIS GUY'S FROM SAN FRANCISCO. NOT THAT THERE IS ANYTHING
      WRONG WITH THAT. 190
  1986 POSTMORTEMS: MANAGER MCNAMARA: OXYMORON
      OR JUST MORON? 194

Chapter 9. Damn Yankees **205**
  EVERY OCTOBER, HE PAINTS THE TOWN BEIGE 206
  I HATE PEOPLE THAT ARE LATE… LIKE THE LATE MICKEY MANTLE. . . 208
  SOME PEOPLE FEEL STEINBRENNER IS THE BACKBONE
      OF THE YANKEES. I WOULDN'T PLACE HIM QUITE THAT HIGH. . . 210
  A VASECTOMY IS NEVER HAVING TO SAY YOU'RE SORRY…
      SO IS BEING A NEW YORKER. 211
  DAMN YANKEES: YANKEE DOO-DOOS 216
  THE EVIL EMPIRE STRIKES BACK: WELCOME TO BOSTON,
      WHERE THE LOCAL TIME IS ALWAYS 1918 220

Chapter 10. Hot Dates, Cool Mates **227**
  OUR SEATS HAD A "FOR SALE BY NEIGHBOR" SIGN 228
  WHERE DID THOSE PEOPLE IN SECTION 35 GO?
      TRY SECTION EIGHT 231
  SILENCE MY SWEET, MY LOVE HATH NO LOGIC. 241

Chapter 11. Fandemonium **247**
  OUTSIDE OF A DOG, A BOOK IS MAN'S BEST FRIEND.
      INSIDE OF A DOG, IT'S TOO DARK TO READ 248
  ROOTIN' FOR THE RED SOX IS LIKE GETTIN' MARRIED AGAIN…
      HOPE WINS OUT OVER EXPERIENCE. 252
  SO SAY YOU ONE, SO SAY YOU ALL: FANDEMONIUM 254
  IN THE FINAL QUARTER OF THEIR LIVES, PRAYIN' FOR OVERTIME . . 265

Preface

"Boston? Oh, no! You're going to hate it out there. The people are cold, almost rude and they are the worst drivers in the world. You're not going to enjoy it at all." That was the chorus I heard at the end of my freshman year at a Midwest college as I packed my bags to go East to play baseball for the summer in the Cape Cod League. Fortunately, my roommate, Matt Storin, was from Springfield, Massachusetts and he calmed me by saying, "If there are any Irishmen left in the state (I'm 100% Irish) when you get there, you won't have any problems!" There were plenty of them in Falmouth that summer; Matthew was right…as were the people who warned about the drivers. I soon found out that stop signs and red lights were mere guidelines and not to be taken seriously.

Don't tell Sox fans that Harry Caray made a St. Louis Cardinals fan out of me as I grew up on an Iowa farm three bottles of Tabasco sauce ago. Cardinal fans take great pride in being universally regarded as the best baseball fans in America by many players and pundits.

I have lived in Arizona the last 28 years. During that period, I had not spent much time in the East until last summer when I did a book on Tom Brady. Two things amazed me during my long Boston-area visit. I had forgotten how absolutely beautiful New England is and I was astounded by the passion and knowledge of Red Sox fans, every bit as passionate and knowledgeable as Cardinal fans. Both teams have one common denominator that puts them over the top: Their female fans are as insightful and well-informed with the same emotional, intense feelings as their male counterparts. Other teams may have wonderful fans of the fairer sex, but none—other than the University of Kentucky basketball fans—can measure up to the Cardinal and Red Sox distaff side.

This book is a real groundbreaker in the sports book arena. Never before has a book like this been published: From the fans, about the fans, for the fans (Thanks Abe). It's the first in an 80-book series that will be released in the next 15 months. From Green Bay to Austin, from Notre Dame to Boston and 76 other places, loyal followers will trumpet their neatest stories about their favorite teams.

As stated on the dust jacket, there have been hundreds of books written about the Red Sox but not a single one about Red Sox fans—until now. From one baseball fan to another, I sincerely hope that you enjoy this unique format.

For some of us, baseball recalls broken glass, broken bats and broken dreams with lingering reflections of a simpler, more innocent time.

For many of us, baseball defined our youth, still overly-impacts our adulthood and is one of the few things, that can make you feel young and old at the same time.

And for all of us, it is—most of all—a game of memories: the transistor under the pillow, sitting outside a small store feverishly opening newly purchased baseball cards, our first uniform, learning to keep score, the dew and mosquitoes, the sounds of the radio or our first big league game. Little did many of us know that baseball would be the best math and geography teacher we would ever have…and none of us knew that the vibrant green of the field during our first major league game would be the lushest green, the greenest green and the most memorable green that we would ever see in our entire lifetime.

Since the age of ten, I've been a serious collector of sports books. During that time—for the sake of argument, let's call it 30 years—my favorite book style is the eavesdropping type where the subject talks in his or her own words—without the "then he said" or "the air was so thick that you could cut it with a butter knife" waste of verbiage that makes it so hard to get to the meat of the matter. Books such as Lawrence Ritter's *Glory of Their Times* and Donald Honig's *Baseball When the Grass Was Real*. Thus, I adopted that style when I started compiling oral histories of the Mike Ditkas and Harry Carays of the world. I'm a sports fan first and foremost—I don't even pretend to be an author. This book is designed solely for other sports fans. I really don't care what the publisher, editors or critics think. I'm only interested in Red Sox fans having an enjoyable read and getting their money's worth. Sometimes a person being interviewed will drift off the subject but if the feeling is that baseball fans would enjoy the digression, it stays in the book.

In an effort to get more material into the book, the editor decided to merge some paragraphs and omit some of the commas which will allow for the reader to receive an additional 20,000 words, the equivalent of 50 pages. More bang for your buck...more fodder for English teachers...fewer dead trees.

Jim Bouton, who graciously gave of his time at his beautiful Massachusetts abode for an interview for this book, perhaps said it best, "For years, we hold a baseball and it ends up holding us the whole time."

And Marty Appel appropriately opined: "Some say the beauty of baseball is that it isn't played by a clock. But there is a timepiece governing it, and it's the timepiece of our lives."

Hopefully, the stories you are about to read will bring back wonderful memories of your youth and growing allegiance to the Sox. Wouldn't it be nice to have a do-over? It just seems that sometimes, as you get older, the things that you want most are the things that you once had.

Go now.

> Rich Wolfe
> Celebration, Florida

Chapter 1

Leading Off

THE FUTURE IS HISTORY

SHAUN KELLY

Shaun Kelly, 48, teaches English and American History to ninth grade Yankee fans in Greenwich, Connecticut. Shaun grew up a die-hard Red Sox fan in Wellesley, Massachusetts.

My mother knew I was passionate about baseball, and when I was eleven years old, she approached the coach of the Orleans Cardinals of the summer Cape Cod League and asked if I could be a bat boy, a ball boy, anything for me to be able to hang around baseball. They said, "Sure!" and, on and off, from 1964 through 1969, I was batboy for the team. My grandfather lived just north of Orleans, in Eastham, and I lived with him in the summers.

We had some very good ball players. Carlton Fisk was our catcher. Pudge's brother, Calvin, was our first baseman. To me, Calvin was just as good as Pudge. Pudge was a nineteen year-old kid—tall, gangly, strong, somewhat raw, but a great guy. There I was, an eleven year-old kid, and he used to crouch down in his catcher's position and have me throw to him.

The Orleans Cardinals and the Chatham Red Sox were rivals, always competing for the same division. We hated everyone from Chatham. Thurman Munson played for the Chatham team. He was from Ohio, but he played in the league because it was the best summer league in the country. He and Fisk hated each other. That's where their rivalry began. I remember how good each of them was. Carlton used to say, "I don't like that catcher from Chatham at all. He's an ————."

In those years, Luis Tiant was one of my favorites. He's still among my top two or three favorite players. I used to love to sit at Fenway and shout, "Lou-ee, Lou-ee!" I was really into that. But Tony Conigliaro will always be Number One. I was Tony C. when I was up at the plate. I had that sort of closed stance he did, and held my hands on the bat the way he did, which was a bit like Pudge's style, too: knees bent; head fiercely facing out to the pitcher; his right elbow was up high in the air, almost like Yaz' except in a right-handed stance, just looking determined and gritty. I was a pitcher, and left-handed, so there was no one on the Red Sox I could really emulate, which is why I always loved **Sandy Koufax**.

I clearly remember Tony's first home run, which was in early April 1964. It was John F. Kennedy Day at Fenway Park, the opening day of the season. It was quite a big to-do. Jacqueline Kennedy, Robert Kennedy, Senator Ted Kennedy, and Ambassador Joseph Kennedy were all there. The Ambassador was in his wheelchair. The nation was still grieving but our grief was so much deeper. In fact, Bostonians have never really recovered from President Kennedy's assassination. Teddy is a joke compared to Jack. I mean, Jack Kennedy was the Prince to us. Many times, I heard Dave Powers, President Kennedy's special assistant and curator of the Kennedy Library for thirty years, say that if Kennedy had lived he would have bought the Red Sox. Powers felt that after his presidency, Kennedy would have dabbled in politics, possibly run as a senator for the Commonwealth of Massachusetts, but eventually he would have bought the team.

I probably saw Tony Conigliaro a good fifteen or twenty times at Fenway before he was hit. I wasn't there that day, but watching him get beaned on television was scary. I thought about it for a long time. I remember being gun-shy at the plate for about a year. Think about Tony Conigliaro. Everything is tribal in Boston, and he's a local kid; he's incredibly handsome; he can hit a ball farther than anyone you've ever seen; he plays a great right field on a level of Dwight Evans, and he's an excellent base runner, which people forget. He's a superb teammate, *and* he can sing half decently and has his own rock 'n roll group. To us kids growing up in Boston, Tony C. was big as the Beatles.

> The freshman basketball team at the University of Cincinnati in 1953-1954 had three future Hall of Famers in three different sports; Jack Twyman (basketball), Sandy Koufax (baseball) and Tony Trabert (tennis).

His big record was called "The Red Little Rooster." It sounded a little like the Freddie Cannon song, "Tallahassee Lassie." I never thought it was particularly good, but it always cracked me up that he made it.

When I watched him get hit, the first thing I thought was, "The perfect season has gone right down the drain." But then I just worried that he wasn't going to live. I've never personally gone as crazy as a Red Sox fan as I did when Tony Conigliaro, in the opening game of 1969, after being away from baseball for almost a year and a half, hit a home run in the tenth inning to win a game in Baltimore. After Conigliaro hit that home run, he ran around the field, jumping and clapping.

Tony made an audacious comeback with the Red Sox in 1969. He basically had a hole in his left eye's vision, so the ball club began a movement in the center field bleachers which became known as "Conig's Corner." Sox fans sitting in the section closest to the center field television camera were required to wear dark clothing in order to help Tony C. with the background when he was at home plate. A friendly, very large usher whom the fans lovingly nicknamed, "The Whale," made sure everyone in the section was always wearing the dark apparel.

For the next two seasons, I sat in "Conig's Corner" almost religiously. Many of us even began to bring an extra white shirt to wear when the opposing team was up at bat. When Tony would come up to bat, scores of New Englanders would put on dark blue or black T-shirts as he approached home plate.

There was one girl—I believe she was from the North Shore—who became the unofficial head of "Conig's Corner." She always had a homemade sign encouraging Tony and his younger brother, Billy. When Tony came out to his usual spot in right field, she would sing out: "We love you, Tony, oh, yes, we do!" Occasionally, Conig would smile at us and wave his cap in appreciation.

When Conigliaro was traded to the Angels in 1971, "Conig's Corner" was disbanded. But when the Angels came east to play the Red Sox that year, nearly everyone sitting in the old "Conig's Corner" section automatically wore dark blue shirts that day. As Tony took his place out in right field in an Angels' uniform, he turned around and waved to us. "The Whale," our old usher, clapped, too.

As play resumed, we could hear that same woman singing, "We love you, Tony, oh, yes, we do…" I remember even "The Whale" was teary-eyed.

Four years later, when Tony Conigliaro made another astounding comeback as the Red Sox Opening Day designated hitter, everyone wore dark clothing in the bleachers. "The Whale" made sure of it. Even today, when I put on a dark shirt, I often think about the courage of the great Tony Conigliaro.

That whole '67 season was written right out of a John R. Tunis novel. I was twelve. When you think about that season, even if the Red Sox win it someday… I've said this before to other Red Sox fans and they all nod in agreement… even if the Sox finally win it, it will not be as magical as the '67 season.

In 1967, I was at Fenway to see the Red Sox win the whole thing on the final day of the season, October 1. That May, I had gone to my dad and said, "Geez, Dad, I looked at the schedule. We're playing the Twins the last game of the year." At the time, the Twins were the crème de la crème of the American League. I said, "I have a feeling that that game will be important."

My dad, being sweet enough, said, "Son, let me call Dick O'Connell." My father and Dick O'Connell, then the general manager of the team, were old buddies from the Navy and were in the same American Legion post in Charlestown, Massachusetts. My father called him and told him about my feeling that the game was going to be big. I had never followed the Red Sox when they'd been in first place or close to it. Usually, they were forty games behind.

O'Connell sent us incredible tickets. We sat two or three rows back, almost directly behind the Red Sox dugout. Of course, I couldn't sleep the night before. I was a nervous wreck. I noticed Sandy Koufax walking close to the batting cage, wearing his blue NBC jacket. The game was being aired on national TV, and this was his first year as a color commentator for the NBC broadcast. Kids began to gather close to the batting circle, putting programs through the batting screen for him to sign. There must have been two hundred kids. I ran down and said, "Sandy." I didn't think he heard me but then he said, "Son, I'll be glad to sign your program."

My happiest ever moment as a Red Sox fan came after that game. The Tigers and California were playing at the same time and if the Tigers had won, there would have been a play-off. About 5:30 in the afternoon, Tiger infielder **Dick McAuliffe** grounded into a double play allowing the Red Sox to win the American league pennant.

I still have the program with Koufax's autograph and when I look at it, I can remember my stomach churning during that game. I was so nervous that by the eighth inning, I stopped keeping score. I wasn't thinking, "Oh, they're going to screw up!" What I was thinking was, "I can't believe my childhood dream is about to become a reality." The feeling was completely innocent, not this fatalistic turn that came about later, in the 1980s. People absolutely didn't feel that way then.

I brought a transistor radio and when school got out I walked all the way home listening to the games. I was a little upset because my parents went to Game 2, which turned out to be the great game of the series because Jim Lonborg almost pitched a perfect game, and Yaz hit two home runs. It's a funny story how they got tickets. Dom DiMaggio is an old family friend because he was a neighbor in Wellesley. I went to school with the DiMaggio kids. Dom called my mother and father and said, "You're the only people who haven't called us for tickets, which is why we're going to give you some."

I was irate at my parents. "Look," I said. "I deserve to go after all these years. You guys are Braves fans." My mom is a huge baseball fan, but throughout the years, she's expressed this New England fatalism in regard to the Red Sox. She's tried to protect me from the

> After grounding into a double play to end the Tigers' pennant run in 1967, Dick McAuliffe went the entire 1968 season without hitting into a double play. Only two others in the history of baseball, with 500+ at bats, have ever accomplished that feat: Augie Galan (1935) and Craig Biggio (1997).

pain and suffering. She'll say things like, "You know, maybe it's not meant to be!" Even when I went to the last game of the season in '67, she said, "Now don't be disappointed, dear, if they don't win. They've had a grand and glorious season."

I cried bitterly hard at the end of that series because I really believed in the dream. As I say to my Mets friends, it would be like if the Mets lost the seventh game of the 1969 World Series to the Orioles. It seemed like the Mets were destined to win, and they did win in five. It seemed like the Red Sox were destined to win, and of course, they didn't.

The Red Sox don't get a break in World Series. We never play a team like the '84 San Diego Padres with ninety-one wins. The Cardinals won a hundred one games in 1967. In '75, the Big Red Machine had one hundred eight wins and five or six Hall of Famers. In 1986, the Mets also won one hundred eight games. And when we go into a World Series, we never go in with a whole team healthy. Tony C. misses '67, so he's replaced by Jose Tartabull. Now there's just a little bit of difference. In '75, Jim Rice was hit two or three days before the end of the season. He missed the play-offs and the World Series due to a broken wrist, and was replaced by Juan Beniquez. And then in '86—and people forget this—the week before the season ended, Tom Seaver, who was our Number 3 starter behind Roger Clemens and Bruce Hurst, got a knee injury and couldn't pitch anymore. We had to go with Al Nipper. Again, there was a little bit of a difference.

My high school, Wellesley High, was twelve miles from Fenway Park, and I used to go every year to Opening Day. When I was a senior, in 1973, I asked my history teacher, Jerry Murphy, who has a passion that is very similar, if not even more intense, than mine, if we should cut school and go to the game.

The idea of asking Jerry to go with me didn't feel strange. It was the Vietnam era. He was **anti-Vietnam**, a very progressive, good old liberal Democrat. I called him Jerry.

> The last major leaguer to lose playing time during a season due to military service was Nolan Ryan of the New York Mets.

All year Jerry and I talked about whether or not we should go. To us, Opening Day is almost like a Druid rite of spring from the old days of King Arthur. The only way to describe it is to say that it's like a festival. It's unbelievable. The whole winter revolves around Opening Day.

Jerry had some time off coming to him, and I was dismissed early and we went. That day, the designated hitter rule was being put into effect; the Yankees batted first, so we actually saw the first designated hitter, Ron Blomberg. The designated hitter seemed odd to watch. The Red Sox had **Orlando Cepeda**, who I considered the enemy because he had been with the 1967 Cardinals.

Jerry was actually the one who taught me about the journeyman Red Sox pitcher, Denny Galehouse, who epitomizes what being a Red Sox fan is all about. In class, we were discussing the Kurt Vonnegut novel, *Slaughterhouse-Five*. The main character, Billy Pilgrim's favorite expression is, "And so it goes!" Jerry brought it up because in 1948, the Red Sox tied with the Indians for first place and had a play-off game. If the Sox had won, they would have played the Boston Braves, giving Boston a subway series. Joe McCarthy, then manager of the Red Sox, was an alcoholic and the Red Sox brought out the best in him. He looked at his pitching staff, held up a ball before the game and said to his pitchers, "Gentlemen, this is a pennant! Who wants it?" The Sox had a great bunch of pitchers: Ellis Kinder, Mel Parnell, Jack Kramer, Joe Dobson, yet who does McCarthy go with but Denny Galehouse, a journeyman middle reliever when there was no such thing. And Galehouse just gets killed. Jerry said "Red Sox fans can interchange Billy Pilgrim with Denny Galehouse. And so it goes with Denny Galehouse." There've been times when I've sat in the bleachers with old-time fans and if someone asks "Who's pitching tomorrow?" one of them will say, "Denny Galehouse." It's a reflex for old Red Sox fans.

Orlando Cepeda used more bats than any player in history. He felt each bat had exactly one hit in it. When Cepeda got a hit, he would discard the bat. He got 2,364 hits in his career.

Jerry and I loved Bill Lee. He was the first decent left-handed starter the Red Sox had gotten in my lifetime. I loved the fact that he was a left-hander and such a flake, such a character. I remember in Game 7 of the 1975 World Series, the TV cameras showed Don Gullett, the Cincinnati pitcher. He looked as nervous as Calvin Schiraldi did eleven years later. He looked liked he was about to die just warming up. Then Joe Garagiola, the announcer, said, "Warming up for the Red Sox is Bill Lee." Lee was clowning around, juggling two rosin bags in the bullpen. I thought, "God, that's who you want to pitch a 7th game."

I played baseball in college at the University of Jacksonville, and stayed down there after graduation, working at a public relations and advertising firm. In the summer of 1978, I decided to move back to Boston because I felt that the Red Sox were going to win the whole thing. I figured I could live in my parent's house in Wellesley, find a temporary job, and watch the Red Sox win. Of course, this was during the worst economic times of the Jimmy Carter administration. The unemployment rate was about eleven percent and inflation was horrific, but this explains how I ended up at Fenway Park for the one-game play-off between the Red Sox and the Yankees on October 2, 1978.

I sat in the bleachers, where I'd sat hundreds of times. Red Sox fans had gobbled up the play-off tickets the minute they went on sale, so instead of there being two or three thousand Yankee fans in attendance, there were very, very few, maybe ten, which was nice because we felt as though everyone was on our side.

Yaz played like a hero that day. Mike Torrez was on a roll, getting out Yankee after Yankee. You could tell he felt like, "Give me the ball and let me throw it!" At that time, the 600 Club had not yet been built so the press box was fifty feet higher. Wind direction in Fenway really mattered. Up until that point in the game, the wind had been blowing out to right field, but it hadn't affected the game that much. With two outs in the seventh inning, two Yankees were on board, and we were thinking, "If Torrez can just get out of this inning, our bullpen will take over. We'll be up 2–0, and God, we'll win the whole thing!"

People forget that Bucky Dent fouled a ball off his foot before he hit the home run. A good five, six, seven minutes went by while he hobbled around. In the bleachers, we were all saying, "Jeepers, come on Torrez, warm up! Keep your rhythm going!"

Then somebody said, "You know, it's like when Tony C. got hit!" Of course, the guy didn't have to say anything after that because all Red Sox fans know that Tony C. fouled off a pitch that Jack Hamilton had thrown right down the middle of the plate before he was hit. Then some guy in the center field bleachers threw a smoke bomb, which completely obscured the field, causing a seven or eight-minute delay. Hamilton didn't stay loose during the delay and when the umpire said play ball, Hamilton hit Tony C. in the face on the first pitch. Red Sox fans always say that if that jerk hadn't thrown that smoke bomb, Tony C. never would have been hurt.

So, now everyone was saying, "God, let's just hope Torrez throws one low and outside." Instead, he threw Dent a hanging slider. I've seen so many balls go to left field that I probably could judge a ball as well as Yaz, at least from my angle, so I figured I knew exactly where it would go. About halfway up, I thought, "Well, maybe it's headed for the warning track!" But as I kept watching, I thought, "My God, it's sailing!" It was like a balloon that someone lets some of the air out. It sailed and sailed and sailed and went all the way. From my angle, the ball seemed to hit no more than an inch over the edge of the wall, so if it had been just six inches lower, it definitely would have been off the wall. We put our heads down and thought, "Oh, God we can't believe it!" Sitting next to me was an MIT professor, a typical professional-type Red Sox fan. He looked at me, shook his head and said, "Pathos!"

What happened was that the course of the wind had suddenly, completely changed in the seventh inning so that just a few minutes before, Dent's hit would have been stopped by the wind. For most of the game, it was blowing to right field, and then it changed completely and blew to left field, which happens a lot in the autumn in New England.

In the ninth inning, Lou Piniella made that incredible play where Jerry Remy, with Rick Burleson on first, hit the ball to right field, and Piniella stabbed it at the very end and prevented Burleson from going to third base. Piniella didn't see the ball until the very last instant, and just made a stab for it. If the ball had gotten by Piniella, Jerry Remy—the Jerry Remy before his knee injury—would have had an inside the park home run, and the Red Sox would have won the play-off game. The sun was so low by that time of day that it was purely a miracle that **Piniella** made the play.

Then Jim Rice got up and scalded the ball to right center field. It sailed, too, but because the wind had changed to left field, it was knocked down right around the 420-ft. sign. Two innings earlier it definitely would have made the bleachers. Then Yaz popped up and the game was over.

I refused to look up to see the Yankees win. I started kicking my empty Coke cup around. I refused to look up and see people leave. An hour and a half or so later, I was still kicking the cup around. A friendly Fenway usher nudged me on the shoulder, and said, "Son, I hate to interrupt what you're doing, but we have to close the ballpark for the winter!" I wasn't the only one still in the stands, but I was alone in that part of the bleachers. I found my way to Lansdowne Street, cut over to Brookline Avenue, and took the Green Line home. It was horrific!

Ted Williams used to come to my college in Jacksonville on his way up or back from Key West, where he had a fishing place. The former Red Sox pitcher, Jack Lamabe was our coach. I had applied to Jacksonville University, knowing that he was the coach and that the school played a lot of major teams. It had always been my dream to play major league ball and I thought in Florida I might have a shot. Lamabe was a wonderful guy and through his connections, a lot of former major leaguers came and spoke to us, people like Robin Roberts, a fabulous, very, very interesting guy; Curt Simmons, the great St. Louis Cardinal pitcher, and Johnny Pesky. But Ted Williams was far and away the biggest name that ever came because Ted Williams was Ted Williams. In 1974 and 1975, he still had movie star good

> When Lou Piniella played minor league baseball in Aberdeen, South Dakota in 1964, the team's batboy was Cal Ripken, Jr.

looks. He wasn't gray yet. He'd take batting practice and hit the heck out of the ball.

One day, Williams was near the bullpen where I was throwing and I said to him, "Mr. Williams, hi! My name is Shaun Kelly. I'm from Wellesley." I said the name of the town because he had lived in Wellesley throughout his playing career. He brightened up. I said, "I've always been a big fan, sir. It's an honor to meet you."

In the big booming voice of his, he said, "Well, kid, what are you, a ——————— pitcher?" I said, "Yes, sir!" He said, "Lefty, right?" And I said, "Yes, sir!" He knew this, of course, because I was wearing my glove. I think, too, he could just smell what a ball player was like. He said, "You throw a ——— slider?" I said, "Yes sir, I try to." "Well, let me see it," he said. So I threw a couple of pitches to my catcher. Williams said, "You know what. Cut that ——— thing more. Show me that ball. Give me that ball. Now make a vee. Now cup it. Put it more in your hand. Lodge it right in there. Don't break your wrist so much. In fact, keep your wrist stiff. Now let me see you throw it."

When I threw the ball, it had more velocity and broke more sharply. He smiled, looked at me and said, "All right, kid, you know what? You go back to Boston and you tell everyone there that Ted ——— Williams taught you how to throw a ——— slider." That's exactly the language he used. Oh yeah, I was in awe!

There's always an edge to the laughter. You try to protect yourself because the Red Sox are going to break your heart in the end. Fenway Park is the only place where on the Opening Day, fans say, "So, how do you think they're going to screw up this year?" In college, I took a course taught by a rabbi on the Old Testament. This rabbi was also a baseball fan. In one lecture, he was saying how Gentiles could be enormously sympathetic to the plight of Jews, but they never could really understand the hardship, the disappointment, the suffering that the Jewish people have felt over the years. He said that's why American Jews feel the way they do. You can sympathize with them, but you can never really completely understand them. You can't empathize with them. I walked up to him at the end, and I said, "Well, Rabbi, I've been a Red Sox fan all my life." He looked at me and he said, "You know what! You still don't quite make it, but you're an honorary Jew!" This goy, at least for a little while, was accepted into the brotherhood.

On the day I die, I don't want my ashes spread on the warning track at Fenway Park, but would rather they just be put in the dumpster in the bleachers with all the other garbage the cleaning crew filters that day. It would be a fitting end to my love of the Red Sox. But I'll never feel like my time has been wasted, because, seriously, most of life is like rooting for the Red Sox. I feel blessed to follow this team, because it is about the process, not about the product. It's about the love of the game. In the end, you don't think about the championships. You just think about the crowd and sharing times with people you love. I'm so fortunate to have seen so many games in the same ballpark through four decades, and that is something I'll never regret. In a way, whether we ever win doesn't matter because I'm going to follow the Red Sox all the way to the end of my life.

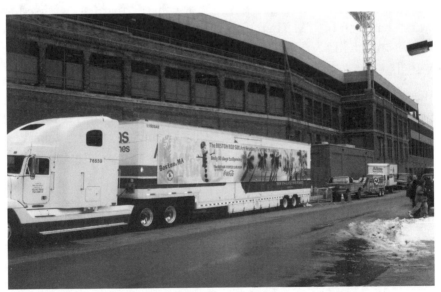

February 2003—Red Sox gear has been loaded, truck is ready to leave for Spring Training in Fort Myers, Florida.

IF THERE WAS A SPONGE THAT CLEANED UP SOX FANS' BROKEN DREAMS, WOOLWORTH'S WOULD STILL BE IN BUSINESS

DALE SCOTT

Dale Scott is a fanatical Red Sox fan. The northern Connecticut native now lives in Raymond, New Hampshire. She is nuts! She is fun!

My first recollection is 1967 when we all started watching baseball. My mother is from Minnesota. The Twins and Red Sox were in a hot race for the pennant so we used to watch baseball on TV. There was only one station then, and the Red Sox were on it. So, if you wanted to watch TV, that's what you watched.

We went for summer vacation to Minnesota to see my relatives, and we got to see our first baseball game. We were living in Hartford, and at the end of that year, my mother said to our Minnesota relatives, "Why don't you come out East, and we'll go to the last game of the year at Fenway?" I'd never been to Fenway.

My cousins came up from Minnesota, and we all went to Fenway Park. It was October 1, 1967. I was thirteen years old. I had been to Boston a couple of times with my sisters because they were going to go to school there, and I just loved it there. My parents took us and we went into the bleachers. I'd never seen anything so green. I was just so amazed because I had only seen Fenway in black and white. As a kid, you walk up, and it was like the Wizard of Oz. You go, "Oh my God. It's in color." It was just like you heard it and you felt it, but you never saw it in color. It was just the most amazing thing I'd ever seen. I just couldn't believe it.

We got in the stands, and we all had the pennants on the sticks. We were half-Minnesota and half-Red Sox. Thirteen of us were there in the bleachers before they had seatbacks. We were all dressed up because back then, you got dressed up when you went out to the ball game. We got the popcorn box that when you took out the end of it, it became a megaphone. I still have mine from that 1967 game. We all had our megaphones, and it was the most amazing game. It's down in history. The last catch was "… and Rico Petrocelli's got the ball." We were just dying. The park, as they say, was in pandemonium—fandemonium!

The fans all poured out onto the field, and this was before they had the horses and all the guards. They started to tear up the field, and they ran to the pitchers' mound. All of a sudden, they had Lonborg up in the air. I'm a kid watching all this—"What's going on?" The people are going to the left field wall and they're taking all the numbers out of the slots on the scoreboard and tore it all apart. I could see in the distance that Lonborg doesn't have his uniform on. It's getting ripped off him. People are screaming. Half my cousins are all crying 'cause the Minnesota Twins just lost. The rest of the family is jumping up and down. We're going crazy.

Afterwards, when we went outside the park, all the college kids around there had torn up all their papers and were throwing them out their windows. I'd been in Boston just a couple of times as a kid, and here was this instantaneous, ticker-tape parade. There are these people running down the streets with pieces of the field. Toilet paper is flying through Kenmore Square. People are honking and walking over cars. Everyone was being crazy. My parents were very strait-laced. But we were laughing and screaming saying, "I can't believe we won." But the catch was, they hadn't really won the pennant unless the Angels won—they had to beat the Detroit Tigers.

We all go off to a very fancy restaurant downtown—Anthony's Pier 4—right on the water. Everyone was in shirts and ties. Everybody goes there. In 1967, everybody had transistors with big nine-volt batteries. They were in everybody's pockets, and it looked like everyone was wearing a hearing aid. Since I was just a little kid, I got to have the transistor and listen to it during dinner, but I was supposed to pretend we're not listening to the radio. My parents figured if I got caught that they could disavow any knowledge of my actions. We have this dinner, and in the middle of it, all of a sudden, the Angels won. The whole restaurant stood up. Now, everyone had been pretending no one is listening to this game, and everyone started cheering the Red Sox. Then, everyone just sat back down and ate. I'll never forget that moment. These days, a restaurant would have TVs on, but back then everyone was pretending they weren't listening…but the whole restaurant was.

When they got to the World Series in '75, I wanted tickets. I found out that the tickets went on sale at nine o'clock in morning—but I had to get to the park. The MTA started at five in the morning. At five in the morning, I got to the MTA when it opened. I'm a college student and usually get up as late as I can, but here I get up, get down there and start standing in line. I'm already down by where radio station WEEI is now at the end of the street. We start waiting. Before nine o'clock, there's such a crowd, that I'm actually being smothered by all these guys around me—I'm only five feet tall. Pretty soon before the gates open, I was just being moved in the mob all the way down Lansdowne Street. I was really nervous wondering if I would ever get to the ticket window, and if I did get there, would there be tickets? I couldn't see, and sometimes I could hardly breath. It was unbelievable. Even though I was in an orderly line, when the ticket window opened, everyone just sort of filled out and I ended up in the middle of this moving mass of people. I ended up getting up to the window and I could get four tickets, two games, standing room only, "Which games do you want?" So I said, "Game 2 and Game 7." I figured at Seven, if they win the World Series, I'm there. If they don't, I've just wasted my two tickets.

Game 2—everything was absolutely wonderful. But, I didn't have Game 6 tickets. They get rained out, and I'm looking everywhere for Game 6 tickets. For three days, I walked around Fenway Park in the rain looking for tickets. I wanted to see if somebody who had gotten rained out would just want to sell a ticket. I'm a poor college student and don't have much money. My sister was with me, and she is going to go to Game 7 with me, using the second ticket I bought. We had a mission to find more tickets. We try and try and the games keep getting rained out, and we're walking around Fenway.

I remember seeing the bus come in with the Cincinnati Reds and Tony Perez, looking sharp in a white suit, getting off the bus. We kept walking around there and couldn't get tickets. We've given up. No one has tickets. Can't find a ticket to Game 6.

I'm in Betty's Rolls Royce, a restaurant, down in the North End. Betty used to come out and sing songs like *Take Me Out to the Ball Game*. She dressed up in a Boston baseball hat. She was a character. She had a yellow Rolls Royce that got the most parking tickets in Boston. She parked it out in front of the restaurant, and the police gave her tickets constantly. They used to show all the tickets there, and it became a big thing in Boston about how many parking tickets Betty's Rolls Royce had.

We were in Betty's and my sister and I were talking about spending three days in the rain looking for tickets and not being able to get to see Game 6. We had tickets to Game 7, but we were so worried about "what if they don't win?" The waiter finally says to me, "Oh, you're fans?" So we started talking to him. He says, "Well, I've got one ticket to Game 6, and I can't use it." I said, "You do?" I had already told my sister that I had twenty dollars on me, and that was it. He goes, "Well, it's a bleacher seat. I'll sell it for twenty." I just whipped the twenty out and said, "Give me the ticket." I got one ticket in the bleachers way up in center field for Game 6. I told people that I had this ticket, and they made so much fun of me. "You just spent twenty dollars for a bleachers' seat!" They were laughing at me.

I went to the game and was so excited. I sat way up in the bleachers and was sitting next to a bartender from the Copley Plaza. It was so great. Everyone had a migraine headache, it hurt so much watching that game. It was just more fun than I could ever imagine. We talked baseball and watched the baseball, and I had never known this guy before. It was like everybody next to you was your best friend.

At the end of the game, I remember seeing Carlton Fisk running across the field out to do an interview at the left-field wall. He was jumping up and down as he was going across. When they were putting the tarp down, he was jumping through the tarp like a kid—like it was waving in the wind. He was jumping all the way through the infield and out through the back. Nobody wanted to leave the stadium. Everyone just screamed and screamed and screamed. We were having so much fun. I can remember, I thought, "Oh, I can't believe that game I just saw." I'm all by myself, and I left the game and thought "I'm just too excited. I'm going to go across this street to Fathers, a local bar in Boston, to get a beer. All the people that were around me were much taller than I am, so I get the beer and look up and the guy that sat next to me in the bleachers was standing next to me. We had left at completely different times and ended up at the exact same place. So we toasted again at the bar, and I then took a taxi home to my apartment on Beacon Hill.

I still have my ticket stubs to Games 2, 6, and 7. Looking back, I can remember knowing it was going to be a special game before I even got into the stadium. If it's any play-off game, and especially a World Series, when you go up to the park during that time, the energy is unbelievable. You feel it everywhere. It rings in your ear when you walk up to the stadium. When you get in it, you know instantaneously you're seeing something special at Fenway. Maybe that's the fun or the charm of it. Any play-off game or any World Series, if you've ever been there, just feels like history from the minute you walk up. It's got an energy you wouldn't believe. Everybody in the park knows baseball. As you walk up, you feel the buzz, you feel the energy—even the people selling the sausage, everything's different.

When Carbo hit that home run, it came right at us, but just a little in front of us. I sat in the bleachers all my life. We "know" when the bat hits the ball. You just listen to it in the park, and you know what's going to happen ahead of time. We all heard it, and your heart is ahead of even seeing the end of the play. That's what it's like to be a Red Sox fan. The ones who really know the Park and know Fenway, it becomes home to you. There's something about the crack of the bat. There's something about the smell of the Park—the ambiance of it. You just know everything that's going to happen, and it makes it feel like home.

My husband at the time wasn't really into baseball so I would watch all the different games. In '86, my husband had gone to bed, and my son was only six months old, and he was sleeping. I'm watching the World Series all by myself. I'm watching—and getting so excited! It was just, "Oh my God, look what I'm about to see." I've never been so excited. I couldn't believe how my heart was racing. It's finally happened! What are we going to do? My mind is going a million miles an hour—it's sort of like before you die, you see a life in front of you. I think before the Red Sox win, for that moment, you see your life flash before you, but it's the Red Sox' life. You're looking at it, watching it, and when "IT" happened, I got up and went across the room. I didn't know what to do. I was so angry. I remember going into the kitchen. I had piled up all the pans 'cause they were drying, and I started to throw them. I'd never thrown anything in my life, and I started to throw the pans across the room. I remember my husband waking up, going, "What are you doing? You're gonna wake up the baby!" I remember thinking, "You'd better hope it's only the baby I wake up 'cause I'm about to kill you. You don't understand." I was crying and throwing. I was so angry. He was like, "What could this possibly be?" He was so dense about baseball and the passion of the sport—he didn't get it at all. And, he was *upset that I was going to wake up the baby!* The baseball goes through Bill Buckner's legs, and he's complaining the baby might wake up! "Let him cry. He'd better get used to it. He's gonna be a Red Sox fan. He was born into it. He'd better start crying now." I told my husband that wakin' up the baby would pale in comparison to killing both of them. If I would have killed my husband that night, I'd probably be out of jail by now. That was a major, major, major inkling that this might not be the guy I would spend the rest of my life with.

Actually Carlton Fisk was my favorite player. I ended up moving to Raymond, New Hampshire where he was living at the time—by accident. I wasn't stalking him or anything. It just so happened that I was in the town and looked at a house and thought, "I'm in the middle of nowhere. Where is this?" The real estate agent said, "Well, do you know Carlton Fisk lives here?" I looked at my husband, at that time, and said, "Well, I don't know where I am, but if it's good enough for Carlton, it's good enough for us."

I moved to Raymond, and I knew that Carlton Fisk lived here. I'd go into McDonalds and they'd say, "Carlton Fisk just left." I went to the florist and they'd say, "Carlton just left. Isn't he such a nice man?" Every place I ever went, he had just left. I used to be a substitute teacher a long time ago. I'm substituting for the second grade class in the elementary school in Raymond. I get to the class early, and Carlton's daughter is listed in the class, and I look at the little table, and it's got her name on it. I remember touching her name thinking, "Oh my God. She's going to be here." Well! She was sick that day. I never even got to meet *her*.

Now all I have left is a cat named Pudge. And he can't autograph ——. He doesn't have a thumb, so he can't write! Here I am the only person in this whole town who was at Game 6, and if anybody should meet him, it should be me. What's up with that?

What I remember most was my mother was the big Red Sox fan, and she used to leave notes for my father telling him, "There's a TV dinner in the freezer. I've taken the kids to Yankee Stadium to see the Red Sox." She'd take us, and she'd get lost in the Bronx. This would have been in 1968-69, when you really shouldn't even be in the Bronx with a station wagon full of white kids. We'd get to the stadium, and she'd say, "Now, don't cheer for the Red Sox. We don't want to get in trouble." So we'd all sit there, and we got so confused 'cause we wouldn't want to let people know we were Red Sox fans.

My parents are gone, and the house I grew up in—I don't get to go to it or see it or be in it anymore so, the family has no place that used to be ours to go to. When I go to Fenway Park, I feel like I'm going home to my living room. I feel like I'm going home, and my family's there. When they tear it down....

WIT HAPPENS

MIKE DONOVAN

Mike Donovan, 47, is a standup comedian. He grew up in southeast Boston, a neighborhood where everybody rooted for the Red Sox. Mike lives in Brookline, MA

It was because I won a coin flip that I was able to go to the final game of the 1975 World Series. My friend and I wanted to go to the Series, but he didn't want to wait in line all night, and I didn't have any money. I said, "If you pay for the tickets for us, I'll wait in line."

I literally waited all night. When I got to the ticket window at nine the next morning, I was told that I could get two tickets for one game and a third ticket for a different game. Hmm. This meant that one of us would have to go by himself.

When I told my friend, we just looked at each other. I said, "You wouldn't have gotten the ticket if I hadn't waited in line, and I wouldn't have gotten the ticket if you hadn't given me the money. So, I think it would be fair if we just flipped a coin for it."

I won the flip. I went to Game 1 and Game 7. I think my most memorable moment as a Red Sox fan happened when the Cincinnati Reds won Game 7 to clinch the championship. I was very close to the field. I had swiped an extra good location, and it was so quiet when they won that I can still hear the slaps on the back. I was at the Bucky Dent game in 1978 when the Yankees won, but there were enough Yankee fans at Fenway when Yaz popped out to Nettles to end the game that there was a little bit of a cheer. When the Reds won in '75, there were maybe a hundred Reds fans in the stadium, and you, virtually, couldn't hear them. The place was stunned. There was no booing. It was probably the longest any group of fans ever stayed right where they were after a loss. Usually, when your team wins, particularly a big game, fans stay around for an extra ten minutes. This time, after the loss, no one left the ballpark.

I remember one Reds fan walking down the street. He looked like a little country bumpkin. He seemed liked a nice, harmless-looking kid, but he got some vicious heckling, and he waved back trying to be cool about it. The next thing I knew, a full beer can went flying at him. It was freshly opened, and the beer spilled out as it flew. Whoever threw it was a pretty good quarterback, and it hit the guy right in the head. It didn't really hurt him, just bounced off. He tried to act nonchalant about it. He was cool because he wanted to protect himself. He acted like, "Yeah, okay!" and kept walking. It was an ugly moment.

I have to stress that I'm a baseball fan first, and a Red Sox fan second. I love the Red Sox, don't get me wrong, but it's baseball that I really love. If the Red Sox disappeared tomorrow, I'd still be a baseball fan. At all times, I keep sporting equipment in my car, including seven bats and loads of balls. I take swings. I exercise with the bats. I still go out and bang the ball around in the summer. I'm more into the action. I don't keep scorecards. I don't keep score of the games. It's a complete waste of time.

The VCR changed my sporting fan habits completely. I used to knock off baseball books like Lifesavers. I'd read three or four a week. My favorite is **Pat Jordan's** *A False Spring* about his minor league career and how he almost made it to the big leagues. With the VCR, though, I'd rather watch an old ball game. I have more control. I never watch the pre-game show, for instance, because I'd rather pop in an old Super Bowl tape for twenty minutes before the game starts.

I have tapes of all the old Red Sox games. In the 1980s, I even taped random regular-season games. I break them out like fine wine. I'll edit them. I make highlight tapes with different themes. I'll mix news, politics, sports and comedy just to please myself. I've made

Pat Jordan is the oldest player in minor league history…he is the stepfather of actress Meg Ryan.

"hits" tapes of nothing but great hits—real rocket hits. They don't have to be home runs; they can just be doubles and singles, or occasionally a line drive out, but not too often does an out make the "hits" tape.

At three in the morning, I might take one out. Every day, I edit for about an hour. This is a hobby. It's all about the action. People will ask me how I spend my day. I tell them I get up in the morning and read a history book for a little while, then I'll go out and shoot some baskets; then I'll go upstairs and maybe stumble over a stack of baseball cards and throw a few out and put a few into some plastic. Then I'll go onto the Internet and maybe read some interesting stats; maybe try to memorize who won the Super Bowl every year. Then I'll edit some old games. A friend might say, "You going to the Yankees game tonight?" I'll say, "Oh, I didn't realize the Yankees were in town." They'll say, "Oh, I thought you were a sports fan?" You see, I don't live for the transactions in the paper, and I certainly don't give a hoot who the general manager is. I never have.

When free agency first came around in the late 1970s, it changed sports in the sense that, for the first time, the off-the-field antics dominated the sports pages. Article after article was about, "What should we do about the free agent clause?" "Do you think baseball is going down the drain?" After a few months of reading that, I just said, "The heck with it. I'd just as soon not know what's going on because they don't call me to find out if they should raise the ticket prices. They don't call me to decide if the third-string catcher should be released. So why should I care?" It would be different if we were being polled, like baseball were a democracy.

As a kid, I never really emulated any one player's style, although I might have imagined I was Yaz or Conigliaro. I played first base in Little League. I was pretty insane in how much I played. I threw my arm out by the time I was seventeen. I pitched half the day against the steps of my house. When the ball hit the corner of the steps and went flying, that would be a double by Reggie Smith, for example.

The kids I played ball with thought we were sophisticated. We'd go to the Red Sox games wearing a St. Louis cap because we didn't want to be gauche. We rooted for the Yankees, if the Yankees were in the

World Series, although we would never have worn a Yankees cap. The kids in my Southeast neighborhood were really good ballplayers. To this day, they are great baseball fans. We felt that when you become too much of a team fan, you become less of a quality sports fan. And so we were real interested in the National League players, too. We'd sit around and talk about guys like Clemente and Koufax, while everyone else was worrying about whether the Red Sox were winning.

I loved Yaz. Yaz, Yaz, Yaz. He's still my favorite Red Sox of all time. I'm a fan of a guy that has a great batting eye. **Tony Gwynn** was a great hitter, but he had about 35 walks a year, so his .330 was really .295. Yastrzemski's .295 was really .330, because Yaz was getting around 95 walks a year his entire career. He had so much style and power at the plate, and that incredible eye, the great glove, great throwing arm, and the great instincts on the base paths. He did everything. I care a bit about a player's personality, but not enough to make a difference. I feel sorry for people who get wrapped up in personality. If you're a criminal, then I care.

Yaz' autograph was the only autograph I ever really wanted. I could meet a hundred movie stars, a hundred athletes, and I could care less whether or not I ever got their autograph. But I wanted Yaz because he was my idol. It didn't matter if it was silly; I always wanted it. I worship Larry Bird, but I don't really care one way or another if I ever get his autograph. Yaz' was just something I wanted so much when I was little. It was like the toy I never got.

I had been doing a road show with Steven Wright in Florida, opening for him in West Palm Beach. I was flying back to Boston the next day and, as I was walking through the airport, I saw this guy walk by. I said to myself, "That was Yaz! I know I wouldn't mistake him. That was Yaz!" I saw him slip into a door of what must have been the Admirals' Club or similar place at the airport where the rich people hide from the plebeians.

The National League team photo shoot at the 1999 All-Star Game was delayed one-half hour because Tony Gwynn was absent. He was found inside the scoreboard at Fenway eating sunflower seeds.

An hour and a half later, I boarded the plane. It was going to Boston. I started thinking, "You know, Yaz might get on this plane." I looked up and down but I didn't see him. Still, I thought, "You never know, he might get on at the last second because he's a big celebrity."

When the plane was 30,000 feet up and we were halfway home, I thought, "I'll make my move." This was before 9/11, when passengers had free reign of the plane. I walked up to the first class section, up to the area where the food and beverages are kept and I looked around. Sure enough, Row 1, Seat 1. He obviously had slipped onto the plane, the last person on at the last second, for special security purposes. I said to myself, "All right, I'll go back and get my game plan together."

I went back to my seat. I just happened to be using a 1989 Ken Griffey, Jr. rookie card as my bookmark. I thought, "I know, I'll try to start the conversation with the card. I'll say I'll swap him the card for his autograph."

So I bagged him. He had this look like, "I'm bagged!" When you're a little bit famous, you love attention. But when you're real famous, you hate it. Most celebrities I've met, hate it if you bag them in public. If they know you, they're cool. For instance, if they see my show, they'll come up to me and talk. Bobby Orr came up to me once and said, "Hey, I really enjoyed the show!" "Thanks for coming by!" I said. But if you bag them on a trolley, their attitude is, "Shoot."

I said to Yaz, "Excuse me, Mr. Yastrzemski, can I have your autograph?" He looked bummed-out. He was signing for me, but reluctantly. Then, I took out the Ken Griffey, Jr. rookie card and I said, "Hey, I'll tell you what. I'll swap you this Ken Griffey, Jr card for your autograph." He looked up and gave me this big smile. "Oh that's all right," he said. He warmed right up. That broke the ice completely.

I started talking to him. I told him, "I'm a standup comedian in Boston. Comedians do benefits for the Jimmy Fund all the time. I did one with Ken Coleman just a couple of weeks ago." And, just when I had him interested in talking to me, I bagged it. I said, "Nice talking to you. Thanks. Goodbye," and I went back to my seat. To me, that was socially preferable. I don't want to be pushy with celebrities. I wanted to leave on a good note, where I'm in control. I turned the table on the scene.

I have a Yaz confession. There was a record about the '67 Red Sox called the "The Impossible Dream." Most of the record consisted of radio and audio of the TV highlights. But in the middle of Side 2, there was a song written by a local disc jockey, that went, "Carl Yastrzemski. Carl Yastrzemski. The man they call Yaz. We love him!" It had a New Orleans jazz kind of sound. It was corny, but everybody knew the song around here. After the song came out, it was always played anytime Yaz was bandied around. When he was really struggling in '71 and '72, when he hit only about .256 and only thirteen or 14 homers, the song played every day. He had some nagging injuries. He had been going through a divorce, and, for whatever the reason, he struggled. Then he started putting up some good numbers again and made a big comeback throughout the late 1970s. He retired in '83 and was inducted into the Hall of Fame. But around '71 and '72, people thought he was washed up; that he was over the hill, and that this was the end of his career.

During those couple of seasons, my friends and I used to sit behind the plate, and whenever he made a bad out, like a routine ground-out to second base, we'd start singing real loud, "Carl Yastrzemski. Carl Yastrzemski," as he trotted back to the dugout. I know I'm a bad boy. I was the big instigator. We used to get big laughs out of the crowd. They loved it because they were frustrated, too. My only defense is that I didn't know then that the players could hear and that they had feelings. They were like gods to me. I'm sure I hurt his feelings. I don't think he lost any sleep, but now I know that they hear the comments. I've been doing comedy for twenty-five years. I hear every heckle. They don't really matter. You're only here in the "now." If you bag Frank Sinatra on the elevator, and you say something jerky to him, you got him. He's yours for that moment because that moment is all you got. So for that moment, Yaz heard us doofuses singing, "Carl Yastrzemski!"

The Red Sox haven't really made me angry through the years like they do a lot of people. They've had a winning record almost every year since '67. Recently I found a note I had jotted down. For a second, I couldn't figure out what it meant. It read, "585 hurt a lot worse than Buckner's error." I scratched my head and asked myself why I had written it down. What does it mean? Then I figured it out. Everyone always says, "It must have sucked when Buckner made that error. Oh, the pain of being a Red Sox fan! The tragedy! The angst!" Excuse me, it hurt a lot worse to have a .500 record in 1985 than it did getting to the World Series and having a catastrophe take place in the sixth game. I absolutely stand by that. I'd rather go to the Super Bowl and get blown out any day, than to finish 8-8.

A nicer memory was being right behind the plate when Clemens struck out twenty. I was the only one in the area where I was sitting that knew nineteen was the record. When he got to eighteen, everyone was asking, "What's the record? What's the record?" I was like the Shell Answer Man. I told them, "Nineteen is the record. Three or four pitchers have it."

All the people tend to remember about 1986 is the Mets' comeback. The Red Sox' comeback was even better in the ALCS. They were down 5 to 2 in the ninth inning on the road. And they were down in the series, three games to one. To me, the Henderson home run was greater than the Buckner error was bad. They were down three games to one. They were on the road. There is nobody out, and they are down by three runs, and they went to World Series. Donnie Moore committed **suicide**.

At the time I saw Clemens take the strikeout record, I was living in an apartment on Freeman Street, very close to Fenway. From my balcony, I could see the lights. With a pair of binoculars, I could read the scoreboard and see what was going on. The only reason, actually, that I lived there was because Tony Armas lived there first. He led the major league in home runs in 1983, with 43. He had 36 home runs in '83 and 43 in '84. He was a good fielder, too, an overall good player. But he wasn't a high average player. I'm all in favor of power. Both his brother and his son played in the majors. Mark McGwire, for

Since 1980, 14 athletes in the four major professional sports have committed suicide.

example, in his last season hit about .190 and got about thirty home runs in just half a season. But if Mark McGwire had been thirty years old and he wanted to do that for my team, play the whole year with .190 and hit fifty-seven homers, I'd put him in the lineup every day. Power wins games. Really in a way, power is underrated.

Anyway, I had been living in Brookline and my girlfriend told me there was an apartment in Brookline that she wanted to move to. I said, "I don't want to move. I don't really love this place, but I don't really like moving. It's a big hassle." She said, "All right. Tony Armas lives there." She knew those would be the magic words. I said, "What? Tony Armas?" "Yeah, Tony Armas. But I know you don't want to move." I said, "Tony Armas of the Red Sox lives in that building?" She said, "Yeah!" I said, "We're moving!" So we moved. I used to see him in the parking lot. I would always know what time he was leaving for the games, and I would "accidentally" pass him in the hall. I never stopped to talk to him, though, because I had a theory. What if he turned out to be a jerk, and then I wouldn't even like the fact that he was living in the same building. So I played it safe. I'd just say "hi" to him and give him a wave, and he would give me a wave back. It was a nice building. Luis Aponte, the pitcher, also lived there. I think Lou Merloni lived there last year, but I'm not sure because I moved out when the rent was about to go up, and I wanted to buy anyway.

Over the years there have been many Red Sox players in my audiences. I met Bill Lee once at a show where I was performing. I always liked Bill Lee. I liked his personality. The management made me mad in the way they treated him.

Lee talked to me backstage, and in the middle of the conversation he said, "...For example, you're left-handed. I can tell from talking to you." I said, "Yeah, I am!" I thought, "Whoa!" I don't know what he saw. He was explaining about how the brain works and how left-handed people think differently.

To tell you the truth, celebrities are among the most difficult audience people in the world. Some of them are very nice, very polite, very wonderful. But a disproportionately high number of them talk during the show, because they are rich, prima donna millionaires. They don't feel they have to shut up because some working class comic is on stage, and they're having a drink. Everyone else in the room will be perfectly polite except for the two celebrities in the back shooting the breeze. This doesn't happen all the time, but it happens enough. It's just like rich people are a tougher audience than poor people, because they are conceited. Also, an audience can be very distracted when there is a celebrity in the room. Unless they notice for themselves, I never tell the audience because for the next seven jokes they'll be peeking at the guy in the crowd rather than listening to me.

Every year for about ten years I used to sneak into the annual Baseball Writers Association Banquet. I'd dress up a little, hang out in the hotel lobby, and when I could see that the dinner and speeches had ended and everyone was mingling, I would slip in and hang out with the players. One time, Jerry Remy gave me base-stealing tips. Another time, I almost spoke to Tommy Lasorda, then decided not to. I used to hate Lasorda for no good reason. I just hated the Dodgers. At this one Writers Banquet, everyone was mingling, and suddenly, Lasorda walked by me. There was this moment when it was just him and me. I had him; I could have bagged him, but I just gave him a look and then walked away because I hated him. It was a passing moment in his life, and I thought, "No. I don't want to talk to you."

I apologized to Bill Campbell, the screwball pitcher. He was the first free agent the Red Sox ever signed. Because of him, the bleacher ticket prices went up from $1.50 to $2.00. People used to post signs in the bleachers: "Get rid of Campbell. Bring back $1.50 bleachers." He threw screwballs almost exclusively, but considering how much money the Red Sox paid for him, he should have been better. A team has to be a little less generous with a relief pitcher because he's often coming in with an out already recorded. For a starting pitcher, a 3.10 ERA is very good, but for a relief pitcher, it should be about a point lower. Campbell was putting up like 3.20 numbers, and they were paying him a fortune. The fans were pretty down on him, and I used to razz him mercilessly. I would be sitting right behind the plate, letting him have it. I'd get laughs from the fans. "Go home and count your money, Bill," I'd yell.

So I apologized to Bill Campbell. I met him at the banquet, and I said, "Listen, a few years ago, when you first came to town, I used to heckle you mercilessly from behind the plate. I've grown up a little and I realize you guys hear it and have feelings too!" I explained how I thought they were gods, not human beings. He was good about it. He said, "The thing you have to remember is that we're all trying as hard as we can."

I just want to go on record as saying that I finally saw ***Field of Dreams***. I think it is the stupidest, most idiotic movie ever made.

> Matt Damon and Ben Affleck made their first cinema appearances as extras in the *Field of Dreams* scenes shot at Fenway Park.

Chapter 2

Father's Day

The Old Man and the Wee
...and Mom Makes Three

IF YOUTH KNEW,
IF AGE COULD DO

BRIAN KILEY

Brian Kiley, 41, grew up in New-ton, Massachussetts and is now the head writer for Late Night *with* Conan O'Brien. *He has recently moved to Irvington, New York, to ease his work commute.*

My father had given up on the Red Sox by the time I was seven or eight, but Ted Williams was still his hero, so he became one of mine. I read Ted's autobiography, *My Turn at Bat*, and just four of five years ago, I got to meet Ted when he was a guest on the Conan show.

His son, John Henry, managed bands and he wanted Conan to book them. The show agreed to let one or two of John Henry's bands appear in exchange for Ted's appearance on the show. Conan is a Red Sox fan. He grew up in Brookline. Conan says he could actually see Fenway Park from his house. He makes fun of himself for not really being a sports fan, and actually, when he talks sports, he does it sort of as though he's character from a Ring Lardner story from the 1920s or 1930s.

It was very surreal. Ted Williams was a living legend, a person from the past, from another era. He moved feebly, so he couldn't be intro-duced as guests normally are, where they come out and walk to their seat next to Conan. Instead, he was brought out in his wheelchair during a commercial and seated next to Conan. When Conan intro-duced him, he was already beside him. Ted did very well the first four or five minutes. I remember they talked about Mark McGwire, but toward the end of the interview, he became a little mixed up.

It reminded me of my great-aunt, Aunt Mae. Aunt Mae was a huge Red Sox fan. She lived to be ninety-seven. The last few years of her life, she was sort of out of it. I remember going to her house and watching a Red Sox game with her and her saying, "I don't know whether Williams is retired, or if he has one more year." At this point, yes, he had retired decades before.

She would also talk about Babe Ruth. In fact, when she got very old, every time you saw her, she had two or three stories that she would repeat over and over, like five times within an hour's visit. One of them was about Babe Ruth. She would talk about how she used to go with her father. They used to have "Ladies' Day." Her dad would take her to the game, and they would go see Babe Ruth. She'd tell how, "if he hit a home run we cheered him, and if he struck out, we booed him!" And she told us over and over again. It became an expression in our house. If someone spilled or knocked over a glass, or something, we'd say, "And they booed him!"

When I was in my twenties, I was visiting my dad, and my grandmother was there. She died six weeks before she turned 100. That day, the Red Sox lost a game to the Brewers, 18-0. I remember saying, "Nanna, the Red Sox lost today 18-0." She said, "18-0! Even I would have stood up and yelled, 'Rascals!'" I just loved the idea that this 100-year old yelling "Rascals" at them would be the meanest thing that she could think of. It was so cute!

I was a Red Sox fan from day one. I turned six during the 1967 World Series, but I have vague memories even before that. Joe Cronin, the longtime Red Sox player-manager, used to go to our church when I was a boy. He told my parents I was a cute little boy, although at the age of four or five, it didn't mean anything to me. When I was a teenager, a guy in his eighties once came to our house, which was a big old Victorian, and told me that in the 1920s, a baseball player named Jake Stahl lived in our house. His brother, Chick Stahl, also played for the Red Sox.

My dad was just loved Ted Williams. It's funny, because my dad is one of these guys that you almost have to think that he doesn't like anybody that is famous. In terms of any celebrity or actors, or whatever, he always seems to know something bad about them, and doesn't like them because of that. He's more negative. He a cynical guy about

World War II, and that kind of stuff. He's suspicious. So Ted Williams is like the only celebrity I can think of that my dad really likes.

My dad is still alive. He worked for the phone company. He was not a Red Sox fan when I was a kid because he had already given up on them. He had some of this knowledge, which I don't know how he had this knowledge, about certain players. I'd be watching the game, and I'd say, "Who's that, Marty Barrett?" And he'd say, "He's got a range of about four feet towards second base." He would know these things about the players. He wouldn't sit and watch a game, or listen to a game on the radio. But he somehow knew things. Ted Williams was the only guy that my dad would tell stories about. Like, he talked about the final game in 1941, when he was technically batting .400, and could have sat out, and played that doubleheader and went 6-for-8 and .406. Plus, my dad was in World War II, and Ted was in World II. He was telling me about how good his eyesight was.

I never went to my first Red Sox game with my dad until last year. My dad had said that his grandfather had taken him to the Red Sox game, so he wanted to take my son, who is turning seven. We all went together.

My dad doesn't really like crowds. The last time he had gone to a game was years ago. He took my oldest sister to a game, and I guess the fans were really hard on Rocky Colavito, who was playing right field for the Indians. They were really harassing him and swearing at him. For my dad, that was the last straw. I've probably been to two hundred Red Sox games, and I would go with my friends; I'd go with other kid's dads; I'd go with my older brother, or my older sister. I think I did ask my dad a few times, but he didn't want to go.

My wife and I have been married ten years, and we have two kids—seven and five. My little girl is less interested. But when she was two years old, whenever I was watching any kind of a game…if I was watching a football game, or a hockey game, or whatever…she would point to the TV and say, "There's Pedro!" She associated any sporting event with that Pedro must be there.

When my little boy was two, he loved Mo Vaughn. No matter who was up, he would say, "Mo!" I remember Will Clark being up, and he's pointing at the TV, going, "Mo!"

When my little girl was about 1½ or 2, she was in day care, and her day care teacher's name was Mo—Mo for Maureen. When the Red Sox were playing the Angels, it was an afternoon game, and we had turned it on to watch. They announced that Mo Vaughn wasn't playing because he was sick. I said, "Oh, Sean, Mo's sick; he can't play." And my little girl was panic stricken that her teacher was sick. "Mo's sick?" "No, no, Mo Vaughn is sick!" And weeks later, she would just suddenly say, "Mo Vaughn sick."

People would ask me my children's names, and I would say, "Pedro and Nomar." I do remember my little boy having a little stuffed Red Sox bear that was in his crib when he was an infant. Nomar is my son's favorite. He is so great! My little boy goes to a baseball clinic now once a week. He definitely loves—he's obsessed with his baseball cards. He came in our room about six months ago with his baseball cards. He would carry them everywhere, and one day he came into our room and weighed them on our bathroom scale. One Saturday morning, we were in bed around 7:00 a.m., and he came in our room and goes to the bathroom with his baseball cards and weighs them.

Sean's fifth birthday was two years ago. He loved Mo, and sometimes when he was batting, I used to call him "Mo Sean." We go to the game, and I had good seats. They were on the first base side. The game was moving pretty quickly, because a five-year old's attention span is unbelievable. The first like five innings or so, he's watching the game and everything is fine. But then he gets kind of antsy. My sister is at the game, and he wanted to go see her. She was sitting in the bleachers. I'm like, "Sean!" We're in these box seats, and to give them up to go sit in the bleachers; but he was insistent so we have to leave these good seats and we go to the bleachers. Rich Garces was warming up. I'm carrying Sean. Sean waves to Rich Garces and says, "Hi!" So Garces waved to him, and Sean was so excited. A minute later, Garces was in the game and the Angels have the bases loaded with nobody out. It as a fly ball to center field. Carl Everett catches it, throws the guy out at the plate. It was miraculous. Then, with two outs at the bottom of the ninth, I said to Sean, "Unless this guy homers, that's the game." Then, Brian Daubach hit a two-run homer to tie the game. We couldn't make the extra innings. That was too much for him. But I was taping the game anyway at home. So we took the train, and then we got in the car and we heard the bottom of the eleventh. They were losing by a run, and Daubach hit a two-run single to win the game. It was just an incredibly exciting game. Even at the end of the year, they would talk about players, and they said that that was the most exciting game of the year. Sean still remembers it. He still talks about Mo.

One time, I mentioned at work, "My dad and I are going to a Red Sox game for the first time ever." People said, "Ever!" They were just shocked. "Yep!" It started out that he wanted to take my son. But there was one generation missing. It's funny, because after my mother died, my dad moved to San Diego where my sister was living. They used to have this deal where senior citizens would pay $6 and they had this package where they'd get six games during the season. They were all these Sunday afternoon games. It was just for senior citizens. So my dad is the kind of guy, he was always ridiculously early for everything. He'd go to church with the kids and the lights wouldn't even be turned on in the church yet. I used to say, "Dad, we're kneeling here in the dark. We could have had breakfast." He's just so antsy.

Anyway, if he had this deal for a game at 1:00, he'd show up at nine in the morning. Well, he'd be like one of the first ones in. This was in San Diego. In fact, one of his friends, they were talking about that $6.00 deal and my dad's friend said, "Yeah, but you have to pay $5 for parking." My dad didn't even know they charged for parking. They thought he worked there. He got there so early, the parking attendant just waved to him on the way in assuming that he sold programs, or whatever. Since he had been there since nine he would get bored, and by the fifth inning, he would go home.

When I went out to San Diego, I finally went to my first sporting event with my dad when I was thirty. I told him, "No, we're going to go at 12:30, or whatever—right before the game starts. And we're going to watch the whole game. We're not going to leave in the fifth inning." My sister and I sort of corralled him. We had to do this. We were joking that this was his first complete game of his life; he actually lasted nine innings. It was funny because we go to the game. I'm with a little kid, and him and his new wife—two older people. I'm more worried about them being antsy. Sean, I knew could last the whole game and be fine and enjoy it. I was worried about my dad saying, "Oh, let's get going!" What happened was after the end of the seventh inning, he wanted to leave, so we go downstairs and him and his wife had to run to the bathroom. So Sean and I were getting an ice cream while we we're waiting. The TV was on there. It took them like a whole inning to go to the bathroom. They just took forever. As it turned out, we didn't actually leave as early as he would have liked. But we were lucky that it was a pitcher's duel. John Burkett pitched for the Sox and shut out the Orioles 4-0, so the game really sped along. My dad hung in there. Like I said, I wasn't worried about how my seven-year old would do; I was worried about my dad.

I DO AND I DO FOR YOU KIDS AND THIS IS THE THANKS I GET

MOM AND DAD

My dad was passionate about the Red Sox, his children and his family. He adored my mother, but adoration and passion are two different things.

My mother would go to the ballpark and file her nails and talk to the other women. She had no interest in the game. If we went to twenty or thirty games during the season, mother would go to two. She just didn't care. She would go only to accompany him. She didn't resent him going. They each let the other do their own thing. She would travel. He wouldn't travel. He'd stay home and go to the track and go to Red Sox games. She would come down to the game in the seventh or eighth inning and we'd go out for Chinese food after the game. We would take the streetcar to the game, but mother would walk because she was a walker, and it was only about two and a half miles to Fenway Park.

My dad and uncles never talked baseball at home. They would talk religion or read Torah. As much as they were tremendous fans, to my dad anyway, baseball was only a game. It was a diversion. It was not real life, not indicative of the real world's harsh realities. We didn't have any Red Sox posters or photos in our rooms or in our home. We just went to the games all the time. It would have been different if I had been the Red Sox mom who had those seats and went with my kids, two of whom, by the way, are Yankee fans.

If there was a play-off game, and it happened on a Jewish holiday, then we couldn't go, and Dad would give our tickets to someone who wasn't Jewish. My sisters and I would try to sneak away and go, and we'd get caught, and we'd lie, and say, "No, we weren't there." He'd look at us like we were crazy. In Yiddish, or half-Yiddish, half-English, he and my uncle would say, "We know you went." I would say, "No, Dad, I was in Temple, but downstairs. You just didn't see me." He would just give us a dirty look and let it go. He knew we were lying. We knew we were lying. He wouldn't beat it out of us.

——ROBERTA MOCKENSTURM, 46, raised in Brookline, MA

My father totally discouraged me from any interest whatsoever in sports, other than the sports that I was meant to be involved in, which of course was gymnastics. That was basically all there was—dance or gymnastics for a petite girl. And I was the first daughter, so he really didn't want me involved in anything where he thought I might get hurt. So what happened was, I was fifteen years old and there was this boy, named Peter. He was the son of a doctor, naturally. He lived across the street. He used to talk about baseball. I knew it was a sport. But he just kept babbling about it one summer. So I decided that if I wanted to get close to this boy, then I needed to learn something about this baseball thing, whatever it is. This was the late summer of 1966. The Red Sox were terrible then. It was brutal. I didn't really pursue them, other than I decided I was going to learn something about it, because I believe that if you want to get know someone, you should find out what interests that person, and basically try to get on their good side.

So, I went home one afternoon, and I asked my father what this baseball was. He said, "It's nothing!" And I said, "Peter really likes it and I'd like to learn something about it." He goes, "It's not for girls!" I was the first Jewish daughter. He doesn't want me doing anything that could remotely be construed as being "tomboyish." He tried to dissuade me from being involved in it at all. I was undaunted. I went to the library, and I basically looked up the baseball rules, the historic references, and of course, there are dozens of books about the Red Sox.

I really did a lot of homework, too. To me, when I opened up a book, and I saw a picture of the field—you've got the diamond, and you've got the bases, and you got the green grass, and the wall. I don't know, there was just something that was so attractive about it. And it just seemed like the field just jumped right off the page.

I basically learned a little bit about it, and then I went home and I said, "Dad, I went to the library and I looked up some books on baseball. I'd like to learn more about it." He said, "It's too complicated!" Then I said, "Well, it doesn't look all that complicated to me." And I started telling him you got a pitcher and a catcher, and you got nine guys. This one hits, and this one catches, and this one throws. He looked at me like he didn't believe that I had actually picked up on it. He could tell that I had at least done my homework and that impressed him, because he's kind of a gung-ho guy himself.

That spring, there were a couple of exhibition games on TV. I had pretty much stuck with it the whole off-season, learning little bits and pieces about baseball. I didn't let the boy that I was interested in know about it, or that I had learned anything about it, because I wanted to know as much as I could, so I could speak intelligently. Otherwise, he would see right through me. Just learning that I knew a couple of guys on the Red Sox and who they were, that wasn't going to help. I had to, basically, say enough to impress him.

The Sox had an exhibition game on a Saturday afternoon. I put it on, and I started asking my father questions, and now he was answering me. He showed me how to keep score. Then I went to Opening Day in 1967, when there were about 12,000 people in the stands. I went by myself. The game started at 2:05. I went to school during the daytime. I got permission from my parents. Brookline High is only three trolley stops on the Green Line from Fenway. So I hopped on the trolley right after school, and I got into the game. In those days, you could just walk right up and buy a ticket. I went to the game by myself. I sat in the bleachers, and the first time I looked out onto the field and saw that green grass, I mean it was just unbelievable. You could almost smell it. It was so gorgeous. But it was cold, of course.

Then I decided to finally spring it on my little friend across the street. We used to sit around talking baseball. The funny thing is I became so obsessed with baseball, that I didn't really care if this guy liked me or not. When my husband, repeats the story he tells people that's when I fell in love with the game and dumped the guy.

——CHERI GIFFIN, 51, Randolph, MA

I talk to my father about once a week. Even now when it's the off-season, I spend half the time talking about baseball with him. Thinking about just having that Red Sox bond with my father and I'm hoping—he's in good health and everything—but I would love to see them win in the next few years because I know that would be one of the greatest moments in his life and definitely my life to this point in time. My parents divorced when I was fourteen so I didn't really spend as much time with my dad as most kids would do growing up. But he would make an effort to go to the baseball games. Baseball kept things together.

——PAUL MALONEY, 27, Financial analyst

Our love of the Red Sox was certainly a shared activity or passion with my father. When I spoke at my father's funeral I mentioned of this. Our house was, first of all, central for a whole bunch of neighborhood boys. My parents were very warm, and it was where we watched the games. We had a decent room to sit. And my parents didn't mind having tons of kids there. We watched games there through the years. Whenever the Sox blew it in the end, my father always said, "You knew this was coming." I used this line at his funeral.

——MARK STARR, 55, Brookline, MA

During the 1967 pennant race, my father and brother were on the front page of the *Boston Herald*. My father was a professional photographer. Several times he took baseball-themed photos of us that ran on the front page. He'd put a Red Sox hat on the dog, or my mom would wear a Red Sox cap and hold a bat and he'd take the photograph.

In those years, my father was probably more of a die-hard Red Sox fan than anybody I knew. He is still a Red Sox fan, and he's still wrapped up in hating the Yankees. He just hates them. He has a violent hatred for the Yankees, like a lot of other people I know. If the Yankees win the World Series, he's mad. When Luis Gonzalez of the Diamondbacks got that base hit, it was almost as though the Red Sox had won the World Series, just because the Yankees had lost. A lot of people I know felt that way. And I know that some Red Sox fans won't be friends with Yankee fans, but I don't feel that way. That would be immature and stupid. I'm a grown man. I have friends that are left-wing radicals, and I'm a conservative. If I'm going to be friends with political opponents, I can certainly be friends with baseball opponents.

——MIKE DONOVAN, 47, Brookline, MA

As the 1967 season progressed, we had a sense of regret that Dad was not here to enjoy this. He had passed away the year before. My Dad and I would talk about everything and share it. I can remember when the Celtics used to play on the West Coast, he used to wake my brother and me up and we would come into his room and watch the Celtics play the Lakers because those games were on TV. That was almost forty years ago. I can still visualize it. I can still feel it. I think because that happened it's not that I remember anything specific but

I do remember as it got into August and September when every day you'd wake up just to see what the Red Sox were going to do today. I can remember often saying, "Wouldn't it be great if Dad were here so we could go through this together."

———ANDY CORNBLATT, 53, raised in Newton, MA

When I was growing up, my dad was the "typical fan." He hated the Red Sox so much that he watched them and listened to them every day and called them everything, but they just tore his heart out all the time. That's how he looked at it unfortunately. They killed him. Actually he didn't die of a broken heart; he had complications from cancer. When he died, I put a baseball hat, a Red Sox hat, in his coffin.

I grew up listening, especially, to the late night games from the West Coast. I would go to bed with the radio on. My dad would always be fussing at them. I remember if they said someone was throwing in the bullpen, he'd say, "Yeah, and I'm throwing here." He was an electric manager at Raytheon. He worked hard. He won awards for attendance—he went in no matter what. He was the tough, exterior kind of guy.

I read *The Boys of Summer* a long time ago, and there's a great quote by Roger Kahn in that you cheer with the team in victory, but you fall in love with the team in defeat. I think that's what the Red Sox are. My father, though, he can't fall in love with the team—he's got to yell at them. Obviously he liked them, or he wouldn't have watched them.

Since my dad knew pitching, you'd think he would have been more charitable, knowing how hard it is. That wasn't the core of mentality of these old Red Sox fans. They not only fell in love with the team in defeat, but they fell in love with the "idea of defeat" and being disappointed. They just didn't want to let themselves get hurt.

My father had tickets through Raytheon behind home plate. I remember the first time I went to Fenway—I think everybody remembers their first time there. You're walking up the runway, and you see the lights and the wall. You see the grass. Really, it's like that color doesn't exist anywhere else—it's so unique. This was a night game. I probably was about ten years old. It was against the Yankees. In the beginning, my dad only took me to see the Yankees. I remember, too, that the fans didn't have that "Yankee sucks," kind of thing going on. It was more of a friendly rivalry because there were always going to be a lot of New York fans.

When the Yankees played the Cardinals in the 1964 World Series, everybody on my street was rooting for the Yankees because they were the American League team. My father just hated the Yankees, and he was rooting for the Cardinals. I remember being on the street and being asked, "Who are you rooting for?" I said, "The Cardinals," because you rooted for who your father rooted for. I guess I didn't really pay attention to rooting for the Yankees ever. I couldn't divide my loyalties.

———**BILL BRAUDIS**, 46, raised in Dorchester, MA

In elementary school, when the Red Sox played on Monday Night Baseball, we didn't have cable back then so they would just be on occasionally, my father would let me stay up a little later to watch part of it. Obviously I couldn't stay up until eleven o'clock, so he would leave a note on the outside of my bedroom door telling me how they did. I never cut school to go to a game, but I did cut work once.

Because of my job with GE, I had moved out of Massachusetts in 1991 to Birmingham, Alabama. I've never been married, so I was twenty-seven and single at the time I moved. I knew I wouldn't be able to watch the Red Sox as frequently, but was sure I'd be able to go to a sports bar and watch some of the games in **Birmingham**. That's when my mother started sending me the Boston papers.

My mother didn't understand my feelings then, and even today, when I get mad at anything like that, she would just say, "It's a stupid game." I moved down South in '91, and my mother, to this day, sends me the sports section of *The Boston Globe* and entire *Boston Herald* on a weekly basis. She knows I'm a die-hard. I usually get them every week. She spends seven dollars a week to send me all these papers, so she really is a sweetheart.

———**WAYNE TUMBLESON**, 39, raised in East Greenwich, RI

The New England Patriots once played a regular-season home game in Birmingham, Alabama, in September, 1968.

My dad was into baseball, but no one is quite into baseball the way I am. In 1975, when the Red Sox were in the World Series, all of New England was into them, but they were really fair-weather. They didn't quite make it, and everyone went, "Oh well!" But in my mind, they did make it because this was so magical. I was six years old. I remember the excitement and everybody being so into it. It never left me. I remember watching games on TV. I remember sneaking and watching them. My parents were divorced when I was ten. I remember my father telling me about baseball during commercials. Then, when my parents got divorced, baseball was kind of like keeping my father in the house. I lived with my mom. My dad taught me how to catch really well.

——JOCELYN SMITH, 33, Hampden, MA

In 1956, my dad and I spent a whole weekend in **Brooklyn** and saw the Dodgers play the Cardinals. The first game I ever saw was the last game of the 1956 season, when the Dodgers won the pennant that day. Jackie Robinson's last game was my first one. PeeWee Reese, Don Newcombe pitching, Campanella—I remember all these stars. At the end of the game, we were walking through Manhattan in the dark, and my father went into a building—I'm eight years old—came out and had a newspaper in his hand which I have right in front of me on my wall. It says "Ty Waterman Homers for Dodgers, Wins Flag in '56." He had it made up. We went on from there. Then the Dodgers moved to L.A. in 1958, and I felt totally betrayed.

The following year my dad took me to Boston to see my first game at Fenway, which was quite a trip. There was no Massachusetts Turnpike in those days. He went with a friend of his who knew Ted Williams in the Korean War and we sat right behind the first base dugout. My father's friend caught Ted's eye right after batting practice and Ted came over to say "Hi." He signed an autograph for me and gave me his bat that he had just used in batting practice. I remember him shaking hands with me. I remember him saying, "Here, kid, would you like my bat?" I was just awe-struck. I used the bat in the back yard for years. It was so big I could barely swing it, as a Little

> Announcer Marv Albert was an office boy for the Brooklyn Dodgers.

League-age kid, but I was very proud of it. It was a Louisville Slugger. It wasn't cracked or broken at all. It had the marks where he had hit the ball. My mom said, "You can't keep that in the house. You have to put that in the tool shed." It rotted over the years. Now, she denies ever saying it.

——TY WATERMAN, 55, Attleboro, MA

My father was interesting. He emigrated from Ireland in 1922. I loved playing ball when I was a little kid. I remember bouncing the ball against the garage door, and against the house, and all that sort of thing. Thinking now as an adult, because I didn't realize this as a kid—my father, God love him, obviously saw my interest in baseball. I think he talked to his friends and co-workers to learn something about baseball. As I think back on some of the conversations, and as I say "God Bless him," he really didn't know too much about baseball. But he tried to show me that he did, which was a lovely thing to do. He'd talk about players. He knew the then-current players, but he didn't know the players who preceded them. We would talk about strategy, and he would always say, "Oh, that's interesting." Now I realize that when he said, "That's interesting," it meant that he didn't understand it. So he made this wonderful effort to encourage my interest in baseball.

GERRY MURPHY, 67, raised in Cambridge, MA

In 1986, Games 3, 4, and 5 were in Boston, and I had two tickets. I wasn't going as a reporter, I was just going. Game 5, I asked my wife, who isn't interested in baseball and was pregnant at the time with our daughter, to come. That was my ulterior motive—I wanted my unborn daughter to be in Fenway Park for the World Series. You've heard of playing Mozart or Brahms for the unborn child? Well, why not Fenway? Why wouldn't it translate as much? I wanted her to get the vibes. My wife isn't interested in baseball at all, but I took her to that game to, in effect, and more important, take my daughter to the game. My daughter is a Red Sox fan, but it wasn't a totally successful experience. She and I will go to an annual game. She's semi-interested. She won't sit and watch with me. She's sixteen now.

I can remember taking her to her first game when she was about five years old. I picked a perfect Saturday afternoon. We live close enough to the park that we can walk there. We got there about one minute before it started so it wouldn't be too long. It was a perfect day. They were playing the Blue Jays. Stewart was pitching. The Blue Jays were World Champions. There were a lot of good things. We sat down, and she looks at me and she says, "Dad, do you mind if I don't watch?" I thought, "I'd like to kill you! You bet I mind, but unfortunately I'm constrained from telling you how much I mind." She was five years old, and I was trying to be more mature than she was. "No, honey, whatever you want to do!"

——MARK STARR, 55, Newton, MA

My dad was born and raised in upstate New York. Originally, he was a passionate National League fan and a New York Giant's fan. He was actually a close friend of Hal Schumacher, who along with Carl Hubbell was the mainstay of the Giants' pitching staff in the 1930s. When dad moved to Boston in 1936, he evolved into a passionate Boston Braves fan, so his heart was broken after the 1952 season when Lou Perini moved the Braves to Milwaukee.

He didn't follow the Red Sox until the '67 season. In the mid 1960s, the Red Sox were horrific. They had Yaz and Tony C., but that's about it. They would lose a hundred games a season. I didn't care. I loved them. My father would say to me, "Why are you watching these guys? They can't pitch; they can't field." He didn't like the philosophy of the Red Sox. He liked the old Braves' hit and run/pitching defense philosophy. Dad said, "The Red Sox don't play good National League ball. They want three run home runs and hope they get enough pitching to beat the other team."

Within a month of Dick Williams coming to the team in 1967, dad was completely hooked because he said Dick Williams manages the team the way it's supposed to be managed. He played National League-style baseball. They sacrificed; they hit and ran; they played sound defense. Dad said they played like the old Boston Braves used to play, so I finally got acceptance from my father. Until he died—thankfully before the 1986 season, which would have killed him anyway, he was a passionate Red Sox fan.

——SHAUN KELLY, 48, Teacher, Greenwich, CT

Chapter 3

There's No Expiration Date on Dreams

Growin' Up With the Sox

DUQUETTE FINALLY SAID SOMETHING GOOD WHEN HE SAID GOODBYE

BILL BRAUDIS

Bill Braudis, 46, grew up in Dorchester, outside Boston. Bill has written for the Dennis Miller Show *among others, and now writes for the animated sitcom,* Home Movies, *which airs on the Cartoon Network. Bill also wrote for the animated sitcom, Dr. Katz.*

As a kid, when I went to church, I used to pray for the Red Sox. That's one thing about the nuns. They were big Red Sox fans. I went to a Catholic school, Saint Kevin's, and in grammar school, we used to watch Opening Day all the time. I remember during a pennant race, one kid had a transistor radio and ran the earplug up his sleeve and into his ear.

They would always have "Nuns' Day" at Fenway. They'd always have a picture in the yearbook the following year of all the nuns. They loved Tony Conigliaro. He was a Catholic boy, handsome, young. He was just the great perfect example. He was like the "Kennedy of baseball."

I grew up directly across the street from a hospital building, St. Margaret's. We were on a hill and directly across the street from our driveway was this huge brick wall with no windows. It was the lower part of the hospital's wall, like the basement. I spent countless hours throwing a ball against that wall. Most of the time I would just use a sponge ball, the heaviest I could find, but sometimes I would use a hard ball, but it would echo too much. It was a Catholic hospital and the nuns would start yelling at me from the windows. These were the nuns who wore the huge white habits. They would open the window and work their head out—straight out. I would pitch against that brick wall, and it had different colored bricks and there was a pattern there that was almost perfectly set up as a catcher's mitt—darker bricks. I would pitch to those and get to the point where, without aiming, I could hit what I wanted to hit. I remember throwing my first curve ball and seeing the thing actually curve, and just being amazed. I would always be a Red Sox pitcher. Growing up, there was really only the Red Sox. You had to almost be introduced to these other teams. There were other kids on our street who were fans of Sandy Koufax. I knew the name but didn't really know who he was.

I wrote a letter to Johnny Pesky, when he was the manager. I asked for autographed pictures of players on the team. Then, I listed all the players, but I didn't know about commas at the time so I just wrote, "and and and." My mother saw this on a half page note. I can remember her telling me about commas. I sent that in and never got anything back. I can remember sitting at the kitchen table writing these players names.

Tony Conigliaro was definitely my favorite player for two reasons. One, because he was, in our eyes, just a great player. Also, when I was growing up, my street number was twenty-five, and he wore twenty-five. I lived on 25 Rowell Street. I just thought it was so cool to have the same number as Tony C. Then my friend across the street had number twenty-four and at the time Lee Thomas wore twenty-four. Lee Thomas was an outfielder, a decent player, but he was just a back-up kind of guy. I was just in awe of it, man, so lucky to have twenty-five. It was desirable to have a cool number of a player. Without having anything to do with it at all, you just took all the credit for it. You could always claim that twenty-five.

I was watching the game where Tony C. got beaned. I remember being scared. Maybe it was a couple of days later when they had the picture and his eye was just so huge and black, it was so disgusting. I remember my mother was explaining to me how it just missed his temple and that he could have been killed if it had hit him in the temple. I remember when I thought, "temple," I thought, "building." It didn't make sense to me.

I remember in 1967, I would go down in the mornings in the summers and get the *Record American* newspaper for my father. It cost eight cents then. My father would give me a dime, and I'd get to keep the two cents. The back page was the sports. It was set up like the New York papers. That's when I fell in love with statistics because I would read box scores right away. We always had just the league leaders, and it was written like a paragraph form. I would read those. I remember in the back of it they had—the Sox had been off the previous day—a cartoon picture someone had drawn of Mike Andrews sitting on the bench with a thermometer in his mouth and sweat pouring off his face. It said, "Mike Andrews has pennant fever."

I loved Mike Andrews, because you loved second basemen. It was a position that was doable for you as a kid. "I can reach first base from there," you know. So I always had an affinity for the second basemen. Also they were always on the small or slighter side and so I liked Mike Andrews, and I was really upset because I thought he was sick. I was saying, "He's sick. He's sick." My mother said, "No, no, no." She explained to me that the cartoon just meant that he was excited about the pennant race.

I remember in '67 watching the last game where the Red Sox beat Minnesota. Later we had to wait until the Detroit game was over before we knew if the Red Sox had won the pennant. It's been kind of overlooked, but it was one of the greatest pennant races in history because I think there were about four teams up till the last week. Actually the White Sox had a tremendous pitching staff. I remember going outside. My friend, who was only four or five months older than me, always had an air about him that he was much older. He walked up to me and said, "Pennant-winning Red Sox." That's all I remember him saying. "Yeah, we won the pennant." I didn't even know what a pennant was. I thought we actually got those flags.

I still remember the excitement in the city with the World Series. Then, you were into it immediately. There weren't all these play-offs. I remember when they had the red, white, and blue banners all around the park. It looked different. It was so great. I wish I remembered more of the games. When I got a little older, I started keeping score. During the '75 Series, I watched the games and actually kept score of the games. Just recently I saw a highlight on ESPN of the '67 Series. It was so much fun to see it again. I remember how close Jim

Lonborg came to pitching a no-hitter. I remember a cartoon in the paper of a little kid writing on a fence, because Julian Javier got the hit to break up the no-hitter. And he wrote, "Julian Javier is a herk."

I remember when I began to recognize numbers that were good and not so good. Especially back in the early 1970s, when I was really getting into it, to recognize that, at the time, a .268 hitter wasn't that bad. Because if you hit .300, that was the benchmark. That was very good.

In the summer of 1971, I got my first Strat-O-Matic baseball game. That did it. I played well over a hundred games by myself. I would play just one game after another sometimes. That's when I really became fascinated with statistics. I just loved it. I would go in hobby shops and find these baseball games and some of them actually were very good. *Sports Illustrated* put out a very good game called Status Pro. It was a very good game done without dice. When I got married, I got rid of all my old games.

Oddly enough, I liked Sonny Siebert, a pitcher the Red Sox got in a trade from Cleveland, and he was *very* happy to be traded from Cleveland. One time, Nolan Ryan struck out a ton of Red Sox. In this game, he struck out three Red Sox on nine pitches. He was facing Sonny Siebert, who was having a very good game, too. He was a good pitcher. I was at a game with my father and my uncle, and he was saying, "Look at him out there on the mound. Everybody is looking at him. Everybody is watching him and waiting for him. How would you like to be that guy?" I remember that. I remember thinking, "Wow. That's cool." Then I followed Sonny Siebert. I mimicked his delivery because, as I recall, he did make a no-windup, and it wasn't that popular at the time. Whenever I pitched like him, I really felt like I was him and could throw it. I actually started throwing a pretty good curve ball at that time. I think Siebert won fifteen games a couple of times.

Anybody can like the marquee guy. Really, as a kid, the number of your house can mean the guy you root for. It's different things that strike you. Adults don't always understand that. Getting Tony C's baseball card. Getting any Red Sox baseball card. Strangely enough, I actually bought one one time from a hardware store of all places. It had Gary Wagner and it was wrapped in plastic. It cost me four dollars for one card. It's from 1970 and goes up until his '69 statistics when he pitched for the Sox and had a 6.19 era. I have it here on my desk.

The entire 1986 season was one of those magical seasons, but '67, wow…though at that time, I was also distracted by my truck—or any toy. My memories of the '86 season are good because they never played that sixth game. They gave up after Game 5. They left. No game. A friend gave me the book Dan Shaughnessy wrote after that season. It opens with Game 6. I started reading the first page, and I shut the book, and I've never read it. I can't. I know what happened. I was watching that game by myself. When they lost, I never felt more like a ball player at that moment because I just shut the TV off and I said, "We'll get them tomorrow. We'll get them tomorrow." I put it behind me as quickly as possible and I did not want to dwell. Dwelling didn't come until later. I just never really did. It was really, really, really painful. It really was. But people forget that the Sox were winning in the seventh game, again, on another Dave Henderson home run. That was the thing. Again, we had the magic of the '86 season—to beat the Angels the way we did.

Then the fate of Donnie Moore after that. I don't want to say we couldn't complain, but we had so many great moments that even losing the way we did…. It certainly never deterred me as a Red Sox fan. The high ticket prices don't deter me as a fan like some people. But, that's me. That's not baseball. Baseball exists without these owners. They don't own baseball. It's there.

My wife is this newly-avid Red Sox fan, and she will start right in with some fan from New York. "Yeah, why don't you buy another pennant? Why don't you just go and buy another pennant?" They'll say, "1918. 1918." "Yeah, why don't you buy another pennant?"

John Harrington drove me crazy when he was running the team. I think it was just the way he didn't do anything. He really remained in the shadows and Dan Duquette infuriated me, too because he was so smug. For some reason, he thought he was the most intelligent man and nobody else could understand baseball the way he could. He just made so many stupid mistakes.

YAZ WAS JUST A REGULAR GUY WHO SOMETIMES WORE A CAPE

LAUREN DOMBROWSKI

Lauren Dombrowski, 46, the co-executive producer of Mad TV, *grew up in the Boston suburb of Lynnfield, and has been living in Los Angeles for eight years.*

My first Red Sox experience was in 1967, when I was ten years old. We lived in a little bedroom community about twenty miles north of Boston. I was hanging out in the house, minding my own business, playing. Suddenly our house just exploded. My father, a marketing executive for GTE Sylvania, was going out of his mind. He opened the back door and all of our neighbors were out their back doors screaming, blowing horns. This huge celebration just erupted. Prior to that point, I didn't even know baseball existed. I knew it was something my father watched on television, and I would leave the room when he watched the games.

I thought, "What the heck is going on?" Then my father lunged back into the family room where the TV was, and I ran to see what was going on. There was Jim Lonborg being carried off the pitchers' mound by all those fans. I learned that we had won the pennant for the first time in decades. That was the Impossible Dream year. Because it had brought my father so much joy, I became interested in it immediately. I watched that World Series with him—a heartbreaking, though, great series.

The next year, '68, was the year my identical twin sister, Lynne, and I became obsessed with the Red Sox.

That was the year of Mike Andrews, Rico Petrocelli, Reggie Smith, and, of course, Yaz. Lynne and I liked watching the game, and we put a scrapbook together. We loved the team, but really we just were in love with these guys. We thought they were cute. We had giant crushes. Basically, for me, it was all about Yaz. I knew that he had a "ski" on the end of his name so that made him like us. I thought he was really cute.

We all felt that kinship with him because he had that work ethic and he was the most tenacious guy. He was so humble. He was like my father that way, and I think that's why I loved him so much. I had pictures of him up in my room.

For our scrapbook, Lynne and I cut out every article about the Red Sox that year. We knew everybody's batting average. We, and the rest of the neighborhood kids, would have carnivals for the Jimmy Fund, an organization raising funds for the fight against cancer. We'd charge five cents for fortune telling, that kind of thing. I remember I got a snake from the kid next door who had a lot of animals, and I was telling fortunes with the snake. The snake bit me, so it was a big, traumatic day. We'd do it because if you sent the money to the Jimmy Fund, Ken Coleman would say your name on the radio, "We received money for the Jimmy Fund from Lauren in Lynnfield." And you would get a signed postcard from Yaz. My sister, who now lives in Carlisle, Massachusetts, just recently found her Yaz postcard. We had those up in our room.

Coca Cola had a contest in 1968 called "Tops and Tips." You sent in an index card with the words "Coca Cola" on it or a label from a Coke bottle. It was a random drawing. If your name was picked, you got two tickets, box seats, to a Red Sox game. You got to meet Joe Foy, the third baseman, and Gary Bell, a pitcher, and have a baseball clinic with them, and two bucks for a hot dog and a coke. That was the prize. I won. My sister sent in my name, and I won. She fell apart. My mother said, "Oh, don't cry. Maybe you'll meet a nice man some day and get married." Lynne said, "Who cares!" And she did meet a nice man and get married—long before I did. My father took the box seats and traded them for four box seats so we could all sit together. So we both got to go to the clinic and meet Joe Foy and Gary Bell. We got to go to the park before anything opened, and we were the only girls there, of course. Joe Foy and Gary Bell came out and they started telling us, "When you're fielding the ball, make sure you get down low here. We were like "What the heck is he talking about?" We didn't care about how to field the ball. We just thought the players were cute. We just had crushes on them.

I remember later reading in **Jim Bouton**'s book, *Ball Four,* that Gary Bell was a huge pervert and they called him Ding-Dong because the ball always hit him in the cup.

Rico Petrocelli we loved. We used to see Rico in church. He lived in Lynnfield and so did Yaz. My sister and I would try to cut in front of people in communion line so we could stand near Rico. We got in big trouble for that.

Much later, I got to meet Rico when I was a young woman, and we did a benefit for the Jimmy Fund. Rico was there. I saw him after the show, and I practically ran over to him. My friend, Barry, was talking to him at the time. He said, "You'll have to forgive Lauren. She's been in love with you since she was eight years old." I said, "Hi, Rico, you still playing the drums?" I knew that he had played the drums in the off-season. He was just as sweet as could be. So I did get to meet Rico. I never got to meet Yaz, who was the love of my life. That may be a good thing because I hear he smokes and is a Republican. You just want to love these guys for what they were to you at the time.

Tony Conigliaro was beautiful, and the guy who lived next door to us, in Lynnfield, knew him. In fact, I think he'd go hunting with him. So every now and then, we would hear that Tony Conigliaro had actually been in the neighborhood. That was extremely exciting. He

> Massachusetts resident, Jim Bouton, conceived a gum product called "Big League Chew" that has been marketed for over 20 years by a major consumer products company.

had gotten beaned in '67 and came back in '69, but it was just so sad. For me, the memories of Tony Conigliaro are just sad ones.

I remember in '67 at school they turned on the TV's so we could watch the World Series. I used to pray that I could meet Yaz and marry him. I did not do that in church, just in bed at night.

I have three men that I've loved in my life. One is Ringo Starr. Another is Dick Van Dyke. And the other is Yaz. I actually got to meet Ringo, and I actually got to meet Dick Van Dyke. Meeting Dick Van Dyke was the most amazing thing in the world. We wrote a sketch, an homage to his show, and he saw it and loved it, so I got to meet him on the set of *Diagnosis Murder.* Those were my three huge crushes in life.

I don't follow the Red Sox every year. Now I hardly follow them at all because I'm out in LA so it's impossible to do. Being from Boston and being a Red Sox fan, it makes you different. They're always in your heart. There's this unrequited love thing that always happens.

I was not able to be there for Carl Yastrzemski Day, but I was there for his very last game, which was the day after Carl Yastrzemski Day. My boyfriend at the time had received two bleacher tickets to that game as a Christmas gift, and he took me with him. We were sitting up in the bleachers. Yaz was running around the field high-fiving everyone, which was something he never did. He didn't give of himself that way. He was just so stoical all the time. On Yaz Day and on that last game, he did that. He came out and he let us give him that love. I was in the bleachers, and I was surrounded by men. There was not a dry eye in the place. Everyone was bawling. And I don't mean teary and, "Oh, isn't this nice." People were bawling and screaming. It was one of the most emotional things I've ever been part of. It was such an incredible experience. It was his stoicism that reminded me of my father, who was very much like that, too. It just gave him so much appeal. The year before he retired—I just felt such a connection with the guy, I don't know why—I was watching the news. All these reporters were asking him if he was going to retire. He was sitting in the locker room. They had the mike in his face, and had him up against the wall, literally and figuratively. The look on his face was like, "Leave me alone." It was never ever about him. He didn't like talking about himself.

My friend, Mike, used to do the most hilarious impression of Yaz. It was the most obscure impression. We'd be in the room together, and Mike would go, "Here's a quick impression. Carl Yastrzemski." And then he'd go, "It's not about me. It's about the ball club." There would be one person laughing in the room and that was me. I would be hysterical. When he and I worked together, he always did that joke. And he didn't care if anyone else got it, because he did it just for me. I loved that.

I was at Yaz Day, and to this day I still have in my office at work a big photograph of Yaz on Yaz Day, and I have my ticket stubs from that game. In my office at home, I have a huge beautiful signed picture of the "happy Yaz," which was in the locker room in '67 right after they won the pennant, with champagne in his hair. He was just so happy. That's all we wanted. We just wanted Yaz to be happy.

But his career just didn't happen that way. I think he struck out his last time up at bat, and he never got the World Series ring. He was a tragic figure that way but he was so tenacious and we just wanted to see him relax and be happy. We loved him so much.

I am married now, and my husband is a traitor. He grew up in Dorchester, MA, which is even closer to Fenway Park than Lynnfield. He likes the Red Sox, and he understands my Yaz obsession, but he actually roots for the **Lakers**, which in my book, is unthinkable. He's been out here in California for about twenty years, and this is where I met him. I don't care how long I've been here, it could be twenty years, it could be a hundred years, and I would never root for the Lakers.

In March 1954, the Lakers and the Hawks played a regulation, regular season NBA game using baskets there were 12' high rather than the usual 10'…the next night they played each other in a doubleheader. True facts, believe it or not!

SHORT STORIES FROM LONG MEMORIES

GROWIN' UP

I went to St. Mary's School in Melrose, a Catholic school. In 1967, I prayed for the Red Sox when George Scott was at the plate with Bob Gibson on the mound. I do remember speaking to God, quietly, out loud. I remember I moved to a little alcove so no one would see me. I was almost afraid to watch.

For years, the Red Sox held "Nuns' Day" at Fenway Park. You would look into the grandstand, and you would see a whole section of nuns in their habits. I don't know whether any of my teachers went or not. I imagine they did, but none of us ever thought of them as having regular lives.

All the kids collected baseball cards, and we also put them on our bike wheels. You'd play this game where you would flip them up against the schoolyard wall. The one that went the farthest won the other person's card. One of my earliest memories, from first grade, is accidentally trading for the Reds team card, giving up a Red Sox player, thinking the Reds were the Red Sox team. I told my older brother that I got this card with the whole Red Sox team on it and not just one Red Sox player. He said, "You fool. This is a whole different team."

I used to spend all my free time bouncing a tennis ball off the front steps of my house. I had a whole league and would play the Red Sox players against other teams. I had all the pitchers' motions down. I would play full-length games. If a left-hander came in, I would throw the ball left-handed.

———JIM DECROTEAU, 43, raised in Melrose, MA

When I was a kid, I played baseball. I think I probably went through everybody's stance, and that probably never helped—especially anyone who had any little unorthodox thing, I immediately adopted it. I remember Reggie Smith, and even Carl Yastrzemski, had their arms way out. We were always taught to keep your shoulder out and level, and they were the guys who had it way different. I remember Dick McAuliffe, who played for Detroit. He was the first guy who had a completely open stance. He was on the left side. Actually, his chest faced the pitcher so that was the coolest thing. Even though he played for Detroit, I still thought, "That's a great stance." Anybody who did anything different stood out. I used to do Tony C's because he had his legs wide apart in the batter's box. It was not easy to do, but I would do that.

——**BILL BRAUDIS**, 46, Television comedy writer

When I was a kid, any time I heard there was a new collection of cards coming out, I bought it. There was a cigarette called Sweet Caporal. One baseball card would come with ten packs of cigarettes. In those days, shop owners got together and decided which store would sell what, so stores wouldn't compete against each other. My father didn't sell cigarettes in his food store, but the store right across the street did. The owner knew I liked baseball cards, and the people who came in to buy cigarettes didn't want the cards so every once in a while he'd call me in and say, "Here, here," and give me the cards.

I have about 35,000 baseball cards. Two or three thousand are probably Red Sox cards. I keep them all in boxes. I'm writing down what's in each box and sealing them with the date so I don't do it twice. The one card I can't find is the Babe Ruth card I got in 1916. It's worth $85,000 according to the latest auction book. There are only about eight of them still in existence. I know I have it. I don't think anyone stole it from me.

——**KEN HERMES**, 95, Yarmouth Port, MA

Baseball cards are a passion that went along with being a Red Sox fan. I went overboard on that. I probably spent more money than any twelve-year old ever. I spent a couple of thousand dollars. I worked and did everything I could to get money for that. I was a landscaper, and this was at a pretty young age, along with a friend of mine. I shoveled snow. I would baby-sit. I had two paper routes. I basically put every dime into baseball cards. I had every baseball card made from 1986 to '92—minor leagues, Cape Cod League, all major league cards. My dad probably thought I was nuts at the time, but my mom would take me to baseball card shows anywhere in New England. I went to shows where you could get autographs of players. I went to baseball card shops. I really spent a lot.

At games, I tried to get autographs. At that time, in the early 1990s, baseball cards and autographs were taking off. It was a cottage industry. And the market was saturated with so many cards. At the shows, it was really tough for a kid to buy even one. Basically, it became an adult game of speculation. You hear about these people who find their cards fifty years later and they can sell them. But they print thousands of these cards now, and they're probably worth three cents apiece for the good ones. My mom was especially supportive of my baseball card addiction.

——PAUL MALONEY, 27, Financial analyst

When I was a kid, I had a couple of teachers who were pretty good Red Sox fans. I remember my French teacher. A friend of mine was originally from Cincinnati, Ohio. He was a big Reds fan. I remember the French teacher saying, "Hey Jamie, why was Carlton Fisk doing this last night?" And he was imitating him doing the gyrations to keep the ball fair. And my friend said, "His jock strap was too tight!"

——BRIAN KILEY, 41, on growing up in Newton, MA

My family lived in a crowded city neighborhood. The school I attended was very close to home. It was called The Gate of Heaven. We kids called it "The Back Door of Hell." All the priests liked the Red Sox. One priest used to tell this story every year about how baseball was popular even in the Bible, because the very first words of the Bible are about baseball: "In the big inning…" That joke got a big laugh in the church.

——MIKE DONOVAN, 47, Brookline, MA

Patrick Reilly

In 1980, when I was ten years old, we were driving back to Boston from Washington, DC, and stopped in Philadelphia for a Phillies game. I couldn't believe it. Mike Schmidt was my favorite non-Red Sox player at the time. I'd never been to a park other than Fenway, so this was incredibly exciting. One of the first things that struck me was that this was my first experience with the Phillie Phanatic. He's driving around in that little motorcycle, he's messing around with the umpires, and I thought that this was just the greatest thing I'd seen. It added so much to the ball game for me. I knew mascots existed, but I'd never been able to see them live. Between the innings is such a dull time—there's nothing going on, so you had the Phillie Phanatic out there then and before the game started. Sometimes, he would be up on the dugout doing his thing, and as a kid, I was sort of drawn to that. I think we even picked up a little Phillie Phanatic stuffed mascot.

I said, "Dad, why don't the Red Sox have a mascot?" His answer was probably the answer I would have given, had I been older. "This is the Red Sox. This is a traditional team. They're not going to have a silly mascot running around." I said, "They should have a mascot called the 'Green Monster.'" He said, "Yeah, that's a great idea. Why don't you write a letter to the Red Sox. You can draw a picture and send it in with some ideas." When we got home, I drew a big, furry, green monster with a Red Sox shirt on. I wrote on the back of his jersey the number '315', not the time but the distance to the left field wall, which was supposedly three hundred and fifteen feet. It says '310' now. They've remeasured it. So '315' was my mascot's first uniform number. He had these big baseball spikes and a Red Sox cap on his head. The funny thing is, years later they brought in this "Wally, the Green Monster." Wally looks a heck of a lot like the picture I drew fifteen years before.

———PATRICK REILLY, 33, Los Angeles, Operator, www.bceaglesfootball.com

The 1967 season came down to the last game, the last day. The Red Sox were playing the Minnesota Twins, and the Detroit Tigers were playing the California Angels in a doubleheader. If the Red Sox beat the Twins, they were assured of at least a tie to win the pennant that year. There weren't divisions then, there was only one league, so if you won your pennant, you went to the World Series. The Red Sox were behind 2-0 going into the fifth inning against the Twins.

As the Red Sox half of the fifth inning began, our friend's sister, Karen, who at that time was maybe ten years old, came wandering in because we were all gathered in this room to watch the game. Basically we were just, "Leave us alone." The second she walked in the room, just to say "hi" or just to see what's going on, the first guy up for the Red Sox, Jim Lonborg, who is the pitcher, bunts and gets on base. It was the beginning of the rally. He does this, and we're cheering. The next batter singles to keep it alive. Again, something positive happens. Now I have a vivid memory of her trying to leave and us not letting her.

Now we're sort of getting good vibes. She stays for another batter who singles or does something. Again, a second good thing happens. At that point, she turns to go and all of us said, "Stay right where you are. Don't move." She stays, and the Red Sox scored four or five runs that inning and won the game. When the inning was over, we let her go. I don't remember anybody physically getting a hold of her because she sort of was getting a kick out of playing with the older guys, but we literally would not let her leave the room. Superstitious we were!

——ANDY CORNBLATT, 53, Georgetown Law School dean of admissions

In 1960, when I was eight years old, I played for the Lady of Hope, our local parish, team in Springfield, Massachusetts. We got the end-of-the-season bus ride to Fenway Park for an outing. Walking up that ramp behind home plate and first seeing the field—that brilliant color and how it looked like a *Sports Illustrated* photo was so vivid. In all of the hundreds of times I've been to the Park since, I still always enter the Park from that same direction because I love that image.

—DON SHEA, on growing up in Springfield, MA

When I moved to Cape Cod, I became very close friends with Robert Ford. We did everything together. We lived eighty-six miles from Boston—we were only eleven years old—but the two of us took the bus to Boston to see a double-header at Fenway Park in 1959. We thought we were so adult. We went to Peroni's Restaurant for lunch and took the bus all by ourselves. In thinking back, my mother was a fairly protective mother and it says something about the tenor of the times in 1959, how innocent and naïve the country was. We went to the double-header and spent all day at Fenway. I don't remember how much it cost, but she gave me ten dollars. It seemed like a million dollars to us. We had some money of our own from mowing lawns. It was one of those glorious moments. I can remember it like it was yesterday. Seeing the green of Fenway Park that first time, coming into the Park, it was just absolutely magical. We bought the tickets for the double-header. It was a beautiful day in June. It was just an amazing experience.

—RAY ARSENAULT, on growing up on Cape Cod

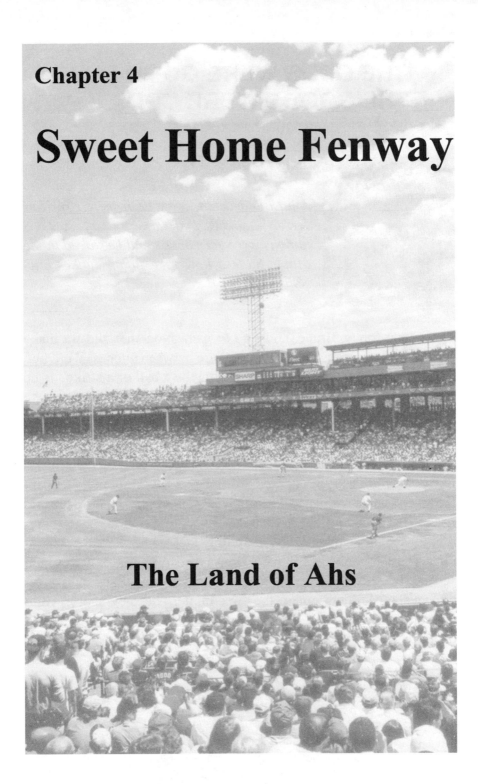

Chapter 4

Sweet Home Fenway

The Land of Ahs

THE ODDS WERE GOOD BUT THE GOODS WERE ODD!

JOHN BENNETT

John Bennett, 34, grew up in northern New Jersey—Yankees and Mets country—but his parents were Vermonters and he's lived in the Maple State a long time. John teaches high school math.

My friend, Bruce, and I go to games together and we make running bets to ease the tension between pitches. We'll bet, for instance, will the next pitch be a ball or a strike? Is he going to hit? Who did the Red Sox get for Mike Stanton the year he was on the team? I might say, "Bruce, 3 to 1, Offerman whiffs," meaning **Jose Offerman** strikes out.

One of my favorite bets happened while we were watching a Mariners-Red Sox game in 1995. The Red Sox had this guy, Vaughn Eshelman. He always had a really good winning percentage and a really terrible ERA. He had about a 5-1 record. His ERA was like eight some-thing—actually 4.85. He'd be incredibly lucky or else, he'd get these junk wins. Meanwhile, the **Mariners** had guys like Griffey and A-Rod. I said, "I'll bet drinks for the whole row that Eshelman does-n't get the Mariners out in the first inning and they score." Sure enough, they did. The Mariners got one run, I think, without even trying. I was off the hook.

> In 1996, Royals switch-hitter, Jose Offerman batted right-handed against Red Sox righty, Tim Wakefield.

> During the Seattle Mariners first year in 1977, they measured the distance to the fences in fathoms. A fathom is 6 feet. For instance, where a park may have a sign that denotes 360 feet, the Kingdome would have the number 60.

Another time, I bet the wrong way on the question of whether Rick Miller is married to Carlton Fisk's sister or Carlton Fisk is married to Rick Miller's sister—I can't remember—but I was wrong, so I lost twenty dollars to him. Actually, Bruce never wants me to pay him the money. He likes holding the twenty or thirty bucks over me. He says it gives him, "a hand over me." I'll often bet against the Red Sox because I figure then only good things can happen. I don't mind owing Bruce five or six bucks if my pessimistic bet leads to a hit.

Sometimes bets become long and convoluted. One time, Bruce and I were sitting in bleachers during the All-Star home run hitting contest. We set up a little bookmaking ring. Everybody around us was from out of town. They had paid scalpers around four hundred dollars for their seats and were having the time of their life. We were laying odds and making "overs" and "unders" such as how many home runs will Sammy Sosa hit? Bruce and I weren't betting, but we were arranging bets and holding money and laying odds for the fans sitting around us. We all had a great time.

Jeromy Burnitz had a really good day. I set the over-under on him low—six home runs for his time up, meaning one guy would guess Burnitz would hit more than six and the other guy would guess fewer than six. Burnitz went way over six. The fan next to us took the over on Burnitz and won all the money from the guy who'd bet against him. It wasn't big money—five, ten, fifteen, twenty bucks. I remember that the over-under for Sammy Sosa was nine. "Nine?" they asked. I said, "Hey, fan favorite, higher spread."

I became a Red Sox fan in 1975. My parents were both from Vermont, and my family spent a lot of time there, especially in the summer. During my summer vacation of '75, I was in Vermont, listening to a game when Fred Lynn hit three homers. I became hooked. I didn't want to root for the Dodgers. My brother followed my father and became a Dodger fan. The relatives on my mother's side were all Red Sox fans. My mother was a Red Sox fan. She really liked Carlton Fisk, partly because he was born in Vermont. The Red Sox were interesting. The Red Sox were good. I made the choice, and I've been with the Red Sox ever since.

Even though I live in Shelburne, Vermont, two hundred miles away from Fenway Park, I still go to a lot of the Red Sox games. In 2001, I went to thirteen games home and away. I went to games in New York City. I went to games in Montreal. Talk about how much of a nut I am—that year, I went to a Red Sox Saturday game against the Mets. Glendon Rusch pitched a one-hitter for the **Mets**. I caught the next flight I could, arrived the following morning in Burlington, Vermont, got into my car and drove up see the Red Sox–Expos game in Montreal later that day. The next two nights, I went to games, too.

If there's a game, I'll be drawn to it. It's like a unique primal calling: There's a game, so I will come! I've stayed home from work to watch a game. I've rearranged vacations and other schedules. I didn't want to go to my college graduation because there was a Red Sox game on television that afternoon, but my family forced me to go. I would get into trouble for sneaking a radio into my room late at night to listen to the West Coast games.

As a kid, I remember the Red Sox always losing in a horrible fashion. Always. I've cried over the Red Sox so many times, I can't cry anymore. There really isn't much that's funny about the Red Sox. Theirs isn't a history with winsome anecdotes like the Mets have or loveable anecdotes like the Cubs. It's mostly about pain and agony and suffering.

I told Fred Lynn years later how I missed his 1975 World Series Game 6, two-run homer in the first inning because some idiot neighbor decided to work with power tools at eight o'clock at night during the game. The tools caused some kind of television interference; the picture was still on, but there was a long line of static. To this day, I don't know what the guy was doing. What, chain-sawing body parts? He was a very strange man.

When the Red Sox lost that Series, it was terrible. Later, in that very long Game 6, I was sent to bed but I remember sneaking out of my room because the Red Sox came up to bat. I listened to Dwight Evans make the big catch and throw it to first base to double-off the runner. I

After the Mets had played their first nine games in their inaugural 1962 season, they were 9½ games out of first place.

remember hearing that Fisk was coming up and I ran into the room to watch him bat. My parents started yelling at me for being out of bed.

At school, it was a tough time with a lot of teasing. The kids were brutal to each other about the teams they liked. As an adult, I understand that things are put on earth for a specific reason: birds fly around and sing, the Red Sox get out ahead early and score, eight guys get on base in the first three innings and they'll get only one more run after that and lose. This is what they do. "TRSB." Stands for "Typical Red Sox Bull———." Hopefully, there will be a payoff someday, but in the meantime, it's part of a puritan work ethic of human suffering. They will be ahead 1-0, their starting pitcher will be doing okay, then they'll tie or make a mistake or someone will make an error, they'll fall behind, the bullpen will come in and instead of keeping the game close, they'll let them get a little bit further ahead until the ninth inning comes. Then, the Red Sox will bring the tying run to the plate, no matter how far behind, especially in a home game on a Saturday afternoon, which is when I go most of the time. They'll make a little joke rally to get my hopes up, and then they'll snatch it away. Dwight Evans is my favorite player because he was the one guy who actually came through with home runs a number of times so we didn't have to deal with "TRSB".

Nineteen seventy-eight was worse than 1986 because I was just a kid, still looking at the world a little naively, and saying to myself, "The Red Sox have the perfect team." Just before spring training, they traded for **Dennis Eckersley**, so they had every piece of the puzzle. They had an All Star at every position. Butch Hobson was batting ninth and had thirty home runs the year before. The Yankees had Billy Martin as their manager, and he was ready to implode at any moment. I felt as long as Martin was the manager, the Red Sox could take them.

Everything was going to be perfect. They were beating the crap out of everybody. After ninety games, they were 62-28. At that point,

Late in his career, Dennis Eckersley was second among all active Major League pitchers, in complete games—even though he hadn't thrown a complete game in eleven years... Eckersley once had 21 consecutive hitless innings...one year he had more saves than base runners allowed.

Sports Illustrated ran an article that included the win/loss records of the four Red Sox aces: Torrez, Lee, Tiant, and Eckersley. Then, it all fell apart. Bill Lee, who was 10-3 at the time, never won another game in a Red Sox uniform. Torrez went like 4 and 12; Tiant only won four more games for the Red Sox. It was incredible how that article doomed them.

What really kills me is that September 7, 1978, that day the Red Sox get destroyed, the day that has become known as the Boston Massacre, is the same sad and inauspicious day that Keith Moon of the Rolling Stones died. He was my favorite drummer in my favorite band. The Red Sox were beaten by the Yankees that day 12 to 1; 13-2 the next night; 7–0 on Saturday, and 7–4 on Sunday. As God is my witness, I still remember those scores because it was horrible! It was a numbing experience. Kids at school were picking on us. We got into fights with Yankee fans—not fist fights, but arguments. There were plenty of times I wanted the fights to come to blows, but I never went that far.

One of my best friends was a Yankee fan and he was horrible. He and I were good friends, but this other, mean side of him came out. He called me up in the middle of a game to yell at me. He was a **Cowboys** fan and I was rooting for the Steelers so I got him back in the Super Bowl, which was nice.

All the Red Sox fans complain about Bill Buckner in the '86 World Series. To me, what killed me worse was the Bucky Dent game in '78 when Yastrzemski fouled out to third to end the game. There were two guys on base, all set up for a rally. All he had to do was get a hit! All Jim Rice, batting before him, had to do was get a hit but neither of them did it! After Yastrzemski fouled to third, I didn't want it to end. It wasn't fair. I wanted a do-over, but that was it. It was over.

I remember thinking then, "This is the way life is. Things are not always going to work out the way I want them to or think they will." I was only in sixth grade. I had thought life was perfect and that everything was going to be perfect from those days forward because the Red

When the Dallas Cowboys Cheerleaders started in 1972, each earned $15 per game—the same amount they receive today.

Sox had this perfect team. They couldn't possibly lose, and yet, they did. There won ninety-nine games and they went home with nothing.

Yankee fans love to talk about '86, but they love to forget about '88. Nineteen eighty-eight was absolutely beautiful because the Red Sox came from nine and a half games behind the Yankees, caught them, and finished four and a half games ahead, which is basically what the Yankees did to the Red Sox in '78. You'll never hear Yankee fans tell this story. Oh, no! They've conveniently forgotten. They can't remember Steve Shields giving up a hit to Spike Owen, or Lee Smith striking out Ken Phelps with three pitches to win a game.

In 1990, the Red Sox were in a heated battle to the end, tied for the pennant. They had a big lead and then blew it. The Red Sox were fighting it out with the Blue Jays. I really hated the Blue Jays. Next to the Yankees, they were the team I really hated. I don't hate **David Wells** now, but I hated him when he was a Blue Jay. He's never been able to beat the Red Sox anyway, but I really just hated him. And I hated Dave Stieb. At the time, I was working a summer job selling sporting goods. We had a lot of Canadian customers, who thought the Blue Jays were so great. It really burned my butt. The Canadians don't even know baseball.

We had tickets for the September 28, 1990 game, which turned out to be the night I almost stopped being a Red Sox fan. My tickets were originally for a Saturday night, but there had been an owner's lock-out which delayed spring training and resulted in the rescheduling of some games. Because my make-up tickets were for a Friday night and we had to work the next day, John and I drove from Vermont down to Boston and back. I don't really recommend this 440-mile roundtrip, where you get home at three o'clock in the morning. I've done it more than once and taught school the next day. There are some things in life you just have to do.

> David Wells paid $35,000 for an authentic Babe Ruth cap and wore it during a Yankee game...Wells and his grandmother use the same tattoo artist....On hot days, Ruth would wear a cabbage leaf under his cap.

We sat in Section 7 next to some Blue Jay fans who were very nice and had driven all the way down from Toronto. It took us forever to get to Fenway because there had been some horrible accident where a car or tractor-trailer had gone off an embankment and pitched thirty feet down. There had also been a fire that night across the street in the souvenir store.

The game itself was a microcosm of the Red Sox history. They had gone ahead like 3-0. Mike Boddicker was pitching against Dave Stieb. I hated Stieb and I was cursing his name and where he had come from because he was such a miserable individual. I remember a game earlier in the year when he cursed out George Bell because Bell had not caught a foul pop and then Mike Greenwell hit a homer on the next pitch. Stieb was taken out, but that's the Blue Jays—the "Blow Jays," as we call them. They're almost better at blowing the pennant than the Red Sox. They blew it in 1987, and in '90, they gagged big time. They won the World Series in 1992 to get off the hook so nobody remembers how they really choked.

I was coming on my darkest hour as a Red Sox fan. The Sox had gone ahead in the game, then they made some errors. They blew the lead. The game tied. They *let* it tie. I was so tired of dealing with TRSB. Nineteen eighty-six wasn't that long before.

I got up from my seat and started to walk out of the park. I went down the tunnel and watched the next half inning. I said to myself, "You know, if I don't go back to my seat, I'm never going to another game again because I'm tired of the agony this team is putting me through." The Red Sox happened to score a run that inning to go ahead, so I figured it was safe to go back to my seat for the top of the ninth.

Larry Andersen was pitching for the Red Sox and he couldn't get the side out. The Sox had gotten him from Houston for Jeff Bagwell because Jeff Reardon had hurt his arm. Jeff Gray came in to pitch even though he wasn't a closer. I guess they figured they didn't need to use Reardon, who was warming up in the bullpen, because he had pitched the night before. They just wanted to see if Jeff Gray could get a couple of guys out first.

Well, Jeff Gray gave up a single and Junior Felix hit a home run. I thought, "These ———, they've done it to me. They have brought me back. I was going to quit on them, then I came back, and now I have to watch this!"

The Blue Jay fans were screaming and yelling. I was just sitting there numb in this horrifying moment. Then Reardon came in and got the side out. It was like the entire Red Sox history in one game. I was sitting there watching this unfold and had the chance to get out, but I didn't take it.

As the Red Sox came up in the ninth inning, I said to myself, "They're not going to put me through this again. I'm just gonna sit here and watch. I'm not gonna say a word. I'm not gonna cheer. I'm not gonna get into it." My friend John was cheering, "This is it." A guy near me, probably in his forties, was praying on a rosary, begging for the Red Sox to come back. The place was jammed, over thirty-five thousand fans were going nuts. I think it might have been the second most attended night game in the history of the team.

I remember the whole inning. Jody Reed got a walk. Carlos Quintana bunted him over to second. Wade Boggs got up and walked. Then Tom Henke, who I hated, a fat piece of ——, came out and I was screaming and yelling at him at the top of my lungs. I'm told Tom Henke is a very nice man, but I hated him because he always shut the Red Sox down. We were screaming at Mike Greenwell, who had been the whipping boy that season because he'd had an off-year, "All right, see what you can do. If you're a man, you'll get a hit right now." And he did. Greenwell got a single. Reed didn't score. He stopped at third, so the bases were loaded with one out.

The crowd was in a frenzy. I'm convinced Henke choked. Ellis Burks, on the first pitch, singled into left field. The Sox could have won the game right there, but Boggs stopped at third. He went halfway around and then went back. The bases were loaded with one out, and who comes up but Jeff Stone.

Stone was a scrub player, a very marginal outfielder who played most of his career for the Orioles. He was picked up in 1990 by the

Red Sox and got up exactly twice as DH that year before being sent to Pawtucket.

Stone was in the game because the inning before he pinch-ran for Dwight Evans. So, Jeff Stone's in the game. They can't pinch-hit for him. They've got the bases loaded against Henke, the best closer. I said to my friend, "Remember **Jeff Stone**?" When he was brought up earlier that September I told John, "He's gonna win a game for them." John said, "Bull ——. The guy stinks. Jeff Stone—give me a break."

The first pitch was a ball. The place was in a psychotic, Nurembergean-frenzy. Then, Henke shriveled up and died. I remember Jeff Stone crushed the ball, or maybe he didn't. Maybe it was only in my mind's eye that he hit the ball that hard. Maybe it was because the outfield was playing in because there was one out and the bases were loaded, but Stone ripped the ball into the corner, and the Blue Jays couldn't get it. They just watched the ball hit the grass, and that was it. The Red Sox won. It was the high point of Jeff Stone's life. That's the thing about the Red Sox. You never know.

I've never been as happy. I've seen a lot of great games, including the Red Sox winning a play-off game in 1999, but that was the ultimate. The place went nuts. I remember the man with the rosary was crying and crying. I remember almost feeling sorry for the Blue Jays fan who had sat near me as he walked out.

Two days later, Jeff Stone faced Tom Henke again and struck out. He didn't make the team next year and his career was over. That hit had been Jeff Stone' shining moment.

If you really want to know hard-core Red Sox fans, ask them if they remember the Jeff Stone game. That game is why I'm a Red Sox fan. It's almost like you don't want the Red Sox to win a World Series. If they did, why would you ever watch another game? What could possibly be an encore? Your baseball watching would be over. Almost-winning is a character-building experience. It really is.

In 1994, six months after the Nancy Kerrigan assault, Tonya Harding's husband, Jeff Gillooly, legally changed his name to Jeff Stone.

DRINK UP...
IT'S LAUGH CALL

JIM DECROTEAU

Jim DeCroteau, 43, grew up outside Boston in Melrose, MA. He now lives in Fullerton, CA, where he does standup comedy when he's not at his day job in customer service.

At Fenway Park, the regular beer vendors know me. Three of them have been there forever, two of them are older—my friends and I nicknamed one of them "Eddie Andelman" for his resemblance to the sports radio host—and one is about my age. We found out the younger guy's name was Leo. Over the years, we'd developed this relationship where they no longer required an ID every time I bought beer. Our relationship consisted of snippets of conversation lasting only the time it takes to draw beer. If I saw them well before game time, we could linger, but once lines started forming, I couldn't chat with them. Two of the older gentlemen were in the movie, *Field of Dreams*, which was partially filmed at Fenway. They're in the scene where Kevin Costner and James Earl Jones get beer and hot dogs. I'll always have the psychic memory of that movie. There's a scene where the character says, "I had a dream I was at Fenway Park last night." I had that same dream myself.

I started going regularly to Leo for my beer, and whatever friend I was with would go to one of the other vendors. At one point, one of the older gentlemen retired, and a much younger guy was moved down to take his place. I started calling him The Rookie, despite his protests that he had been working for years in the bleachers. It was like he had to work in the bleachers eight years to get where he was. I gave him a hard time. I would tease him about his lack of experience and how his line moved slower because he was the rookie.

Anyway, the beer guys one night switched from Bud to Miller Lite. I really don't like Miller because it was owned by a tobacco company, which I hate, Philip Morris. Every once in a while I started going up to the other beer stand, to a Bud vendor at the top of my section. This happened until one game, out of pure habit, my friend steered us towards the "Leo" stand. Much to my surprise, he had recognized my absence. He said, "You've been going to Mike down in 101, huh? It's because we switched to Miller, right?" I felt like I had been caught cheating on a girlfriend. He didn't really know, but he speculated. Then, the guy who was The Rookie was up there at that stand, and I tried to hide from him, and he saw me. I was busted. He gave me this look. It was just so funny. The next time he was just giving me such a hard time. Since then, they switched back to Bud, and everything has gone back to normal.

In high school, my friend, Bill and I would take the subway to Fenway and sit in the bleachers. To this day, he also remembers trying to study for tests while we watched games. During one game, I remember helping him with chemistry, and he wound up getting a better grade than I did, which made me furious.

I began doing comedy in graduate school. I got into the finals of the Stitches Comedy Riot with WBZ Radio, and then the finals at the Paradise Theater, and I started getting work after that. A few of my early jokes were about the announcement made at Fenway Park that "anyone going on the field would be arrested and prosecuted." I did this little joke about someone in a jail cell with murderers and rapists and the guy who ran onto the field: "What are you in for?" "I killed six people. What's your life sentence for?" "I stepped on the field at Fenway." The joke spoofed the announcement because it was an empty threat; nothing serious was going to happen to a person who ran onto the field.

I did an impression of Sherm Feller, the P.A. announcer at Fenway for many, many years. Feller was an interesting guy. He also wrote the pop hit song, "Summertime, Summertime." At the time I began doing his impression, there was a controversy because someone had brought an inflatable doll to Fenway Park and had tossed it around like a beach ball. We did an entire Fenway Park sketch where we had a family trying to watch the game and drunken guys behind them eventually throwing up on them. Sherm Feller would make announcements like, "Objectionable items are not allowed in the stands." I would be more specific: "Ladies and gentlemen, boys and girls, we want a safe environment at Fenway Park. No objectionable objects will be seen in the stands. This includes inflatable dolls, —— extenders and the XY —————."

One time, the Red Sox made me really angry, I had worn shorts on a hot night and had lost my key. I knew it had probably fallen out of my shorts because that had happened before. I didn't realize the key was missing until I left the game, and when I tried to get back into the service gate, the guards wouldn't let me. I said, "Have someone come with me. I'm not going to steal anything. I'm a season ticket holder. I just want to go to my seat and look for the key." They wouldn't let me. It took me about twelve minutes to convince the guy to let me run back to my seat. I was so upset because, as much as I love the team, the Red Sox are so arrogant because they're sitting on a gold mine. They can do anything, and the fans are still going to come back.

I wrote a letter to management after I found out that I hadn't been offered a 600 Club ticket when I should have been. This was after the 1994 season. I had become friends with the novelist Bob Binstock, known as RC Binstock, just from being fellow season ticket holders. He's even made me a character in one of his novels. One day, he asked me if I had gotten my 600 Club ticket. I said, "No, what are you talking about?"

Because of the strike in 1994, there had been no World Series. Normally, if you've paid money for potential play-off games, the team asks you whether you want the money refunded or "rolled over" to the coming season. In '94, several regular season games weren't played and I requested a refund. I don't like the idea of the Red Sox making interest off of my money.

Anyway, it turned out that the Red Sox gave ticket holders who let them keep the money, a free game in the 600 Club. I said, "Oh, they're not letting me have a game at 600 Club because I asked for a refund of games that weren't played." I was furious.

I called the Red Sox on the phone and talked to the secretary. I said, "I think this is so unfair. You have a strike. Baseball's public relations is at an all-time low, and you're alienating one of your best customers. Why would you do this? The 600 Club isn't full. There's no reason why I shouldn't be sitting up there spending money on your products, buying food and beer?"

She said, "No, it's not that. It's just we wanted to reward the fans that stuck with us." I said, "How am I not sticking with you by getting a refund for something I never got to go see." I told her I knew John Harrington, who at the time was the CEO, and John Buckley, who was the vice-president. She said, "What do you want me to do?" I said, "I want to talk to John Buckley." She said, "Oh, you can't talk to John Buckley." I said, "Really? Well, tell them both that a fellow BC alum is very upset." She said, "Oh, you went to BC."

Within two minutes, I had my tickets. My telling them I went to Boston College totally turned the conversation around. I was offended, yet felt good. Watching the game from the Club hasn't been that popular. I wouldn't want to do it regularly because you watch the game behind glass. They've renamed it the 406 Club because that's Ted Williams' batting average. But it's too big. It looks almost like a spaceship has landed.

About ten years ago, before the "Save Fenway Park" group was founded, I prepared press releases for a group I was going to call "Friends of Fenway to Save the Park." Fenway Park is absolutely my favorite place in the world. I would like to see the Red Sox keep it. If I got married, I'd want to get married there. I probably want my ashes spread there. I'd like the seats to be more comfortable, but it brings back so many childhood memories. I remember being dragged along on my sister's date that wasn't supposed to be, and I remember being there many other times with my family. In '67, I remember studying chemistry there. In '75, I recall the game when Jim Palmer went against Luis Tiant, and the Red Sox won 2-0, in what was one of the best games ever played in Boston.

The first time I went back to Fenway after having moved away, it was really, really strange. The intensity at Anaheim is nothing like it is in

Fenway. I was shocked at the 2002 World Series and play-offs when the people here in California finally started cheering. I thought, "Where have you people been?"

I think the 1999 All-Star Game was the most exciting time I ever had at Fenway. It wasn't really a victory but the combined experience of Fenway Park, Ted Williams being there, Smash Mouth playing in the bullpen, and the home run contest the day before was so incredible. The baseball show now put on for every All-Star game was being held at the Hynes Convention Center. I may have been thinking at that point that the Red Sox really were going to get rid of the Park, and it's not quite going to be the same at a new place. The Fleet Center had opened, and you could see how different the Celtics-Bruins experience was.

Four or five times a year, I have access to tickets that are five rows from the Fenway field. I love to give those tickets to people when I can't go and then wait for the phone to ring and the person to ask, "Where did you get those tickets?"

Usually, I give these tickets to friends in the Boston area who I know will enjoy them. Once, I gave them to friends from my fantasy baseball league and they took a woman, also in the league, whom I don't know very well. Evidently, the woman was very excited. I told my friends, "Now you've spoiled her. You've done what I did to my nephew, which was take him to his first game using those tickets. Now, he gives me a dirty look when he sits in my otherwise very good seats."

Though I now live in California, I still buy the whole eighty-one games for the Red Sox and sell the tickets for the games I know I won't be able to make. Last year, I got back for twelve games. I have my season tickets for the Red Sox, Angels, and the Lowell Spinners.

When I went back to Fenway, I found that it was so much more intense. I had forgotten about how even a regular season game back there has this electricity that doesn't exist in California. It's hard to describe. The first year I was out here, I had just moved west a week to ten days before what would have been Opening Day. I missed it so much that now I make a point of going back to Boston for Opening

Day. I still schedule my vacations around trips back to Fenway. I don't know if I could have moved to California before the Internet, since I wouldn't have been able to keep up with the Sox.

Back then, World Series games were played during weekday days. At school, they brought the black and white television set into the classroom and let us watch the game. That affirmed the importance of Game 7, that they would take time out from the school day to let us watch, because this was an environment where you didn't drink from the water fountain without permission. It was such a restrictive environment. My theory as to why the priests gave out the report cards as opposed to the nuns is that not only did the nun know you did well or poorly, but God's Messenger himself was handing out the cards.

Because I was a teenager in '75, the World Series loss to the Reds was so disappointing. Everyone thinks of the Red Sox as choking in the big games, but that's really not true. In Game 6, they won the game when they had to win. Both in '75 and in '86, the National League team won 108 games, back when winning 108 games was a lot more impressive than it is now, with the disparity in teams. I think of that story that Peter Gammons refers to: The guy, who years later in the bar, picks his head up from his drink and just says, "They never should have pinch-hit for Willoughby." That had been the game-turning event in the Game 7 of the '75 Series.

I think the angriest the Red Sox ever made me was in 1991. I had picked up a friend at four o'clock in the morning because we wanted to go to Baltimore to see the Red Sox play a doubleheader. They were in the pennant race, and it was the last year before Memorial Stadium was to be torn down.

The Red Sox lost the doubleheader. Joe Morgan, the manager, insisted on using the overused Greg Harris as a reliever for both games, as though he only had one pitcher to use. We left the doubleheader and started driving back to Boston. We had planned to stop halfway to sleep, but we were so angry we drove all the way home. I dropped him off at four o'clock in the morning. We were pounding the dash, "How do they expect to win just using one relief pitcher so much? They have to use somebody else, or they're not going to go anywhere." We kept saying we'd stop up ahead but we never did. When we got home, we realized we had just spent twenty-four hours driving to a baseball game and back.

To be a Red Sox fan in California is lonely. It's very strange. It's interesting, over in Anaheim, there were big crowds when the Red Sox or the Yankees played there, but the seats were filled by Red Sox and Yankee fans who migrated here. Those were the few times when you would get a little bit of a rise out of the Anaheim fans. When the Angels fans realized there were more people rooting against the team than for them, they were too intimidated to do too much, but at least they were incited enough to show more support for their team.

On occasion, when Angels fans have found out I am from Boston, they talk to me about the Dave Henderson home run in '86, which to them is the same as the Bucky Dent home run is to us. The Red Sox come back like that and then they let you go. There's just no passion in Anaheim. During the World Series, the television newscaster had every bit of Angel memorabilia you could think of. Then they ended the report with, "Sadly, Bob won't be going to the play-offs this year as he gave up his season tickets just last year."

I've had great luck in the two day jobs I've had. Years ago in Boston, I worked for the Red Cross right across the street from Fenway Park. My current job is across the street from the Anaheim Angels' Edison Field. Now I have people calling me from Boston telling me I had to move three thousand miles to win my World Championship.

Some fans think that most of their Red Sox memories are good, and I think that's a good attitude. The "woe is me" sometimes gets to me a little bit. Maybe it was in 1986, when I was starting to be an adult, that I felt, "You know, I've got to live my own life. I've got to accomplish things in my own life and not live a hundred percent through these people." I knew the Red Sox were only going to disappoint me. Since then, I don't take the games as seriously.

Watching the Angels fans last year, even though they had some traumatic memories from 1986, I never got the feeling like I do in Boston that we're waiting for the other shoe to drop. They were enjoying it for what it was. I envied that.

BAND IN BOSTON

John Lincoln Wright and Jay Martell

JOHN LINCOLN WRIGHT

John Lincoln Wright was born in Boston to an old Yankee/Irish family. Now 55, John has been a professional musician for thirty-eight years. He's made several baseball records about the Red Sox and Yaz.

The first game I went to was against the Washington Senators. Believe me, there were plenty of tickets available. I saw Frank Howard hit one over everything. My grandfather listened to all the games all the time on an old Crosley radio. He'd keep a simple score sheet of every game. I suppose it was my grandfather that gave me the love of the game. He was a man of few words. He just listened to the games and didn't really talk about the individual players. It was sort of his solace for a couple of hours in the evening.

In the late 1960s and early 1970s, as their promo, Channel 38 played my rendition of a **song** that my college roommate wrote. It went like this:

> *"It's summer again up in Boston. The Red Sox are play-ing today.*
>
> *Once that first ball has been tossed in, another game gets underway.*
>
> *I always sit up in the bleachers. Get such a wonderful tan.*
>
> *I scream and I yell like a madman. So the Sox know I'm their biggest fan."*

Phil Rizzuto is the only baseball person to earn a Gold Record…his game calling was in the background of Meatloaf's *Paradise by the Dashboard Lights*. Rizzuto was the first mystery guest on *What's My Line*.

My roommate had started a band called the Beacon Street Union, part of the ill-fated "Boston Sound." They were trying to make Boston bands like the San Francisco kind. We weren't ready, but we did it with aplomb. One of our records got banned here because it talked about a stabbing. We did this little country song. I left rock and roll and was going into country music, which was a smart idea for Boston, right?

> *"With two outs, the bases are loaded. Three balls and two strikes is the call.*

> *The crowd is now standing and cheering 'cause Yaz hit one over the wall.*

> *Now it's the end of the inning. The Sox are ahead twelve to ten.*

> *I'm so glad when my home team is winning, and I've got pennant fever again.*

> *Hey, hey, Red Sox, we're all here to lend you a hand.*

> *Go, go Red Sox, the best dog-gone team in the land."*

I did some other baseball songs. When Oil Can Boyd was with the Sox, I thought he was going to be the big deal.

> *"Meridian, Mississippi—the land of Satchel Paige*

> *He's making noise all through the Bigs and the mound down in Fenway.*

> *He's racking...*

You know, he used to have all the names for his pitches: the Dead Red, the Big Yellow Hammer. He was a real Mississippi-style baseball guy. I thought he was gonna be a big thing. I loved watching him. I used to go down and see him in spring training. I saw him a couple of years ago up in Lynn, Masschusetts, where he was playing in the Northern Independent League. He was playing there and threw a one-hitter his first time out. So I went up to see The Can. He had a big bunch of lumbering linebacker-kind of infielders behind him. The fastball wasn't quite there. I got a chance to talk with him and get a ball from him. I loved The Can. He was some kind of character. I brought him a box of the records.

The problem with the Red Sox is not the Curse of the Bambino. It's the provincialism of everybody—the fans, the management. It's a very provincial place. People have a tendency to overrate it—America's Greatest City, Land of Harvard University, the Home of the Revolution. People forget, they still can't beat the Yankees. The Yankees don't care about the Red Sox. The Red Sox care about the Yankees. We get very provincial here about our teams and tend to overrate mediocre players and underrate pretty good players.

I don't think the park helps them a whole lot. People say, "Oh, get a big right-handed slugger like a Jack Clark." My National League friends call me and say, "You're getting Jack Clark. He's been done for three years. Why are they bringing him in for big money? He did nothing here." And Don Zimmer saying, "Oh, Bob Bailey, he's going to put balls over that wall." Well, he never did. He struck out three times in a play-off game. And we don't even want to talk about Luis Aparicio.

As a kid, I followed the Red Sox casually. Communications were different in those days. We didn't take a daily newspaper once we moved to Maine. I went to BC in 1965. I think what really sparked my interest, as with everybody here, was that '67 season. I used to go to Fenway, because in those days you could get the bleachers for fifty cents. You'd stick a beer in your pocket. The '67 season really cemented it for a lot of people here who hadn't been paying much attention to baseball. From there on, I don't know if I've missed fifty games on the radio or the TV. I do every game. If I'm playing a gig, I go out in the truck on my break and listen to ball games. I just really like it. My wife thinks it's kind of a waste of time that should be spent for better and more productive uses. She'll say, "How come the game's on all the time?" I'll say, "That's when they play them, honey, they play the games at dinnertime."

Connecticut is divided as far as Red Sox fans, but from the northern part of the state all the way up to the top of New England, it's Red Sox Country. I've even listened to Red Sox games in Nova Scotia because the radio signal would travel right across the water. That's why there are a lot of fans in New Brunswick and Nova Scotia because it's a clear signal right across the Atlantic Ocean up into the Maritimes. There are an incredible number of Red Sox fans up on coastal Maine to New Brunswick and Nova Scotia. I've heard people say they've heard them in Newfoundland.

I don't know the players. I had good advice from a good friend years ago. He said, "If you love baseball, you don't want to know the players. Know the game, but you don't want to know the players." It's very disappointing.

Bill Lee used to come when I was playing in Harvard Square with my country band, John Lincoln Wright and the Sour Mash Boys. We used to play in Harvard Square all the time. We were a hot item in Cambridge in the 1970s. Bill Lee used to come down there with a couple of other ball players who I won't name. Beside the stage, there was this alleyway. They'd all go back there with some of the sports writers and smoke dope and listen to the music, and a good time was had by all. I don't really know him, but that was a funny bunch of guys. They were called the Buffalo Heads. They hated Don Zimmer because these were guys who hated authority figures. But Lee was a Yankee-beater. He had some wonderful games against the New York Yankees. As a left-hander in Yankee Stadium, he was great. He was the hippie.

I've always loved the team, but never loved the ownership, and I'm holding my breath on this new ownership. I think they're show horses, not work horses. I don't think they have enough money to keep up with the thing. They overspent. They can't build the park because they don't have enough money. They spent three-quarters of a billion dollars to buy a horrible baseball park. It is not this "little lyric bandbox of a ball park" that John Updike describes. I went to a game last year, and I went to standing room only, the seat was so bad. I couldn't see a pitch until the third inning. I just said to my friend, a producer from Nashville, "Let's go up to standing room so we'll actually get to see the game." Fenway has got a lot of problems.

In other places, the city will foot the bill for a stadium, but that's not going to happen here. They'll give them roads, and they'll put power lines in for the infrastructure. They wouldn't do it for the Patriots. The Patriots wanted to be in South Boston. So, they stayed in Foxboro and built their own stadium. It's a ripoff for the taxpayer. If you can't afford the team, well…. Other than bragging rights, there's no tangible asset for a community to have just eight football games a year in a half a billion dollar complex that the people pay for.

About ten years ago, I got a call from an agent down in Rhode Island who wanted me to sing the National Anthem at Fenway on the day they were burying the Curse of the Bambino. At the time they booked the thing, the Sox were about eleven games up in first place. They brought Babe Ruth's daughter down from New Hampshire. They had all the announcers, Ken Coleman and everybody there. They asked me to sing the Anthem. I said, "Oh sure." They had me come over to the park on a Tuesday to just do like a sound check in an empty park. They said there would be a lot of festivities going on on the field. I had to bring a tape of the song in case they wanted to use recorded music, which most people do. I, with my bravado, said, "Come on. I do this for a living. I can do this." So they said, "Okay, great, that will make it easier if you can sing live."

They called me over to the park to check the sound delay, which is a second or two as it reverberates around the stadium. So "the rockets red glare" is sounding while you're still at the "twilight" or whatever….

So I get up that morning. I'd worked the night before. Truth be told, I was probably a little hung over. It was a very humid day with a fore-cast of intermittent showers. I said, "Well, I'll just walk over to the park. I'm only about a mile and a half from Fenway." I would just walk across the Charles River and head down to Fenway, which is what I do when I go to the games.

All of a sudden, I start to get anxiety, which I never had in my career. All of sudden, I'm getting an anxiety attack, hyperventilating, because I was going on the field to bury the "Curse of the Bambino." As a baseball fan, it's easier to be a passive fan than to go out near the mound to sing the Anthem. It was a nationally televised game. They had all these ceremonies, but then there was a little rain delay. So now I'm getting nervous. It's an hour after I'm supposed to do this thing—a long delay. Now I'm starting to get sort of asthmatic. I'm having hyperventilation.

The groundskeeper there, a crusty old guy, Joe Mooney says, "Why don't you go sit in the dugout, kid? You're looking a little pale." I'm trying to drink a beer or something to see if anything will get my metabolism going. So here I am sitting in the Red Sox dugout, the home dugout, and Mo Vaughn is next to me. Mike Greenwell was still here—all these guys. I'm sitting in the dugout, and I can't even enjoy the moment because I'm panicked. I'm just sitting there trying to do the deep breathing that you learn, meditation style. Then the guy says. "It's about time to go on. Make sure you take your cowboy hat off."

So I went out to do it. I literally thought I was going to collapse. I was standing there. I opened my mouth to start singing and I said, "Please, God, not now. Not at this stage of my career. Don't let me hit the deck." You know how you can get faint? Well, I managed to get through the first couple of lines. I knew if I could get through a couple of lines of the thing, I have a good voice. I can sing strong. If I get through the first couple of lines, I'll be fine. I'll have my breath. I'll have my confidence. That was my scariest time in a thirty-eight year career—being on the field at Fenway Park singing the **Anthem**. By the end I was fine. I even put a yodel in.

I've played to a hundred thousand people. I've played to five people. But going on the field at Fenway Park was a daunting challenge—to carry on my shoulders, to sing the Anthem, and to bury the "Curse of the Bambino." I got through it, but it was frightening.

What they had planned for the ceremony to bury the curse was a few speeches, and Babe Ruth's daughter was there to root the Red Sox on. I think they had Laurie Cabot, the "Official Witch of Salem," casting spells. They had booked this when the Red Sox had a healthy lead in

> Before Super Bowl XI, there was no national anthem. Vicki Carr sang *America the Beautiful*.

the division. By the time the game came around, the lead had vanished, of course. They were a few games back by the time they got to do this thing, and I think they finished nine or ten or eleven back.

The maddest the Red Sox ever made me was that sixth game in 1986. I was at my house and had already opened a bottle of champagne. I was on the telephone with all my friends, talking about we we're supposed to do when we win—dance in the streets, or whatever, and I ended up wasting the bottle of champagne. I dumped it out. That was the quintessential humiliating moment for Red Sox fans history.

The phones just went dead after the error. Nothing. Everyone just put the phone down, and I didn't hear from some of these people for months. It was taken very hard up here. The next day, I turned the radio on again and I saw them winning in the seventh game. It was such an anticlimactic thing. And I will mention for my guy, Oil Can, bad manager, McNamara, a drunken Marine. I have tapes here of post-game shows. I think Ken Coleman was the announcer of Oil Can clinching the pennant. He won the big games to get them into the play-offs and get them in position for the World Series. He was hot as a pistol at that time. McNamara promised The Can that he would let him have a start in the World Series. So The Can is pumped. Oil Can was the only guy that would have had the mojo in this town to break that thing, and instead they went with Hurst on two days' rest, instead of letting The Can pitch in the seventh game. He could have done it. I know he could have. He was pitching great. McNamara wouldn't let him do it. Instead of letting The Can start, and if he was too hyper, and he was getting banged around, then you go to Hurst. Seventh game, everybody is available is what the baseball rule is. If it's one inning, if it's two innings, whatever it is, everyone's available. But they didn't give Can the shot. I'll go to my grave believing that he was the only one who had the **Mississippi** mojo that would have brought him over the top.

The posted speed limit on the Ole Miss campus in Oxford, Mississippi is 18 mph. So designated because that was Archie Manning's number when he quarterbacked the Rebels in the late 1960s.

FOR FEAR IT WOULD GO ON HIS PERMANENT RECORD

Patrick Fitzsimmons

Patrick Fitzsimmons is thirty-six years from old from Brockton, Massachusetts, now living in North Easton, Massachusetts.

When I was in the sixth grade, a buddy and I skipped out of school one day. We took the train into Boston from Brockton and ended up getting off at Kenmore Square. We're young, don't know what's going on, we wander around, and there's Fenway Park. We'd heard about Fenway Park. As we're walking around the outside the Park, we just keep pushing on doors and windows and none of them open. All of a sudden, a window opened up, we looked down in there, and it was a concession storage area. The Red Sox were not at home at the time.

We climbed in through the window and got down in the storage area. We go out into the stadium. We're wandering around. All of a sudden, a security guard sees us. We didn't even know security guards existed. We took off running. We're running around what would normally be a concourse at most stadiums, and we ended up in the bowels of the stadium where the seats are. This old security guard is chasing us. We're zigzagging in the rows of seats. We're young, and we're scared, and we're running fast, but we're running out of breath. We had visions of going to jail and being kicked out of school and being excommunicated and going straight to hell for breaking and entering Fenway Park. The guard was yelling at us, but we could tell we were getting further and further away from him because we couldn't hear his voice as clearly. We turned around. He'd had to stop and sit down in one of the seats. He was totally winded. He was a fat, old guy. We were just dead tired ourselves. He just screamed at us, "You guys can't be in here. Get out of here now." We screamed back at him, "We don't know the way out." He's huffing and puffing, sitting there, and he gasped, "Take that next tunnel, go straight ahead and keep going and don't ever come back." We did. We were still shakin' when we got back to Brockton. Of all the times that I've been to Fenway Park over the years, that was easily the happiest I've ever been leaving the Park—not even if I were leaving after the Sox had won a World Series.

Many years later, my wife was having an operation at a hospital not far from Fenway, and it happened to be Opening Day. I had a lot of time to kill and decided I would walk down to Fenway and suck up the ambiance of Opening Day. I'm standing down there by Yawkey Way, really enjoying myself, watching people come for Opening Day. I started talking to this guy who was a few years older than I was, a well-dressed guy, just standing there. We're just shooting the breeze, and he said, "Are you going to the game?" I said, "No, I don't have a ticket." He said, "Well, I'm waiting for a buddy of mine, and if he doesn't show up, you can use his ticket." His buddy never showed, and we go in. It's not like we're sitting in the nosebleed section, we're going in right behind home plate, and we're going down lower and lower. Pretty soon, we're only a few rows from the field. As we go in there, everybody's waving at the guy and calling his name. I'm thinking, "This guy's a big shot, whoever he is." So we're sitting there, and we're really getting along well, and all of a sudden we start talking about the pitching staff. I happened to remark how much I detested a Red Sox pitcher named Matt Young. The guy couldn't throw to first base. Every time he threw to first base, he'd throw it in the stands, he'd throw it down the right-field line. He just couldn't throw to first base. He was driving us nuts. I proceeded to just royally rip Matt Young. I noticed the guy kind of recoiling a little bit. Then for the next inning or two, he never said a word to me. Finally I said, "Did I say something that bothered you?" He said, "Matt Young's a great guy. He was my college roommate."

I said, "Can I buy you a beer?" By the end of the game, we were even.

JUST A TEENAGE CRUSH ON FENWAY PARK

CHARLIE BUSA

Charlie Busa, an executive with Stored Value Systems in Louisville, Kentucky, almost fit the perfect description of a die-hard Red Sox— in the worst way imaginable.

It was opening day in '75. For Red Sox fans, it's always "next year." That was "next year." We knew 1975 was going to be a good team. You just wanted to be there for Opening Day. It was the first Opening Day I'd ever gone to. My two brothers, two cousins and two friends and I got permission to skip school. We were going to get bleacher tickets, which were pretty cheap back then. It was a typical, opening-day, bleacher crowd, not for young kids like we were.

The gates were late opening, and everyone was getting pretty rowdy. You could hear in the background, some of the older attendees at the game, probably college kids, were getting a little drunk back there and were starting to rock some cars. It was pretty ugly. We kept getting pushed and ended up at the front of the line. Out there in the bleachers, back then, the gates rolled up. The crowd heard the gates start to open, and they all started pushing forward. The gates rolled completely up, and—so I wouldn't get crushed up against the gate— I kind of ducked and I fell. There was a big pig-pile, and I was at the bottom. At fifteen, I was pretty little, probably ninety pounds, soaking wet. I lost my brothers and cousins and didn't know where they were, and I was having a difficult time breathing. I really thought I was going to die. I was really scared. I just knew this was "it." It got worse in a big hurry. It felt like the top of my head was going to explode.

Some guy, and I have no idea who it was—I tried to look for him afterward—saw me turning purple. I remember him grabbing me by my arms and pulling me out, and he ran me to the first aid room. I really think that if the man had not grabbed me and lifted me up, I would have been dead. I couldn't breathe. I was trying to take breath in and it just wasn't coming in. He thought I was dead. I had broken every surface blood vessel in my body and all the blood vessels in my eyes. After first aid, they sent me over to Childrens Hospital to get some internals checked out. I ended up at the hospital and didn't get to see any of the game. I was there all the rest of the day and got home about dark. I looked in the mirror and did not recognize myself. My eyes were all full of blood. They stayed red for three months, and I had to wear sunglasses for all that time. It was my last year of junior high, and for a going-away present from junior high, Clark Junior High School gave me a free helicopter ride into Fenway Park for opening day that following year.

I played football in high school so I did feel a little bit of a reaction from that pileup at Fenway. It was kind of a bizarre feeling—I didn't want to be at the bottom of a big pileup in football so I switched my position from tailback to split end.

You see the rushing crowds at rock concerts on TV, and it's scary. You see the people dying in the fire in the night club in Rhode Island a few months ago, and see the trampling, and it's just awful.

That gate is not there any more. There used to be four gates in the back in the bleachers, and now there are only three. They blocked it off, and I don't know why, but it's not there.

❧ ❧ ❧ ❧ ❧ ❧ ❧ ❧ ❧

Bo Jackson's real name is Vincent Edward Jackson. He was named after Vince Edwards who played the title role in his mother's favorite TV show, *Ben Casey*.

FENWAY PARK—THE LAST REFUGE OF SCOUNDRELS

GERRY MURPHY

Gerry Murphy, 67, Wellesley, MA, retired in 1998 after teaching high school social studies for forty-one years.

My father took me to my first game in 1944. I'll never forget it. Tex Hughson pitched. I loved Tex Hughson. It was the last game that Tex Hughson played before he went off to military service. I thought it was great! I found out that his first name was Cecil. I thought. "Wow, what a great name!" It was just tremendous!

Interestingly enough, that was when I became a Red Sox fan. I first became conscious of baseball and players in 1942. I just became fascinated with names. Spud Chandler—what a great name, Spud! And Sig Jakucki, a mediocre pitcher for the old St. Louis Browns; and King Kong Keller—oh, my gosh! What a name!

We sat between home plate and third base and watched Hughson pitch. I do remember the park and the signs out in left field and around the park. Lifebuoy Soap; Gem Blades…Lifebuoy Soap, that goes way back. I don't think they make it anymore.

When I got a little older, I worked. On Saturday and Sunday, I would stand in the middle of Inman Square in Cambridge, at the old Liggett Drug Store and sell Sunday newspapers from six to nine in the morning. I would use that money to go to the ballpark, sure.

I used to go out with my friends, and we got hot dogs and Richardson's Root Beer outside the park. It would cost a nickel. I remember that, five cents for root beer. I don't recall about the hot dog. My mom didn't pack me a lunch. I didn't want her to.

In those days, you could go into the park two or three hours before the game. We'd watch batting practice, and buy a bag of peanuts for a nickel. Eat the peanuts, then eat the sandwich. By then, the game was ready to start. But it was so much fun to see those guys belting the ball over the wall.

After the game, some of them would talk to us and sign autographs. Now the interesting thing here was that the Braves players were there, too, but I was really enamored by the Red Sox. The Braves players were much friendlier and not only did they autograph for us but they spent time with us. But I absolutely felt I was a Red Sox fan because they had the big home run hitters; they had the nicer ballpark. The Red Sox were a more exciting team. They would win 9-8—you know, American League baseball. It didn't bother us that the Sox players didn't sign autographs as much, but I do have one memory of Johnny Pesky signing autographs and rubbing the top of my head. "How are you doing kid?" he said. I went, "God, I'm in heaven!" Oh boy, I was eight or nine years old. It was a thrill. "Hey, Johnny Pesky touched my head!" Everybody says he's a wonderful guy. He certainly appears that way from what little I know of him.

We used to talk to some of the players. During batting practice, we'd be down there trying to get autographs and some would come over. Another player I liked a lot was George Metkovich. It started because of his nickname, "Catfish." He gave me his autograph, and we chatted a couple of times. One time, he said, "I remember you!" I don't know if he did or not, but he said he did. I loved the nickname, "Catfish" Metkovich. We were at batting practice and we were down at the railing around first base or third base, and some of the players would come out of the batting cage, and we'd talk to them and yell to them. Most of them ignored you, but Metkovich came over.

Often in my years of teaching, I would use baseball as an example of something that happened in politics or in history. I would always make references to baseball. Occasionally, some of the females would say, "Mr. Murphy, can't you make a reference to opera?" I said, "No, baseball is important!" And then the boys would say, "Yeah, baseball is life!" And the girls would say, "Oh God, here we go again!" I was always doing that sort of thing because baseball is a metaphor for life. Or life is a metaphor for baseball.

If they win, that will be nice, but if they don't, that's their destiny. Really and truly, that's how I feel. I've come to grips with it. I feel a lot better about it. I haven't been in therapy to attain this; I got there all by myself. But it took me about fifty years to do it.

I've sworn the Red Sox off more than once. After '86, for the first two or so months of the '87 season, I didn't pay any attention to them. Casual; nothing; didn't watch them on TV; didn't listen to them on the radio. I thought I was over my addiction. I wasn't. That's why I've said, "How many times now, that you've said the heck with them?" Obviously, it's a character flaw! Maybe it's genetic. I don't know what it is. Human beings, what do they call it—the "Stockholm Syndrome." You know it dealt with the people who were held hostage by somebody, and they try to befriend that person and get them to like them. Maybe there's something to that. Hostages start identifying with their captors. Maybe it's the optimism, the naivete; maybe it's self-flagellation. They'll get me interested and excited again, and then they'll disappoint me.

I was up in St. Louis for the first time visiting my son, David, and we went to the ballpark. In the second or third inning, I said, "Why don't we get something to eat." So I stand up, and this young woman comes down to me and says, "Sir, we'll get that for you." I said, "What?" I paid her the money and she got the beer and the Coke. Later in the game, I turned to my son, and said, "I'm just going to walk around the park just to get a different perspective."

Out in left field I was talking to the fellow sitting at the gate. In order to get into the lower seats, you had to walk past the security person. I said, "I'm here from Boston." He said, "I've been to Fenway Park." I asked, "Could I just walk down here for a minute?" He said, "Oh sure!" So I go down there and I look at the perspective, and I come back to his point. And I said, "Thank you very much." He said, "You're from Boston right? Do you want to feel at home?" I said, "What?" He said, "I've been to Red Sox games at Fenway Park. Would you like to feel like you are still at Fenway Park?" I said, "Yeah!" So he screamed, "Sit down, you bum!" I said, "Oh, thank you! A touch of home!" It was his impression of Fenway Park, "Sit down, you bum!" Those Midwesterners are obnoxious in their politeness. I'll never get used to that. I treat them respectfully because of that.

The romantic part of my nature says let Fenway Park be. There is the intimacy of the park. The seats are uncomfortable. There is gum that was there in 1944. It's the environment, the atmosphere.

When it got a little slow at the park, my friend and I would play games. Okay, we'd have to come up with a player like say, Dewey Evans. Then we'd have to come up with a player with the last name that began with F, the next letter. It didn't only have to be a Red Sox player, any major leaguer—whoever played. And we would get into some esoteric names. We did this a lot, but one thing stands out to me. He thought he had me one day, and he said "I." The loser had to buy the other guy a hot dog. I said, "Clarence Iott." And some fan sat up in back of us two or three rows. He says, "I've been listening to you guys. Who is Clarence Iott?" And it started a discussion.

I'll tell you who Iott was. He was a virtual non-entity. He pitched for the old New York Giants for about six weeks. His first game he ever pitched in the major leagues was a shutout. He was gone quickly. You're talking to somebody who ate, slept and drank baseball as a kid. I read *The Sporting News,* I read everything. I'm getting old and forgetful because the synapses don't work as well as they used to, but I had an incredible memory. His nickname was "Hooks" Iott. He pitched for the New York Giants, got three wins.

But the point that I was making is that it got other people involved. People were listening to us. This happened often when we went to Fenway. And this was my logic: the point is that intimacy, that terrible seating. People around could hear your conversation, and they'd join in. Nobody objects. It's just a fun thing. My one lasting memory that always comes to mind first, when it comes to Fenway Park, is that. At Fenway, they're not talking cooking recipes or whatever, and they are not talking Patriots. It's baseball, absolutely. People jump in and out of the conversations. It's terrific. It's at its best. That's why I love the game, and I love the atmosphere and everything about it.

A LOT OF OLD PEOPLE LIVE IN FLORIDA...WITH THEIR PARENTS

DON SHEA

Don Shea, 51, is the present CEO of City of St. Petersburg, Florida, Downtown Partnership, an economic development group.

When I was younger, I imagined that I was in the Red Sox lineup. I'd try to be like Yaz. I'd hit a homer to the opposite field to win a game late against the Yankees. I just admired him. He worked really hard. He was Catholic. Later when I played, I played first base for a while and I wanted to be "not" like George Scott. If you needed to ground into a double play, he was your man.

The spring of '75, I went with a buddy of mine from graduate school. We sat in the bleachers there, as we frequently did. We happened to sit next to a couple of guys who were just recent college graduates, in fact they'd graduated a couple of weeks earlier from UCLA. Their summer trip was to visit every Major League ballpark. They were in a Volkswagen bus, a classic thing of the mid-1970s, going from ballpark to ballpark. They had elaborate charts showing the schedules of all the teams so they could be sure whenever they arrived in a given city that the team was at home. That's something I've always wanted to do ever since I saw those guys. In those days, you could go to the Fenway bleachers with no money, after your dollar to get in, and get fed. People were passing around spaghetti dinners. It was a festival. Particular if the story got started that, "Hey, these guys just got here from UCLA and they're on this incredible summer trip and...." They'd start passing over the spaghetti and bread. It was great. Now the teams just want to make all that money from the food so you can't even sneak in a spaghetti dinner anymore!

I always felt like, no matter where you were in Fenway Park, Luis Tiant was going to look you in the eye at some point in the game because of the way he wound up. He had a commercial for a company called California Paint, which was a paint dealer, not a manufacturer. I remember that in his broken Cuban English, he would say, "I am the big job pitch, and taking it from me, California Paint…."

I was in Fenway one day on the rail just outside the Red Sox dugout near Heinz Kluetmeier, a photographer for years and years with *Sports Illustrated*. He was doing a feature on Bill "Spaceman" Lee. Early in the morning before anybody ever got to Fenway, Kluetmeier had him out there on the mound wearing a NASA spacesuit, winding up. That picture made it around later, but nobody at Fenway saw it that day. I was sitting next to Kluetmeier, and this guy's got a motor winder on and is really going through a lot of film. I say to him, "Boy, you really are using a lot of film." He looked me in the eye and said, "Tomorrow, I'm flying first class to London, all expenses paid. Film is cheap, compared to time." I loved Lee. I liked the fact that he was irreverent, and he drove Zimmer out of his mind. Reggie Cleveland, Ferguson Jenkins and Bill Lee had this group of malcontents. Zimmer referred to them as the "Buffalo Heads." That was enough for me. I loved the guy. He won seventeen games three times in a row. He put the numbers up in a pretty respectable way. Then he dabbled in some stupid, stupid things like that Leephus pitch. He just didn't care enough about the things that you're supposed to care about.

People bring a lot of beach balls to the bleachers. One time Bob Stanley was out in the bullpen, and he got so irritated when a ball fell into the bullpen. He took a steel rake—the pitchers used to grow tomatoes out in the bullpen—that was out there and in slow motion slays the beach ball by bringing this rake up over his head and chopping down like a guillotine on this beach ball and threw it back up into the stands.

THEY TOOK THE "UGH" OUT OF DOUGHNUTS

BILL SILK

Bill, age 59, and his wife, Ellen, won a Dunkin' Donuts contest in 2002...the prize? A trip inside the Green Monster. They reside in Milton, Massachusetts.

Your dream, if you're a Red Sox fan, is to get inside the Green Monster. Dunkin' Donuts had a Sports Dream Contest, both last year and this year. You can buy coffee and you get pull-offs, or you can send your name in. I sent my name in and was fortunate enough to win. We went out to Fenway Park along with Jackie MacMullan, who writes for *The Boston Globe*—who grew up in a suburb of Boston—Westwood. She always wanted to go to the Green Monster. The former ownership wouldn't let her go. She tried for ten years. She was all excited. She was finally out there. She was as bad as we were. She had to do a couple of interviews for TV. We went out to the Green Monster, and it was interesting. Out in the outfield, they've got this brown substance, which looks like dirt, but it's not; it's sort of like a wood-chip substance. My wife and I went into the Green Monster, and it's made of sheet metal—the **scoreboard**. You hear a ball hit off that, and it's unbelievable. You go in, and there's a step, and you can look out through the slits in the scoreboard. You're at eye-level with the grass—unbelievable view. You can move around. They have the slits at different positions on the outfield. You can walk around and get different views of the ballpark. It's just absolutely

The Philadelphia Athletics moved to Kansas City in 1955. The A's bought the scoreboard of the Boston Braves and utilized it until they moved to Oakland in 1968.

unbelievable to see. Brian Daubach was playing in left field. We said, "How you doing, Brian?" He would talk back to my wife while we were out there. He was a nice guy.

On the inside, it's bigger than you think, and it's in better shape than you think. The concrete was reasonably new. The two young fellows, both nice guys, who are out there, have been there for years. They have a wealth of knowledge. They went to school at University of New Hampshire. There are slots for you to drop the score down into. During the inning we were out there, there was no score, and I got to drop the zero down through the slot. It was quite a feeling to do it. Inside there they have the signatures of Ted Williams, Ken Griffey, Jr., Mickey Mantle and other great ball players. We signed our names inside on the concrete, up where the ceiling would be, the concrete girder. It was just a great experience.

These guys who work inside us told us that a number of years ago, when Ken Griffey was with Seattle, they got a call during the game from the press box that all the out-of-town scores were wrong. Evidently, Griffey had changed them during outfield practice, but they got all the heat. They were wondering what had happened. The next day, Griffey came over to them and said, "Hey, did you get a call from upstairs yesterday?" They said, "It was you. It was you!" He was laughing around with them. I guess he's quite a jokester.

After we were out in the Green Monster, we went back in that garage door that opens in the outfield there and they had seats for us up behind home plate in the grandstand. It was very, very nice, a great experience. Everybody was good to us. They took us on a tour of the press box and the broadcast booth. All my friends wished they could have won. They wanted me to enter them this year, so I did.

What's interesting is my wife, Ellen, won this year's Dunkin' Donuts contest. She got to go and skate with Joe Thornton, captain of the Bruins. She got to go in after one of their practices.

We *love* Dunkin' Donuts.

BITS AND BITES, BEGGED AND BORROWED

FENWAY PARK

Every year I bring my oldest boys with me and a couple of friends and we go on a road trip to a different ballpark. We were at Fenway for the first time. They have these old urinals there that are just troughs. I turned around and there was my seven-year-old son trying to wash his hands in it. He had never seen one before. "Wow, look at this big sink!" he said. I said, "Sean, don't." Too late! That's my Fenway memory.

———PATRICK HOGAN, 44, Brooklyn, NY, Yankee fan

Jimmy Hain

If you were to come into my special room in my house, you'd sit in an old Fenway bleachers seat and you'd hang your coat in Luis Tiant's old locker. I got that in the early 1970s through a friend who had gotten a tip that Fenway Park was being remodeled. He and I went over to the ballpark and my friend "sold" himself to the grounds keeper.

The seats and some old lockers were stacked in a pile. I asked the guys from the grounds crew, "Where are these going?" One guy said, "They are going to the dump." I said, "Could I get a couple?"

The guy said, "Haywood Sullivan, the general manager, is coming in and you'd better not get caught in here." At the time, I worked for a construction company. I called up the office and was able to get a truck. My friend and I took five or six sets of the bleacher seats and two lockers. The seats had been broken up so they were only two-attached. I took a bleacher seat and a locker to my office, and when people came in, they'd sit in the bleacher seat and hang their coat in the locker.

The locker I have has a cigar holder in it. It's a standing metal locker. The legs are about four or five inches off the ground and there's metal, woven, fence-like wire on each side and a metal tarp, a shelf and a couple of hooks. The cigar holder is plastic. The guy at Fenway told me it had been Luis Tiant's locker. I wish they had left the nameplate on it. The guy said the only Red Sox players who smoked cigars at that time were Carl Yastrzemski and Luis Tiant.

——**JIMMY HAIN**, 71, Medfield, MA

Duffy Lewis played left field for the Red Sox in the early 1900s, and there was this little cliff, really it was about three feet of dirt against the wall that people called Duffy's Cliff. When Fenway Park was originally built in 1912, somebody made a mistake on the measurements, and the wall didn't come down to the grass, so they built up this mound of dirt and sod. Someone always had an excuse for why it was there, but they didn't remove it until they remodeled Fenway Park.

——**KEN HERMES**, 95, raised in Roxbury, MA

Here's a funny story. And it really embodies what a Red Sox fan is all about. In 1988, I went to a game in early April. I had spectacular seats, which I normally don't have. But I was in the second or third row, right by the coach's box, first base side. There were a couple of close plays early on in that game that were called against the Red Sox by the first base umpire. So I turned to my friend, and I said, "Geez, let's look up that umpire's number because he's starting to really bug the crap out of me." So we looked up his number in the scorebook, and by God, it's Larry Barnett! Of course, he's the umpire who decided that there was no interference in the 1975 World Series. So I waited for it to be very quiet at the ballpark. Dwight Evans, of all people, was playing first base. It was his second-to-last year with the team. And it was just a perfect moment. There was a real quiet settling over Fenway. And I shouted out, "Hey Larry, I still think it was interference on **Armbrister**!" Well, everyone around me started to laugh. And I thought, "Okay, that was a pretty good line!" And then I noticed Dwight Evans starting to chuckle to himself. And then Barnett started to laugh.

The inning finally is over. Barnett slowly walked near to where I'm sitting, looks up at me and says, "Cripes, you guys from Boston—

> Catcher's interference is called approximately ten times during a major league season. Batters interference with a catcher is called approximately twice per year.

you got memories like elephants! Won't you ever give it up?" I looked at him and I said, "Never!"

Earl Weaver used to talk about Fenway being the only place that he ever managed where sort of the whirl of the crowd could be heard when there would be a ground ball to shortstop in anticipation of a double play. He said, "Most of the time, most people aren't paying attention, so it would happen and then everybody would applaud, but Red Sox fans would start to applaud before it actually happened."

——SHAUN KELLY, 48, Teacher, Greenwich, CT

Fenway Park is probably my least favorite part about rooting for the Red Sox. The ballpark is cute, and I love going because I can see all my friends walk by all the time, because everybody's so close, But I would like a new one. I'm not married to Fenway! My husband hates Fenway. He doesn't like to go with me. It's crowded. The seats are uncomfortable. The fans are obnoxious. There are about 4,000-5,000 really bad seats. There are seats near poles; seats in right field that actually face the bullpen; they don't even face home plate. Yeah, way in right field, those seats are terrible.

——ARLENE CROTTY, 51, Atlanta, GA

Fenway Park is expensive. Partly, it's just old Fenway Park, which is just my favorite ballpark. It's just a wonderful ballpark. I think people arc willing to pay for the experience. Maybe even these days, the sense that it won't be around that much longer. I think John Updike got it just right. Lyrical band box where everything is in sharp focus; everything is close. There's no parking, you're so close to the field and you seem so much a part of the action. And the Green Monster, which is a kind of legend! I like the old antique quality of it too. You really feel like you're back in the 1900s or something. Inevitably nothing lasts forever. It's getting pretty creaky and rusty. I'm sure they'll tear it down.

——JOHN GORDON, 57, Mystic, CT

In 1969 when I was 14 years old, I had the chance to go to an Orioles game by myself, but the astronauts were expected to make an afternoon landing on the moon and I didn't want to miss it. There was this incredible anticipation about whether the landing was going to be successful or not. That was high drama at the time.

I decided to go to the game, but in the back of my mind I kept thinking, "I should be home watching the lunar landing on TV." All of a sudden in about the middle of the fifth inning, the P.A. announcer came on. He deliberately dragged out the words, "The Apollo astronauts…" There was about ten seconds of silence. Everyone in the stadium was saying, "Come on, come on, spit it out!" "…have made a successful landing on the lunar surface." People cheered for twelve minutes. I have never in my life seen an ovation like that. Nothing has ever come close. I'm getting goose bumps just remembering it. The place went berserk. There was a sold-out crowd; it was a sunny afternoon. It was really amazing. The cheering never stopped. No world championship has ever gotten an ovation that long.

———MIKE DONOVAN, 47, raised in southeast Boston

When I had a summer job at the then-First National Bank of Boston, I remember sneaking out one or two afternoons from work to go to a game. I had this job that had me in multiple places, which was great. I had multiple floor responsibilities. That's where I met my friend, Carl. We were both in this summer job program there. We did not quite understand that if you go watch an afternoon game at Fenway, you will come back quite sunburned. It became very hard to explain that.

———MARK STARR, 55, Newton, MA

You can't talk about the Red Sox in Fenway Park without mentioning the Citgo sign. It's a fixture that's been there since I can remember and maybe even my mother will be able to tell you when they put it there. You can see the Citgo sign from hills all over the city. You know where Fenway Park is because you can see it.

———JANE WOYCIK, 38, Westwood, MA

I didn't find the Yankee fans offensive in New York, but I find them extremely offensive in Fenway Park when I watch a Red Sox-Yankee game, actually to the point now where I would rather not go to a Red Sox-Yankee game anymore. I tend to always be surrounded by really rude loud abusive people from New York. I sit behind home plate in the grandstand seats about ninety-five percent of the time, along the aisle on the left side of the screen. It's where the wheelchair section is. I know where to go to get those seats. I don't buy those seats. I never sit where I buy a seat. I usually get moved two or three times in a game when people who have the seat I'm sitting in find me in their seat. But I do get a good view of every game. Most people who go to

Fenway in seats like that don't own the seats. They're jumping around. There are no ushers in the grandstands. There are no rules.

I do think the Red Sox fans are extremely intense. They follow the pitches. I sit by home plate so I'm watching people who are really watching the game, in my opinion. There's so much electricity in the air most games that aren't blowouts. I can come away from a game almost having a headache because of the intensity of a Red Sox game. The fans are into it. They are extremely knowledgeable fans. It's not what I would call a relaxing experience. It's more of a tense experience. As I grow older, I find myself wanting to go less, not more. I'm growing older, so I look around and I don't see fights anymore and I don't see as much drinking anymore. That has definitely improved. They don't allow beer after the bottom of the seventh, and at least behind home plate it's really pretty civilized now.

———TY WATERMAN, 55, Attleboro, MA

I was the one who tried to take the Coke bottles down from Fenway Park. In March 1997, the Red Sox allowed Coca-Cola to place ridiculous, giant Coke bottles on a light stanchion over the left field wall. On April 9, two days before the Fenway opener, I snuck into the park, waited until about one a.m., and climbed up with a hack saw and an adjustable wrench. The reason? Principle. Fenway Park is the oldest ballpark in America. It's been called a Mecca. Baseball is America's pastime, and we have a responsibility to preserve what is sacred. Would we allow Coke bottles to be put on the steeple of the Old North Church, or on the masts of Old Ironsides? Or how about in the hand of the Statue of Liberty?

Now, six years later, Fenway has been littered with a ridiculous, giant exploding Hood Milk bottle on a right field stanchion, a Fleet Bank MPH sign on the center field light stanchion, and there's been talk of McDonald's giant golden arches behind home plate! Integrity and principle are being ruled by economics.

———NAME WITHHELD BY REQUEST

It took me a long time to understand why the Red Sox had so many batting champions and why Fenway Park is such a hitter's park. Back in the 1950s and 1960s, the Red Sox had these lumbering players who could hit it out of the park. I wondered if it was because the park was smaller than others. I was thinking about it terms of, "Well, gosh, the right field is still 340 feet and it's 370 in center field," and so on. I didn't realize the affect of the tiny little foul areas, so that all those foul balls don't get caught as they do in a big stadium. Therefore, the batter has an obvious advantage, over playing in, say, Dodger Stadium.

——ROBERT BELL, 57, Williamstown, MA

I'll never forget when Tony Conigliaro got hit by the ball. August 18, 1967. I was there that night and I can still hear the sound of it, like something hitting a piece of metal. I was on the third base side in what they now call the upper boxes, about fifteen rows behind, almost in line with the on deck circle. The fans stood motionless. People didn't open their mouths. Everybody just stood there in silence. I don't think the fellow who was with me and I said a word to each other for fifteen or twenty minutes. I thought Tony was gone. The pitcher walked about halfway to the plate and a couple of the players stood around him. It was like the day the world stood still! What a player!

When my wife and I were dating—going to the ballpark would be the first place to go. I was such a sports fan, and you'd go through and push through the crowd and go down to get a hot dog. There was something about the crowd at Fenway Park always moving around. You go into some of these stadiums and places today and they're just wide, wide concourses. To me, it was a romantic place. One thing about Fenway Park, and I hope they really don't change it, it draws you together—you're always crowded. You're always in a crowd, where you're standing to get a hot dog, or standing to get in the men's room, and there's a crowd at that street there, and you always stand there and all of a sudden you say hello to somebody and the next thing you know you're in a discussion about the ball game. It gives you a feeling of "being there."

——JIMMY HAIN, 71, Retired construction estimator, Medfield, MA

The people who sit next to us, I adore them. We have a bond. We share games. She was sitting on the edge of her seat praying during Derek Lowe's no-hitter. She took a picture of exactly how I felt. Then she took a picture of us. We were glowing. I have that picture. We are glowing like candles.

I've never once said, "Yankees suck" in public. I've never been rude. I've never pushed. I've never said anything to a gutter mouth, scumbag who might have sat behind me. And I've had really disgusting people sit around me. I've really had some really tasteless people sit around me. That kind of Red Sox fan is out there. They are out there, and they are disgusting. They are loud, and they are rude. But I don't think they are real fans. I think they are drunks who have nothing better to do, who happen to have some money in their pocket, or maybe were given a ticket. Neither my husband nor I drink. That's why I love the people next to us. They don't drink either. It's funny because they don't chant gross things.

——JOCELYN SMITH, 33, Hampden, CT

Sometimes my buddies and I like to play "mound ball." It's a game that we play between innings after the third out is made. Whoever has the ball, whether it is the outfielder who catches the third out, or the catcher has the ball because it was a strike out—they always toss the ball back to the mound. Everyone antes in a dollar. So the more people you have, the more money in the pot you have. If the ball is thrown back to the mound, and it lands on the mound, the person who is holding the money gets to keep it. If it rolls off the mound, or if it doesn't go to the mound, or say the catcher just tosses it to one of the umpires, or the umpire puts it away and they pull out a new ball and give it right to the pitcher—then the money is passed to the next person. And it's always every half inning, where it's, "All right, it's third out, let's see where the ball goes!" So that's one of the games we play at Fenway. You start with $3 or $4, and sometimes it gets up to $20-$24.

——SCOTT GREENE, 32, Nashua, NH

I went to the game where Dick Pole was hit in the face with a line drive. They used to have these 75-cent general admission seats, for kids if you were under sixteen, during weekday games. But they were in the grandstands, Sections 1–7. It was during the day. It was afternoon games, so I'd go with my friends. I was about thirteen. We would sneak down into the box seats. One game, I remember we went to in '75, they were losing 6-3 in the ninth to the White Sox. It's funny how you remember these things. With one on, and one out, they just rallied with just one single after another. They won 7-6. The funny thing was, the White Sox brought in Goose Gossage, and then the last batter—Rick Burleson hit a line drive, and the White Sox shortstop jumped. He was six or eight inches away from it when he leaped, and it was over his glove for the winning hit. It was Bucky Dent who was the shortstop for the White Sox. It was so ironic, to think later of those two guys. We went crazy. To be losing by three runs in the ninth, and have this amazing comeback. It's incredible.

——**BRIAN KILEY**, 41, Writer, *Conan O'Brien Show*

When I was about twenty-one, I worked at a department store called Sims. I called in sick and a buddy and I went to an afternoon game. Back then, the Sox played a lot more day games. We went in to the game. I had a particular boss at the time who was really strict. He used to keep a little black book. If you made any type of mistake, he would jot it down—if you had excessive tardiness, or whatever, he would make little notations in this book.

I had kept in touch with my friends from Sims, and years later, we were out one night with the assistant manager at the time I worked there. The manager who had documented everything had been fired or left the company, and this friend had gotten hold of the little black book. In the black book was the notation that I had called in sick to go to the Red Sox game. To this day, I have no idea how he found out. I was not with another employee from there. I was with a friend who had nothing to do with Sims. It reminds me of the Ferris Bueller movie.

——**WAYNE TUMBLESON**, 39, raised in East Greenwich, RI

There's a website called "Sons of Sam Horn," and my name on that is "Zupcic Fan" because the Red Sox had a player name Bob Zupcic. He was a fairly good hitter, and I was at a game with my friend, Vinny, and my youngest daughter, Laura, who at the time was about eight. Laura never talks. She just sort of sits around and listens. At a game, Vinny and I would be chattering away, and Laura would just sort of be there. She probably went through the entire nine innings without saying a word. It's the last of the ninth, and it's a tie score, and Zupcic comes up. It would be impossible for me to convey to you how unusual this is, but Laura suddenly screams out, "He's gonna hit it over the Green Monster!" And Vinny and I look at her like, "Where the heck did that come from?" The next pitch, Bob Zupcic hits it over the Green Monster and the Red Sox win the game. All these people are slapping five, and they're carrying her around on their shoulders.

I always refer to it as the only purely psychic experience I've ever believed in my entire life, because I'm telling you, there is no way this kid would ever have yelled that kind of thing out! I talked to her about it, and she said she had no idea why she yelled it out. She hardly ever pays attention to the game. It was unbelievable! That was my most memorable experience at Fenway.

——BUD POLLAK, 56, Norwalk, CT

One of the things I love about baseball, the game, are its possibilities for narrative and its narrative beauty. It's a game of individuals—individual confrontations and the accumulation of individual stories. I love to read about games in the paper and articles almost as much as I like to watch them. I like to hear how people express themselves.

Sherm Feller had a unique voice on the Fenway P.A. system, somewhat deep. He spoke in a kind of deliberate way. He had this inimitable fashion with which he introduced players. If Jim Rice was coming to bat he'd say, "Now batting for the Red Sox, left fielder, Rice—Jim Rice." "Or, Yastrzemski —Carl Yastrzemski."

Feller retired about ten years ago, and I don't think he's still alive. One of my fantasies is that when I retire, I'll go apply for that job. I don't know a lot about Feller, but I do know that he also was an author who wrote the book for some Broadway shows.

To me the Red Sox are inseparable from Fenway. For me, Fenway Park is a kind of holy place. I don't want it torn down.

——REVEREND CARL HEICK, Minister, Centerville, MA

The first time I ever went to Fenway Park was when I was maybe five or six. I remember sitting somewhere on the first base side in the grandstand because I could see the Citgo sign. It was at night and I thought it was so cool. I'm a little 5- or 6-year-old kid, and I see the sign lighting up and the triangle closing and opening. There were so many people and I had never seen that many people. It was just my dad and me, and I remember that I was so overwhelmed that I was scared and crying. That's my only recollection of my first game.

A few years later, in 1982, I was eleven, and I remember Carney Lansford had won the batting title the year before, which was a big thing, because he was the first Red Sox right-handed hitter to win a batting title. In 1982, he was going for an inside-the-park home run and he slid into home plate, got hurt and left the game. An unknown rookie came in to take his place at third base, and that was Wade Boggs.

——SCOTT GREENE, 31, Nashua, NH

My family builds our trips to Boston around going to Red Sox games. I try to go late in the summer or early in the year, hoping they'll be in the play-offs, hoping I can go in September or October to the ballpark. I love going early in the year, in April or May. I love those early games when it's anyone's bet, and it's fresh and new. A lot of my love for the Red Sox—and I get emotional when I think about it—is that I love Fenway Park. I think it's one of the most beautiful places in the world. When you walk up, it's so dirty and so old, but so pure. You walk out and see that field and see how small it is, as though you can touch the other side. I love that ballpark. I definitely don't think it should be torn down. I see the practical side that it needs to be torn down, that there needs to be something else. But, no, I think baseball is being destroyed by these "super parks." The fun's being taken away. I love Fenway Park, the way it looks, the way it smells, the way it feels.

——ROBERTA MOCKENSTURM, 46, Clearwater, FL

When I was fourteen years old, I knew a guy named Tim McAuliffe, who had a sporting goods business in Boston. McAuliffe supplied the uniforms for all the major league teams at that time. One Saturday, I went into the store to buy a baseball or a glove from him. He said, "You got a few minutes, Jimmie?" I said, "Sure." He said, "I'm taking all the Red Sox jackets over to the ballpark in my beach wagon. Could you help me?" I said, "Sure."

When McAuliffe and I finished unpacking all the jackets in the locker room, he said to me, "Here. Why don't you take one home for yourself?" I took the jacket home, and then because of my good grades, I was allowed to start going to ball games.

I wore that jacket to my first Opening Day game fifty-seven years ago. As life proceeded, I went to my second Opening Day, and third, and now I've worn it for fifty-seven straight Opening Days. I only wear it on Opening Day. It has a royal blue background with maroon and black trim and the words, "Red Sox" on one side. The old-fashioned jackets were reversible, gray on the inside, so you could turn it inside out and wear it on a damp day.

On my fiftieth Opening Day, the scoreboard went blank at the top of the sixth inning and then an announcement appeared in which the Red Sox thanked me for being such a supportive fan. I have a big photograph of the scoreboard.

——JIMMY HAIN, 71, Redfield, MA

A group of about thirty comedians used to get together and go to a game, usually the second or third game of the year. Opening day would be sold out. Game 2 would be serious Red Sox fans. It would be a day game. It was very sparsely attended early in the year like that, and it's freezing. I can remember, we would have ridiculous chants when a batter was up. I remember thirty of us chanting, "Hit the ball with the bat!" It was totally juvenile!

For some reason, I can remember in the seventh inning stretch everyone singing "Delta Dawn." I have no idea why. Someone started and everyone just joined in. But Mike Donovan, a really talented comedian, wouldn't sit with us. And even when we'd go with just four or five comedians, Donovan didn't like people talking during the game. He's a real serious baseball fan. If it was between innings, you could talk with him. But he didn't like to talk during the game.

——BRIAN KILEY, 41, grew up in Newton, MA

In 1982, I had a brand new custom van, best car we've ever had. The maiden voyage was to take the neighborhood kids to a ball game at Fenway Park. We loaded them all up, threw them in the van, and we must have had half a dozen or more. We get to the park. I hate Boston traffic. We could park in one of those parking places next to the park, but you never get out, and it costs you twenty bucks. Brand new van—they'll ruin it. So I told my son he was in charge, gave him tickets, and told him to take the kids in and find their seats while I go park the new van. I dropped them off at the front gate.

I went in concentric circles around Fenway Park for about half an hour. I wound up out by BU, which is probably a mile from Fenway Park. By then, it's almost game time. I stopped at a light, and there were a couple of guys with brown bags waiting for the subway. These guys knocked on the window. I rolled it down, and they said, "Hey, where you going? Are you going down to Kenmore Square?" I said, "Yeah, I'm going to the ball game. I'm trying to find a parking space." He said, "Mind if I get a ride?" I said, "No, hop in." So these two guys jump in, the door is open. I'm at a subway stop. Next thing I know, he's calling everybody over and they're getting in the van. The guy was a funny guy, to begin with, no question. He's inviting everybody in. He's a hot ticket. I don't know what's going on—people are climbing in. As it turns out, we finally got loaded up, closed the door, headed down, and I dropped them off right at the front gate to Fenway Park. They're laughing and joking and drinking their beer on the way down— had a wonderful little time. As they left, the guy said, "Hey, all you people in the back there, I want you to drop a buck on the seat on your way out." They all pour out like clowns in a circus car and there are all these dollars on the seat. I pick them up—

twenty-seven dollars. I had twenty-seven people in that van. They were crammed in like sardines. One good turn deserves another because, lo and behold, I turned the corner and right there— probably the number one parking space at Fenway Park—some girl was pulling out. I wound up with the number one parking space, went into the park, and "bingo" first pitch. Didn't miss a pitch.

When the first guy had gotten out, he said, "All right, after the game, we'll plan to meet you right here." I thought, "You've got to be kidding." But there they were…I made only six bucks on the trip back to the subway…same twenty-seven people, and the kids got squished… and loved it.

————JACK REILLY, 62, Andover native

Recently, I drove a guy from San Francisco by the park—he wanted to see Fenway Park. I told him that he was going to be surprised. When he's thinking of a ballpark, he's thinking about Pac Bell or Candlestick. For all of Candlestick's problems, you knew as you approached it, it was a ballpark. You see it from the highway coming around. So I drove up there, and I pulled to a stop, and the guy said, "Why are you stopping?" I said, "You see that red brick factory?" He said, "Yeah." I said, "Look up top what it says over the big gate there." He said, "THIS is Fenway Park?" I said, "Yeah, this is Fenway Park."

Everyone who goes there for the first time has the same experience. You go into this red brick place and you're in this kind of dark, dingy kind of place—it feels like you're in the bowels of the earth. You walk and finally come to a ramp and you walk up the ramp and, oh my God, all of a sudden this carpet appears before you. There's this big wall off to one side. That's the real fantasyland for me is walking into that park. Every time I see it, the thousands of times that I've been there, I'm still reminded a little bit of what it was like that first day when I was seven or so years old when my father took me there. I went there thinking we were going to see a playground of some kind. When you come up and out of this darkness into that magical place, it's an unforgettable experience.

——**DICK FLAVIN**, Retired media personality

I think it would be fine to put seats on top of the Monster. In 1991, my editor at the Globe said, "Why don't you write a piece about the city or just call it 'On Boston,' and we'll put it out front." So on opening day in 1991, I wrote a piece that said, "Tear Fenway Park down. Move somewhere else. It should be downtown, near the train station, right near everything." I got a lot of mail in brown-wrapping paper, red crayon, that sort of thing. "You are going to die." John Harrington, who owned the Red Sox then, didn't object because he was trying to get the city's attention to move, but the Red Sox were kind of passive on it, and the city didn't care, so it looks like they are stuck at Fenway for a long time. Boston is a very tight, small city. It's forty-six square miles, and there's no room.

——**MARTY NOLAN**, Former Columnist for *The Boston Globe*

In '87, which was the seventy-fifth anniversary of Fenway Park, I was running a summer institute for the Fulbright Commission for English teachers from around the world. Part of it was at the University of Minnesota, but a lot of it was a tour of the United States. The last stop was Boston. I was in charge of forty of these teachers. We got to Boston in August of '87 and were staying at the Park Plaza Hotel. There was this big bag of keys that I had to get out to them. Normally, I would be careful and efficient and go through and make sure they were in the right room. But we got to the hotel at about one o'clock, and the game started at one-oh-five. I had no idea whether it was a sellout or not. I just grabbed the bag and started throwing the keys at them and said, "You're in Boston now. You're on your own. I'll see you at dinner."

I raced upstairs to my room, tore off my clothes, put on a Red Sox shirt and Red Sox hat, jumped in a cab, got to Fenway about one-fifteen, one-twenty. Game had already started, and I had no idea whether or not I could get a ticket. It was a beautiful Saturday afternoon. There was a man outside selling a ticket. I'll never forget. I said, "I need a ticket. How much is it?" He said, "It's fourteen dollars." At that time, that sounded like a hundred dollars—fourteen dollar ticket—I never heard of a fourteen-dollar ticket. A baseball game might cost three dollars. I said, "Is it that good?" He said, "Trust me. This is the best seat you'll ever have in your life." I took a chance and bought it—for fourteen dollars. There was a season ticket, and it had the owner's name on it, del Negro.

I get in and I'm looking for the seat. It was in the first row overlooking the Red Sox on-deck circle. My only lament is that I had no camera—I usually take a camera to a game. I was five feet away from the Red Sox as they were in the on-deck circle. Before or since, I've never had a seat like this. All the people around me were very interested in me because apparently the previous week there had been a story about Mr. del Negro. He was a man from East Boston. He had not missed a game in forty years. The Globe had done this big profile of him and how he was "Mr. Red Sox" but he had gotten ill and his nephew was out there selling this ticket. I sat in Mr. del Negro's seat. The Red Sox won the game 14-2. They had a rookie catcher who never amounted to much, but he hit two home runs that day. It was as good as baseball has ever been for me—that August day in 1987. I still have the seventy-fifth anniversary of Fenway Park T-shirt. I can't fit into it anymore unfortunately, but my daughters wear it from time to time. I've been back to Fenway many times since then, but I don't know that anything will ever quite match that afternoon in 1987.

———RAY ARSENAULT, Directs Honors College at a southern University

My son, who is thirty years old, and I were at the last play-off game in 1990 when Oakland beat the Red Sox four straight. As we were leaving Fenway Park after the game, my son turned to me on the stairs and said, "You know, dad, I think in order for you to be at a Red Sox World Series, I'll have to dig you up from the grave."

———JIMMY HAIN, 71, Medfield, MA

Chapter 5

Playin' Favorites

Heroes, Like Memories, Never Grow Old

THEY MIGHT BE SLOW,
BUT THEY HAVE BAD HANDS.

DAVE MULVEY

Dave Mulvey, 46, of North Attleboro, just completed his sixteenth consecutive Fantasy Camp with former Red Sox stars.

Dave Mulvey (left) and Carl Yastrzemski

I had no idea what to expect going there for the first time. If you're a first-time camper, it's about thirty-five hundred dollars, plus your air-fare. The one Larry Marino runs, Sports Adventures, is about the cheapest one going. There's another one sponsored by the Red Sox that's approximately the same price that just started this year.

The first year I was able to go was '88. The first time you go, you figure it's going to be a one-shot deal. Before the week was over, I'd made my up mind I was going to go back, and it's been sixteen years. The first one was in Winter Haven. In '94 we moved over to Fort Myers.

Dick Radatz was fantastic. The first time I ever saw him was going in to Winter Haven, and I was a little late the very first day back in '88. I had never been there before and I got lost between the airport and the hotel. By then, everybody is inside. I don't know anybody. They're all inside the bar. They were all crammed in there. I go walking in—I figured that's where the crowd was so that must be all our people. The only stool open at the bar was next to Dick and Gary Bell. So I just sat there at the bar stool, and he's telling stories. They were having a beverage special that night, Mudslides, and he was pounding them down two at a time. Next thing you know, he reaches over and introduces himself. He asked me if I was with the camp, and I told him yes, and that it was my first year. He puts his arm around me, and that was it. We wound up closing up the bar that night. Dick and I have been friends ever since. I talk to him quite often.

We didn't get out of the bar until close to two o'clock. A lot of times back then, we'd mill around by the pool. They'd let you stay out there all night if you wanted to, which we did a few times. You have to be up early in the morning. I probably didn't get a whole lot of sleep that night anyway. It just got better every day since.

The next morning we do what we've got to do and we have our game, and I go back to the hotel. At Winter Haven, they had a main area where everybody congregated, and it was all centered around the pool and the lounge was off to the side. I come walking over to the pool area and there was a girl down there. Her ex-husband was one of the campers. She had been a Penthouse "Centerfold of the Month." She goes by the name of Dominique St. Croix. As I'm walking down by the pool, she's walking up out of the pool. She's got probably the skimpiest string bikini on you ever saw in your life. She was just gorgeous. I'm looking, and I said, "This is one of the campers?" Right then and there I knew I was coming back the next year. Ted Williams wound up being there that year. He latched onto her like a tick on a coon hound. They were almost inseparable the rest of the week. I've got pictures of them together.

That was how it started. This was my first full day down there. The second day was just as interesting. Bill Lee drives everywhere he goes. Bill is a baseball junkie. He's going to die playing baseball. He travels all over the world. If somebody says they've got a charity softball game, Bill goes. If he can drive, he drives there. He picked up this guy he knew and they drove from Vermont to Winter Haven, Florida, a two-day drive. Bill Lee's wife, Pam, was very pretty. She's lounging by the pool. This friend of Bill's is going around video taping everybody. I guess he kinda zoomed in on Pam a little bit. There was a setup in the lounge where they used to tape certain games during the day, and they would show them in the lounge at night. This guy puts his tape on the VCR at the lounge—it took about six people to hold Bill back. Bill wasn't too happy about the whole situation.

Now it gets to the end of the week, and the camper team plays a game against the pros. It just so happens this guy's team comes up. Bill Lee is playing in the outfield, and Dennis Bennett was pitching. This guy that was traveling with Bill comes up to bat, Bill comes dragging in from center field, and back then Bill could still throw pretty good. He's since hurt his arm, but then he could still throw hard. We're all saying, "Oh no, Bill's going to hit him. He's gonna hit him." Bill calls everybody in off the field, like Satchel Paige once did. They basically just laid down on the field. We just figured he was gonna smoke this guy. Even the camp director thought Bill was going to hit him. Bill just threw three fast balls down the pike. This guy struck out in three pitches. Bill says, "That's it." Bill jogs back out to center field and the game just went on.

Now, you've got to remember, these guys have got to ride all the way back to Vermont together. This guy came back to the camp for some years after that, and I don't ever recall them being close after that, but I don't think there was any other problem. That was Bill Lee's way of saying, "Okay, you did what you did, and I did what I did, and it's over."

The two main people that I really wanted to meet that first year were Bill Lee and Luis Tiant. Luis was everything I thought he'd be, probably the funniest man that ever lived. He's non-stop. He's a riot. I wasn't overly impressed with Bill Lee. He was in a world of his own back then. He was pleasant enough with everybody, but Bill's on his own plane, and you had to be his type of person back then, and I wasn't that crowd. Bill and I have kind of gotten friendly maybe the last five years. He was always nice to me, don't get me wrong, but it took that long for us to warm up to each other. I consider him a good friend now, and we'd all miss him if he wasn't at the camp.

We have a Hall of Fame, and you have to go a minimum of ten years to get in the Camp Hall of Fame. We have twenty-four people in the Hall of Fame with three more going in next year. That's twenty-seven people with a minimum of ten years. We have forty that are there five years or more. I think that's what's kind of different about our camp, compared to a lot of the others. Other camps don't really get a lot of repeating campers, for whatever reason.

Gary Bell and Dick Radatz have a kangaroo court they run a few times a week. Basically you get fined for certain things you do during the week. They'll get guys for wearing their wedding rings out in the field. Or just for doing stupid things. We had a camper one time, and it was real hot in Winter Haven, he was an older guy, and he had false teeth. He got heat stroke and threw up—he threw up his false teeth. In the process, he caught them. They fined him ten dollars for retching his teeth, but they gave him a five-dollar refund for catching them. That's the kind of things you get fined for down there, and there are a lot of strange things that happen.

You don't tell Gary Bell or Dick Radatz anything. If you do something stupid, you don't tell them because you're going to get nailed for doing it. I happened to be on Jose Santiago's team in that first year. He wears a partial plate. Jose was eating, and he thought he swallowed his teeth 'cause he gets done eating, and they're gone. Well, that was it. This happened the first night of the camp.

We were in a big room and they're up at the podium doing their fines. I'm sitting with Jose Santiago and Luis Tiant every night. Luis was just hysterical. So, they're having a nightly Jose Santiago "teeth update." Jose had to go down and get X-rayed to see if he had swallowed them. The doctor told him that if he did swallow them, he was going to pass them sooner or later. One night Radatz said Jose's ass ate his pillow. Every night, it got crazier and crazier and crazier. It just got to the point that almost the whole kangaroo court would be these jokes about Santiago's teeth. His wife goes to do the laundry at the end of the week—there are his teeth in his shirt pocket.

When I started going to the camp year after year, my friends were a little bit jealous and they thought I was a little bit crazy. By the end of the first year, I knew I was coming back another year. Then by the end of the second or third year, I knew I was going to keep going back as long as I could. Now it's just gotten to the point—I've made so many lifelong friends down there that there's no way—if I had to go in a wheelchair, I'd go in a wheelchair every year. That's just how good this is.

We just can't say enough about Larry Marino, the guy who runs the camp. About six of us were sitting by the pool one day, and we are all bombed, and Larry is there. One of my buddies has played semi-pro hockey in different countries. He said, "The camp's great, and I couldn't imagine having a better time than down here. Wouldn't it be kind of neat if we could put together a trip and play somewhere else at some other time during the year?" When he said this, I was just thinking maybe he was talking Arizona or somewhere else in the United States. Larry said, "Where would you like to go?" Mark said, "I don't know. I've played hockey in Europe." Larry said, "Tell you what, give me a couple of weeks after the camp, and I'll get back to you guys. Just let me know who'd be interested."

Larry used to be involved with Team USA, the Olympic baseball team, several years ago so he had some contacts over in Europe. He went home and made a few phone calls and about three weeks later, he calls us, "We've got a trip to Italy put together." That year we went over and played in Rome and Anzio and Naples. We played three years in a row. In 2000, we were in France, we saw the Concorde crash. We were the next plane in line from the Concorde on the runway at Charles DeGaulle Airport.

Before I began doing this, I had met a few of these guys here and there. I've always been into collecting baseball memorabilia and had met them at card shows. But that's one of those deals where you pay to get their autograph, you only have thirty seconds with them. But, did I ever think I'd be sitting there talking to my heroes on the phone? I just applied for a part-time job at McCoy Stadium with the Pawtucket Red Sox this year. Johnny Pesky was my main reference. I never, ever would have thought it. I never know when a day goes by, Johnny might call or Dick or Gary Bell.

Back in the early 1990s, Bobby Doerr called me. He was coming to town for a baseball card show, and he wanted me to come over and see him, have breakfast with him. I was planning on going to the show anyway, and he calls me up out of the blue, so I go down and meet him at the hotel and he buys breakfast. We must have sat there for three hours just talking baseball. He was asking me about the camp because he hadn't been there in a couple of years—seriously unbelievable. There are still days I still have a hard time believing this—even after sixteen years, I still have a hard time believing that it's come down to this—that I can sit and talk to these guys just like they're somebody off the street, like somebody I've known for years and years and years—a regular blue-collar worker. It's amazing.

George Scott was the worst I ever saw. He's not even allowed back at the camp anymore. His first year at the camp, he was trying to charge campers for his autograph. He's absolutely worthless. The last year he came to our camp he wouldn't even suit up and go out on the field with his team. He'd sit in the clubhouse all day. He was probably the only one I ever met that I could care less if I ever saw again. The sorry thing about it was I remember him playing, and he was one of my heroes, when I was a kid—great ball player, great first baseman, but absolutely worthless. I have nothing good to say about the man. I really don't—everybody I've ever met says the same thing.

Yaz was there in '91; he was paid to be there for the week. He might have spent a total of a day and a half there. He'd go out and do whatever little bit he had to do, very personable, take pictures with you, sign autographs, but then he'd go out fishing with his buddy who ran the clubhouse. I can't really say anything bad about him, other than he wasn't there as much as he should have been. The first year, the day he was leaving, he sets up a table in the locker room, and he sat there until he signed everything anybody wanted to have signed.

It should not have surprised me. I had been in a bad car accident back in '82, me and my family, and I spent nine weeks in the hospital. We had gotten burned in a car accident. The first time I got to meet Carl was in '82 when he was doing a card show in Boxboro. I was just out of the hospital and was still bandaged up pretty good. I was a mess. I stood in line for three hours to get up to him, and he was just rushing everybody through, signing and rushing everybody through. I was in line with my brother, and he was in worse shape than I was. When we got up to the table with Yaz, he stopped everything. "What happened to you? Do you want a picture taken?" Well, even if we had a camera with us, we wouldn't have wanted our pictures taken at that time. He must have kept us there for twenty minutes. Now everybody is complaining in line, and I couldn't really blame them. I mentioned that to Carl when I saw him again at the camp in '91, and he remembered it. He was great, asking how I'd been since then.

Without a doubt, we veterans go out of our way to make the new guys welcome. If they don't have a good time, we don't. Sixteen years of it, and I've probably met thousands of different people, and I don't ever recall anybody, anybody, having a bad time down there. It gets better because Larry tweaks things a little bit over the years, but I can never remember hearing anybody say they'd never come back again.

(For more information, log on www.sports-adventures.com or call 1-888-901-7529.)

Two Red Sox #7s: Dom DiMaggio and Trot Nixon

YASTRZEMSKI—GREAT NAME IF YOU'RE PLAYING SCRABBLE

RAY FOSTER

At 62, Ray Foster remains an ace pitcher on St. Petersburg, Florida's Half Century Club, but this retired Topsfield, Massachusetts truck driver grew up in Hamilton, about thirty miles north of Boston.

Back in the 1950s when I was a teenager, there was a place in Fenway Park where the ballplayers used to drive in, park their cars and then walk into the stadium. Us kids could stand right on the street and put our hand through the wrought iron fence and players like Dom DiMaggio and Billy Goodman would stop and sign autographs.

You could always tell when a big shot ball player arrived because he'd drive the fanciest car of the time—a Cadillac or similar model. But I always remember that Ted Williams drove a '49 Ford convertible. He would just park it, get out, and wouldn't stop to talk to anybody. He would buzz right by and walk through the gate. That was Ted Williams. Everybody would say, "Look, he's driving a '49 Ford and all the others have the Cadillacs." It was quite a thrill for a youngster to see something like that. Ted had an aura about him. People would say, "There's Ted Williams. There's Ted Williams." Everything would stop when he showed up.

Growing up, I always wanted to be Sammy White, the Red Sox catcher throughout the 1950s. I thought he was as good a catcher as Yogi Berra. He was an average hitter, nothing outstanding, but I just took a liking to him because I played catcher from Little League through high school.

Carl Yastrzemski will always be my number one favorite player. In 1967, he won the Triple Crown, and I was so excited and proud of him. In those days, when I'd go to Fenway Park, every time Yaz came to bat and his name was announced, there was a girl, probably in her twenties, who sat off to my left about two or three rows behind me, and she would stand up and ring a big bell—dong, dong, dong, dong, dong. Then she'd sit back down and hold her head down. She'd only do it when Carl Yastrzemski came up to bat. I became so curious. One time, an usher came by and I said, "Is that girl here all the time? Why does she do that?" The usher said, "Well, believe it or not, she's blind." I could not believe it. I said, "Are you serious?" He said, "She comes here every once in a while, and she sits there. She's blind, and she's a great fan of Carl Yastrzemski's. She just likes the atmosphere of being in Fenway Park."

Around that time, the Red Sox had a sales slogan on the radio like, "Being there is half the fun." It made me think of that blind girl because just being there was definitely half the fun for her.

Carl was always loyal to the team. I thought he was a great teacher. He taught players how to play the left field wall. I just admired the man especially when he got older. His knees and legs were bothering him, but he still played. I remember one time during his last season he got a hit and stretched it into a double. People gave him a standing ovation because he could barely run at that time.

I have the tape of his last game at Fenway where he ran around the outfield. I can watch that tape now, and it still brings tears to my eyes every time. I've always thought if someone asked me who I would like to meet in my life, it wouldn't be a president or someone like that. It would be Carl Yastrzemski. He was the greatest ballplayer I think I ever watched.

QUICK HITS AND INTERESTING BITS

HEROES

I remember my first disappointment in baseball was when I was about eight and my father took me to see Bill Monboquette and Earl Wilson. They had been twenty game-winners for the early Red Sox. My father and I were going down to the Commonwealth Armory and he said to me, "You can't meet them, Mike, but I can get you to see them. They're going to give a little speech." We went and saw them and on the way home, my dad kept asking me, "What's the matter, Mike? You seem like you didn't have a good time." What I never told him was that I was shocked that they didn't have their uniforms on. I thought ballplayers existed in their uniforms.

——MIKE DONOVAN, 47, Standup comedian

I'm absolutely amazed at Pedro Martinez. Pedro Martinez, to me, I'm watching one of the two or three greatest pitchers in the history of baseball. I just feel so fortunate. Some day people will look back and realize just truly how great he is. I'm not sure we realize this now. I've watched him evolve last year into a real pitcher. He was careful with his arm because he thought he might hurt it. I don't think he really threw the ball as hard as he has in the past. Nevertheless, he's evolving and becoming more crafty and using a variety of pitches, changing speeds. He's a real gentleman, too, from what I can tell, as an individual. We're watching not only a Hall of Famer, we're watching one of the great Hall of Famers. He's been playing since the early 1990s, so if he plays another year or two, he should make the Hall of Fame. He's the one that I most enjoy. His comments about Mike Piazza in spring training, 2003…wow!

——TY WATERMAN, 55, Social worker, Attleboro, MA

Jimmy Piersall was one of my favorites. In my opinion, he was the player that invented backing up on a fly ball, trying to get to throw the guy out from third to home and running in and catching the ball and throwing it at the same time. My dad even noticed it. He'd say, "Why is he backing up? Why isn't he coming in to catch the ball?" Piersall would go back, then he'd run like a son of a gun, catch the ball, and throw it while still running forward trying to get the guy out from third to home. I really do believe Jimmy Piersall invented that move.

——RAY FOSTER, 62, Retired truck driver

Carlton Fisk was an endearing character when I was in high school and was loved by a whole swarm of teenage girls. Some of my friends, who were much more avid baseball fans at that point than I was, had posters of him. My cousin, Maria, when Tim Naehring was playing third base in his first season for the Red Sox, went with several girl friends to a game. They had seats right behind the visitors' dugout. They were yelling at Tim, taunting him in a teasing way, telling him that he was a great player, and that they wanted to go out on a date with him and things like that. He actually was interviewed that night and remarked about how surprised he was that he had developed such a big fan base already.

——JANE WOYCIK, 38, Westwood, MA

After I saw Babe Ruth play in the 1918 World Series, every time he was in town, I'd go watch him because he was my hero. I remember him as a pitcher because had every kind of pitch. He had an overhand curve that dropped down fast and cut off the knees of the right-handed batters. He just had everything. I remember him as a batter because he hit prodigiously long balls to the right field, and he used to rap them off that wall. I remember this clearly.

——KEN HERMES, 95, born in Roxbury, MA

Around 1990, I went to Fenway with a boyfriend to see a game. We got there early. They said, "The game doesn't start for another hour. We're going to have a little Old Timers game before. I thought, "Oh, that'll be fun." Since not many fans were there, we could sit wherever we wanted to, so we went and sat behind the Red Sox dugout. They started introducing guys. There were guys from my era, like Rico, Mike Andrews. I thought, "Oh my God. They're not…. They won't, will they?" And sure enough they called his name, Carl Yastzremski," and he walked out. He didn't wear the uniform. He never wore the uniform at these things. It makes people mad, but who cares. He —— rose petals, as far as I'm concerned. He walked out and I'm screaming, I'm crying, "I love you." My boyfriend loved baseball as much as I do, so he just loved it. He used to get me Yaz shirts and hats for presents.

—————LAUREN DOMBROWSKI, 46, TV comedy producer

I have a scrapbook filled with clippings from the 1970s up until the mid-1980s, especially if it pertained to Carlton Fisk. A guy I used to work with at the Celtics got me Fisk's game jersey when he was with Chicago, autographed by him. He also got me the original seat back to seat Number 72 from the old Comiskey Field because Carlton wore Number 72 when he played for the White Sox. He had Fisk autograph the seat back, too. I keep both of them in my office. They're awesome. When my wife, Carolyn, and I got married in 1991, I put the jersey on, put my Red Sox hat on, and danced with my mom to a recording by John Kiley, the former Fenway Park organist, of "Take Me Out To the Ball Game."

About six years ago, I actually got to have dinner with Carlton Fisk through a mutual friend, Jack Fox, who had business dealings with Fisk down in Florida. Fox is the owner of Fox Toyota in Providence, Rhode Island, and Fox Toyota used to be a sponsor of the Celtics. Jack and I have stayed friends through the years, and one day he told me that he was having dinner with Carlton Fisk in Providence, and that I should come on down.

It was great! I told Carlton how much he meant to me, how I appreciated the sport of baseball and how he approached the game. He shared some of his own memories with me, and then he started asking me questions about the Celtics, which was really fun.

Rather than me just talking to him and praising him the entire night, he asked about **Larry Bird** and Red Auerbach. He told me about how much he loved Red. He told me that basketball had been his number one sport, that he had been a basketball star up in New Hampshire, and that he always wanted to be a draft pick of the Celtics.

—————JOE DURKIN JR, 39, Boston Celtics Director of Corporate Sales

Larry Bird is from French Lick, Indiana, as is former Sacramento Kings coach, Jerry Reynolds. Reynolds once had a heart attack during a Kings' game. While writhing around on the floor, he was given a technical foul by the referee, who felt that Reynolds was trying to "show up" the officials.

Luis Tiant is my all-time favorite player. God knows how old Tiant was. He was older than I think everyone knew he was. That's typical for the Latino players, the Cubans. He pitched a hundred and fifty six pitches in a World Series game. Today, they take 'em out at ninety. In Game 5, of either a play-off or the World Series, a hundred and fifty six was a gritty performance. He gave up nine or ten hits, but he toughed it out. Everybody still loves him and the line of cigars he's selling, El Tiante Cigars. I just loved him because he was just so much fun to watch. He loved what he was doing, and he was all business on the mound even though he'd be laughing. I remember in the World Series, he got a base hit. He hadn't been to the plate because of the DH rule all year. He got up there and put a ball through the hole. They had him chugging around third base. He scored a run. That would have to have been '75.

——JOHN LINCOLN WRIGHT, 55, Musician

Ted Williams cut store ribbons for me two or three times. He was a quite a guy, talked baseball a lot. He was my third favorite player of all-time after Ruth and Fred Lynn, who would have been a superstar if he hadn't made the mistake of leaving Boston for the money.

About two years ago, Ted came to my house with Johnny Pesky because someone told them I was sick and laid up. Ted looked awful old to me. I'm ten years older, but I thought he looked older than me. I had last seen him about ten years before. How he aged! His face had been almost without wrinkles, and then it was all wrinkles.

We talked quite a while. He kidded me about going out and playing ball with him and Pesky. He said we should start a team of our own. These fellows do a lot of good that never gets into the paper. Pesky is a heck of a nice guy. He goes overboard to help people, and I don't think he gets any credit at all. He doesn't brag. I hate guys like **Barry Bonds** who wants to be cheered every time he makes a play. Guys like that spoil baseball.

Like Carl Yastrzemski. I think he was terribly overrated compared to Ted Williams and Fred Lynn. He ran bad. He wasn't so hot. Fred Lynn was a better fielder. And Fred was a better hitter when he

In 2002, Barry Bonds received 68 intentional walks...eight came with the bases empty.

was with the Red Sox. Carl is another one of those players who reminds me of Barry Bonds. He was his own hero. He probably was better than I thought he was, but I just didn't like the guy.

——KEN HERMES, 95, Retired, Yarmouth Port, MA

The boys knew I was really into baseball. I'd talk about it. I read everything I could about the Red Sox. And I knew how to read box scores. We'd play Frisbee baseball in the neighborhood, and there would be more boys than girls. I was always the shortest and the smallest and the lightest, so everyone thought they picked who were the good players. But I was perfectly happy with being Dwight Evans. Oh my God, yes, I emulated Dwight Evans. I was Dwight Evans. I liked him because he kind of had the same batting stance as I did, kind of like the bow-legged thing. And they said, "You're just going to hit a pop-up anyway." And I said, "Well Dwight Evans hits the best pop-ups. Guess what? You're going to score on my pop-ups, because I'm going to hit a sacrifice fly." And I could make the best catches too.

——JOCELYN SMITH, 33, Physical therapist

Besides Ted Williams, I loved Dick Radatz, The Monster. He was also a god to me. I wish I knew him personally. I listen to him all the time on the radio even now. He's a radio commentator, and I've never met him. He was the most intimidating pitcher I ever saw in my life, and here he was playing for this really mediocre-to-lousy team. He could strike out Mantle any time he faced him. He was death on the Yankees. It didn't matter whether the Red Sox were in ninth or tenth place, the only thing that mattered was when they played the Yankees and Radatz had their number. He had this tremendous side-arm, almost underhand pitch. He came at you sideways. I don't think I ever saw him throw a changeup and curve balls would be rare. He was six feet-six. He would come at you a little bit like **Drysdale** did but even more intimidating.

——TY WATERMAN, 55, Attleboro, MA

Don Drysdale said his most important pitch was his second knockdown one because it told the hitter that the first pitch was not a mistake.

My father knew somebody who knew somebody who knew the Red Sox doctor, so I got an autographed baseball. I still have it. My daughter made a little special mount for me. I also have my 1957 Ted Williams baseball card. So we have a little shrine. When I was ten, I "wrote" a book about Ted Williams and stitched it with colored pipe cleaners. I called it *The Ted Williams Story*. I got the text from a series of 1956 and '57 cards that were all about Ted Williams and his life. I taught myself to type, and I typed up the entire thing on the back, so I had a consecutive biography. I memorized all his stats. It was as if I was living in the 1940s in my head. I still resent the 1941 and 1942 and 1947 MVP awards that went to Yankees when they should have gone to Ted Williams.

I tried to pretend I was Ted Williams. My father and Ted Williams get mixed up in my mind in who was having the greatest effect on me, because they were roughly the same age. Ted Williams was born in 1918; my father was born in 1916. Both of them were kind of volatile; could be high-tempered.

——ROBERT BELL, 57, English professor, Williams College

I contribute to an organization called the Friends of the Hall of Fame and every year my friend and I go to the Hall of Fame induction. It's a good weekend. We watch a AA game, the induction ceremony, and then, the Hall of Fame game. My friend and I also go to Oneonta, the Yankees affiliate, which is just outside of Cooperstown, where the team plays in the most dilapidated stadium I've ever seen in my life.

The day following the induction, there is a special round-table discussion with the inductees, which ESPN2 has broadcast a few times. One particular year, the discussion had a 1975 theme. Carlton Fisk, Tony Perez, and Sparky Anderson participated. About seventy-five to a hundred people attended.

Fisk told a story that epitomizes the Red Sox-Yankee feelings I have, although Fisk was with the White Sox when this happened. Deion Sanders was at the plate. He popped up and didn't run out the ball. Carlton Fisk went up to him and said, "Don't you ever do that again, or I will kick your —— right here at home plate at Yankee Stadium." Deion said something like, "The days of slavery are over." Fisk said, "This has nothing to do with that." Then Fisk said, "I should have just left the Yankees to their misery."

I grew up when the Yankees weren't winning, so I don't I have the jealousy that people claim New Englanders feel. But I think that story captures what Fisk, coming from New England and having been a Red Sox is all about.

——JIM DECROTEAU, 43, now lives in Fullerton, CA

In the 1970s, Yaz was one of my favorites. As a player, he was very classy in the extreme. In 1978, when everyone else collapsed and seemed to give up, the score could have been 10-0 against him, and Yastrzmeski was still giving everything he had. I remember him with great affection and respect.

I went through a cycle with George Scott. He was one of my favorite players when he was first with the Red Sox, but then he turned into sort of a lump. People blamed his wife's cooking but I don't know. He did put on a lot of weight in a hurry. He had been wonderful to watch, a very graceful, quick player, and then in a few short years he became a totally different physical type.

The Spaceman, Bill Lee, was also one of my favorites. He was a great character and a very good pitcher. He always came out with great quips. He seemed more intelligent than the average bear. I always preferred him against Don Zimmer, although Zimmer seems to have improved with age. Zimmer turned out to be a very smart guy, although we didn't know it in 1978, which is the year that Red Sox fans identify with. In '78, Zimmer had this old "Gas House Gang playing with pain" psychology, so that by the end of the season his players were run ragged. They fell apart. Dwight Evans was in right field having trouble seeing straight. He was having dizzy spells. Zimmer kept telling him, "Go play. Go play!" He accused Dwight of being a California cream puff because he wanted to sit the game out once in awhile.

The saddest case was Butch Hobson, who had bone chips in his elbow. He was a terrible, sore arm fielder who could not throw the ball, but because Zimmer was such a tough "play with pain" kind of guy, he kept Hobson in. Zimmer did not treat his players well, and the fans mostly took the side of the players against him. They tended to sympathize with Bernie Carbo and Bill Lee against Zimmer. It was a counterculture thing. Nineteen seventy eight was still close enough to the 1960s that Bill Lee came off as a counterculture type while Zimmer was seen as "Old School."

————JOHN GORDON, 57, Mystic, CT

Ted Williams was probably my first sports hero. As a kid, I played all kinds of fantasy games. I ran dice games or card games that I created, and ran whole Red Sox seasons. I wasn't interested in anyone else playing. I didn't have any interest in the White Sox or the Yankees. It was just the Red Sox. The game, which was a pure game of odds, was always weighted in the Red Sox favor. If black cards were the Red Sox and red cards were the Yankees, the Red Sox got two extra cards or something like that. I wasn't interested in having any eighty-one and eighty-one seasons, or back then it would seventy-seven and seventy-seven. I wanted them to be powerhouses.

————MARK STARR, 55, Newton, MA

Years ago, I taught a standup comedy class at the Boston Center for Adult Education. One of my students worked for the Jimmy Fund. One night, while the students and I were out having beers after class, I told her that her boss, the executive director of the Fund, former Red Sox second baseman Mike Andrews, had scarred me for life. She said, "What do you mean?"

I told her that 1967, the year the Red Sox won the AL pennant, was my first year following the team. I remember crying as Bob Gibson struck out George Scott to end Game 7 of the World Series that year. Everyone in my family went crazy watching the Sox lose.

Each one of us was identified with one of the Red Sox players because there were nine people in our family. It seemed natural since there are nine players in the field. Each of us was like the player's individual fan club. My mother was George Scott, the 230-pound first baseman. I was Carl Yastrzemski, and my brother Joseph was Joe Foy. If Yastrzemski got three hits in a game, I would have gotten three hits that day. I could mimic Yastrzemski's stance exactly. He would come to the plate, take his left hand and hitch up his belt. He'd very carefully reach over with his right hand with the bat and touch the outer corner of the plate, and then he would do a little windmill action with his right hand. His left elbow was very high up before he took the swing. In later life, after hearing more about his personality,

I began to learn that these people are human beings, but I always loved Yastrzemski as a player

Anyway, in 1969, I went to a week-long Red Sox baseball day camp in Winchester, Massachusetts. Red Sox players were brought in every day to teach drills. I was ten years old and it was the highlight of my life at that point. Carl Yastrzemski, in the batting cage, lined one that almost hit me even though there was mesh between us. We got baseball tips about keeping your glove down and standing back and shifting your weight when you're hitting.

Mike Andrews and Rico Petrocelli, then the team's shortstop, were teaching infield play. They told me that on the double play, the second baseman or the shortstop doesn't really have to have his foot on the bag, that it just has to be in the neighborhood. I was ten years old and I remember thinking, "What?" I don't remember ever believing in Santa Claus, but I thought, "What do you mean? That's the rule. How can you say that?"

You have to remember these guys are gods to us when we're little. What Andrews and Petrocelli said stuck with me so long that when I met this student, I said, "Your boss scarred me." Well, she went back and told Andrews. He sent me a letter in 1999. He wrote, "Jim, Laura tried to explain to me how I traumatized you as a youngster by teaching you the phantom tag. Had I known it would leave such lasting scars, I never would have taught it to you. Of course, this is the first case I have heard of this in our twenty-four years instructing thousands upon thousands of campers this highly professional technique. So, I have decided to dismiss it as just one very disturbed young boy. Seriously, I hope life is treating you well."

I wound up sending Andrews a big contribution to the Jimmy Fund, saying, "Hopefully, this will bring closure to the matter."

——JIM DECROTEAU, 43, Stand-up Comic, Fullerton, CA

Somebody wrote an article about Carl Yastrzemski in *American Scholar*, the Phi Beta Kappa journal. It's a very good publication, not really scholarly, but it has a highly educated audience. I don't know if the person who wrote this article was an academic, but in the early '80s, this person wrote an article about Carl Yastrzemski which asserted that Yaz was as good as Ted Williams. I thought it was remarkable. Of course, I loved Yastrzemski, but there is no comparison. So I sat down and I wrote a letter to the journal, making the simple point that Yastrzemski's great golden year in 1967 was an average year for Ted Williams. Williams had twenty years that were as spectacular as '67. My letter was published.

———ROBERT BELL, 57, raised in Belmont, MA

Let me tell the Johnny Pesky story. This is actually a famous one that Pesky has told over the years. I've heard it several times at various Red Sox functions. Right after the 1946 World Series, he goes back home to Oregon completely bereft. And he has to come back to Boston that December for a function. But he decides to go to the BC–Holy Cross football game. Now back then, BC and Holy Cross were actually big time in football, and they were playing a nationally ranked game at Fenway Park. He decides to wear sort of an old cap and dark glasses, and come to the game incognito, because, again, he didn't want to be recognized. Late in the game, a guy for BC punts the ball, and a guy from Holy Cross who is catching the ball, fumbled it. BC recovers. And everyone is swearing!"

All of a sudden, some leather-lung ten or fifteen rows behind him stands up and shouts out, "You should have kicked it to Pesky. He would have held on to it!" When that story is told now, people crack up! And Pesky is laughing when he says it. But there's the classic thing. You see, we bring the Red Sox history to all of our other games. It's because we are a baseball town, and we started with the Red Sox. The Celtics can win sixteen championships in thirty-two years, but you're still a baseball town. You still sit there and you'll say, as Larry, and Robert and Kevin are doing their thing down on the court, "Cripes, why can't the Red Sox be like this." You'll never say, "God, aren't the Celtics' great!" It always goes back to the Red Sox.

Now when you think about it, the Bruins won a couple of Cups in the 1970s, the Celtic's won a ton after 1960. As baseball fans—the other major sport is football—and nothing else really counts. And that is the attitude of most Bostonians, that, "yes, we have hockey in our blood, but still hockey and basketball are minor sports compared to baseball, which will always be number one."

———SHAUN KELLY, 48, teacher, Greenwich, CT

Rico Petrocelli was my favorite player. I imitated his stance when I was a kid. He had this habit. I can still see the way he would kind of hold his bat, and move his upper torso, almost robotically. He moved front to back, and it was almost swaying like a porch swing.

———BRIAN KILEY, 41, raised in Newton, MA

My favorite player was always Jim Rice, just because he could hit the ball as far as the eye could see. I'll never forget when Rice was the guest star on the TV show, *The Baseball Bunch*. It was my favorite episode. They did this skit where he hit a ball and it kept going and going and going and the San Diego Chicken kept running after it.

The Baseball Bunch was a show that Tommy Lasorda used to be part of. It was on every Saturday morning. They would have the guest stars give lessons on certain skills—an outfielder would show how to catch the ball, a power hitter would show how to really hit with power, and a pitcher would show all the different types of pitches he had. It was a kids' show and Johnny Bench hosted it. Tommy Lasorda was the Wizard who came out in a turban. Johnny Bench wore his Reds outfit. They'd have a different ball player on every Saturday, and I remember the one Jim Rice was on. They filmed him on a Little League field and he hit a ball that just kept going. They just showed the **San Diego Chicken** running through the streets, downtown and then along the beach, and he just kept running for the ball.

———SCOTT GREENE, 31, raised in Burlington, MA

I'm one of the one million or more New Englanders who will tell you that they were at Ted Williams' last game—but I was there. I remember it because it's the only game I ever attended with my mother who is not a baseball fan at all. I don't even remember why she took me. It was the only professional baseball game she ever attended in her life. She is still alive, and if I told her about it, she would say she remembers going to the game, but I really doubt she does remember.

The reason I remember her presence is I remember asking her why Ted Williams was not playing any more because he was removed after his home run. I guess she understood why because I remember her explaining to me that it was important for him to finish his career with a home run. She was in touch enough to know that.

———CARL HEICK, 51, raised in Wellesley, MA

The San Diego Chicken grosses well over two million dollars per year for his personal appearances.

One of my favorite Yaz playing moments was when he made a catch that is now long forgotten in, I believe, the 1968 All-Star Game in Washington. He robbed somebody of a home run by making one of those over the fence catches and pulling it back. I loved the fact that it was a great catch in a game that nobody remembers. It was a meaningless game, even though it was an All-Star Game. Also, I have 500 at bats of Yastzremski's on tape. For a couple of years in the 1970s, Manhattan Cable, you should pardon the expression, carried WSBK-TV in Boston, the Red Sox station. This is reel-to-reel tape, which I transferred to VHS. Every time Yaz would come to bat I would tape it. It's all on one tape. I hardly watch it, but I watch it. Yaz threw out Reggie Jackson at second base on a ball hit to left field. And Reggie just said later that he had no idea that Yaz could make that play. I love that!

I still play every week in a league in Central Park. I have my own team. I've played for thirty-three seasons, fast pitch softball not arc ball. So it's pretty competitive. I stand like Yastrzemski. It probably ruined me as a hitter, but that's my tribute to him.

——JEFFREY LYONS, 59, New York City

Dwight Evans, by far, is my favorite Red Sox player of all time because if he didn't do the famous catch, the famous home run would have never happened. No one ever talks about the catch he made in the eleventh inning of Game 6 of the '75 World Series. Remember, if he didn't do the catch that created the double play, the game's over. It would have never happened.

——JOCELYN SMITH, 33, Hampden, MA

Tip O'Neill was a great, great Red Sox fan. To go to a baseball game with Tip O'Neill was really something. He had a great mind for numbers. Long before it became fashionable, Tip O'Neill would know the pitch count. You'd go to a game with Tip, and he'd be scoring the game. All of a sudden he'd say, "You know, this guy's starting to get a little tired, he's thrown a hundred and five pitches. You'd say, "What the hell are you talking about?" He'd say, "Aren't you paying attention?"

About fifteen years ago, they have a big charitable event in Boston honoring Ted Williams. Tip was there and he found himself in the Green Room along with Ted. They had this grand conversation, and Ted, at one point, said, "Tip, was there anything in politics that you regretted not having?" Tip said, "I was a pretty lucky guy. I got to go places I never thought I'd go. And to see places I never thought I'd see. No, nothing in politics that I regret. What about you Ted, anything in baseball do you regret not having?" Ted said, "Yeah, Larry Doby's ———." Tip was just dumbfounded…and then let out the loudest roar you've ever heard in your life.

———DICK FLAVIN, a fine Irishman from Quincy, MA

Dick Radatz was such a funny guy. They should have him on television. He was so good. He has so much knowledge. He's forgotten more than most of these guys on television know, or ever learned.

One day at the camp, we were eating breakfast, and I was sitting there with Radatz and some other guys. This old fellow came walking up with a cane. He must have been in his late eighties or early nineties, and he was really hobbling along. He stops by the table and Dick chats with him for a few minutes. As he starts to walk away, Dick says, "How's the boy doing?" The guy says, "Good, good, the young boy's doing good." I turned to Dick and said, "What's that all about?" Dick said, "See that guy over there. He's seventy-one years old. That's his young one." True story.

———JOEL LEAVITT, 73, Red Sox Fantasy Camper, 1992

After the 1986 season, I met a guy who started a Bob Stanley Fan Club. A friend of mine introduced me to him and I was able to go to the Club dinner held in a Methuen, Massachusetts restaurant. In spite of a lot of people blaming him for giving up the ground ball that Mookie Wilson hit through Buckner's legs, the dinner was great, and Bob was very gracious. The guys in the Club were truly his fans. I had to leave early because I had to do a show. Stanley's wife told me a dirty joke. She said, "You can use that if you want." Of course, I don't use other people's jokes or jokes from the street.

———JIM DECROTEAU, 43, Standup comedian

I think Ted Williams is so special in the minds of so many Red Sox fans because he followed his own charge, he followed his own code, he was a tough guy who did it his way—Boston's a tough, gritty city filled with disagreeable people because of the weather or whatever. They don't like to take any ——— and they like somebody who won't either. When the sportswriters beat up on Ted, that didn't hurt him. It hurt the sportswriters. I think it's right that he didn't tip his hat—well, so what!

——MARTY NOLAN, Columnist, semi-retired from the Globe

Right around St. Patrick's day, the Red Sox make single-day tickets available after their season ticket allotment is all subscribed out. I remember standing out on a pretty cold day on Jersey Street, now Yawkey Way, in March of 1982 and buying ten or twelve tickets for the last game of the season on the theory that would be Yastrzemski's last game. We were right. By the time the game came around, everybody wanted those tickets, but we had them.

That game was kind of surreal. There were sort of hushed tones for a while. People were wanting to say farewell, but not wanting it to end. He took this kind of bizarre victory lap around the field when the game was over. The only time I ever talked to him was at a game in Fort Myers. He wasn't very talkative. He had a good ability to sign his name, which is not an easy thing to do with his name, but to sign it and talk to someone else while looking you in the eye. I thought he was sort of full of himself, but he gave us a lot of memories. Given my age and vintage, he was really important. When he was succeeded by Jim Rice, some pundits said, "It's like they've got a hundred-year plan in left field—Ted Williams for twenty, Carl Yastrzemski for twenty, and here comes Jim Rice, who's got all the talent in the world and will be around for twenty. Yaz was one of those icons that you never get over. I don't remember seeing people crying, but I just remember that it was spooky quiet for long stretches, people knowing this was something they were never going to see again and having very fond memories of some of the drama that Carl Yastrzemski had put in their lives.

—DON SHEA, St. Petersburg, Florida

Chapter 6

I Saw It On the Radio

I Never Met Ned Martin,
But I Knew Him All My Life

TURN YOUR RADIO ON

ANDY CORNBLATT

Andy Cornblatt, 53, is the Dean of Admissions at Georgetown Law School. Perhaps his job preparation came from his long years living in Newton, MA as a die-hard Sox fan.

In 1967, my world began. My identical twin brother and I were at this perfect age. We had suffered a little, not dramatically; I don't want to overdo this. But, in '67, there were so many times following the Red Sox between 1960 and 1966 when we were between ten and sixteen when we would say to each other and to our friends, "Wouldn't it be great if we really were in a pennant race." It would have been great to win the World Series, but just be in the pennant race so the games mattered in August and September. For those years, when the team wasn't very good, there were no meaningful games in August and September. There were no pennant races. They were thirty-forty games out.

The tendency is to glamorize, because the people talking about this are my age or a little younger or a little older and it just hasn't been fifty years of drama. It's been thirty-six years of real ups and downs. You go back to 1946 when Ted Williams played. I wasn't born yet. I know about it. I've read about it, or I was told about it, but it wasn't part of my life experience. My Red Sox experience began in 1967. I think for everybody at that time, it's almost impossible to capture the sense of exhilaration that was going on throughout the city then.

Wherever you would go then, that's all people would talk about. It wouldn't just be people who were fanatics like me—it would be casual fans, women, too. My mother was caught up in it. The kids my age were caught up because every kid was. The girls were caught up in large part because one of the first matinee idols they had was Tony Conigliaro, who was this local kid from Swampscott. He started with the Red Sox when he was nineteen, hit a home run in his first game.

He recorded songs! He put out a record, "Playing the Field," and "Why Don't They Understand?" was the flip side of it. This kid was good looking, local so he talked like everybody up there talked, with that accent. And he was a great player, too. Nice Italian boy, humble kid. All the women just thought he was fabulous and terrific. Then on August 18, 1967, he got hit in the eye by a pitch and we kept on moving forward, but that was a very traumatic moment.

The one thing that is striking about 1967 that is almost impossible to explain to my six-year old son: That is, most of these games weren't on TV back then. There was no cable. There was no satellite. There was no nothing. What you relied on was the radio. Some of my best memories of 1967 were listening to the Red Sox play on radio, particularly when they were away. My brother, Bruce, and I would sit upstairs and we'd put on the radio and maybe we'd do a little homework and maybe we wouldn't. We would follow every single game. The Sox would go to Cleveland. We knew who was pitching for Cleveland. That was what you did at night. You followed them.

We were listening to the game when **Conigliaro** got hit. We just held our breath. It's hard to remember because now you see every game. You not only see the game, but you see the replay of the important things twenty times. If you missed it, watch it on SportsCenter twenty times. In many ways, it's what makes radio so much more vivid than TV in an odd way because in your mind's eye, you're picturing what this looked like. No one was telling you because you couldn't actually see the picture. So, of course, we were horrified. We were sixteen and didn't have the bigger picture of the tragedy although that grabbed you for a moment. But then you worried, who was going to play right field? At that age, it was all about winning, and winning the pennant. Were we older, I'm sure we would have felt more for the family and would have felt all those things that grownups feel more.

The very, very first moment of excitement when it felt different was the very first game, the opening game, at Yankee Stadium and Billy Rohr was pitching. He was going for a no-hitter. He was a rookie. It

In 1971, Tony Conigliaro screen-tested for a role in *The Godfather*. Al Pacino got the part.

was the first game he ever pitched. I can't recall if it was the first game of the year or whether it was the first away game. I think it was the first game of the year. He got to the ninth inning and Yastrzemski in left field made a spectacular catch. This game was a game that on Opening Day everybody gathered around and if you were lucky enough you went, of course, but if not, we all listened on the radio. It was a school day so we were in school, but I can remember listening on that hidden transistor radio. In between classes, we would listen. Everybody in school was sort of paying attention to this, even the teachers. We would get out of school about two or three o'clock in the afternoon. Of course, the game was still going on then, but it would be toward the end of the game. We were in Newton South High School and we were all standing outside. A bunch of us just gathered around this radio listening to what was going on, again visualizing that the medium of radio is different than TV. Ken Coleman was the radio announcer, along with Ned Martin. He was terrific. He was excited but always professional. He captured the sense that—first of all, I don't think any rookie pitcher had ever pitched a no-hitter in his very first game, but it was against the **Yankees**, and it began to signal the importance that maybe this had never happened to us before. Maybe something that never happened to us before was about to happen. That's the sense you had listening to this. He was exciting. The moment was exciting. They were beating the Yankees. Suddenly, it occurred to you, "Oh gosh, so this is what it feels like to be in the eye of a storm, this wonderful storm that you could feel something brewing.

Bruce, my friend Mark, and I were all counselors up in a camp, Indian Acres, in Fryeburg, Maine. This was the summer of '67, which anybody who grew up then knows what that means, the summer when the Red Sox were in the pennant race—finally. Up there, transistor radios did you no good, and there were no TV's, so we relied on the kids in Mark's cabin. These were eleven-twelve year old kids who got to go to the Science Shack and built a radio. It was as basic as could be. Fortunately for us, Mark's kids were very good at this. We had a science counselor. They had a transmitter. They didn't build it from scratch, but they put together a radio with the help of the science counselor that

> John Elway, Deion Sanders, and Billy Cannon, Jr. were signed by George Steinbrenner for the Yankees and given $100,000+ bonuses. All three quit baseball for the NFL.

was a real radio. No one really had one, for whatever reason. These kids brought it back to Mark's cabin and we would all—remember we were the counselors—gather round and listen to this home-made radio that these eleven and twelve-year-old kids built during science at this athletic camp. We picked out these kids who loved science and they created this radio. The kids, who are still my friends, have memories of sitting around that cabin listening to Red Sox games.

Our evenings and our Saturdays and Sundays—because those are the day games they usually played—our sense of this was just listening to these games. It was an eight-week camp. Their parents would come to see their kid and most of the dads would check with us to see if we had any Red Sox scores because that's what people were talking about. That's what it was about. We would gather and listen and cheer and it would be what you would do.

This was the summer of Yastrzemski, when he was almost super-human. I'm sure by now you've heard the stories, I wasn't there, but people wouldn't go into Sumner Tunnel. That year every single time it mattered, he always performed and succeeded. He was remarkable, remarkable. It's impossible to describe. He was coming up with bases loaded, and, of course, if you go into a tunnel you lose reception on your radio. The cars were backed up because no one would drive in the tunnel for fear of missing what Yastrzemski would do. The front car just sat there and wouldn't go in until they heard. Of course, they didn't stay there the whole inning, but because it was Yastrzemski and because it was a critical moment of the game, no one moved.

Long after 1967, when the rabbi would say, "Now let's have silent prayer," I can remember silently asking the "Big Guy," "Just once, what do you say? What do you say? How about us doing the Red Sox right?" And I do that now, for goodness sake.

The next moment that's vivid to me is 1978 with Bucky Dent. By then I was twenty-eight years old and had gone through my share of heartbreak with females. But you don't know what heartbreak is until you are sitting in my living room with my younger brother and other friends watching that game unfold. Part of it was that it was such an odd season because the Red Sox were way ahead, and then they collapsed. The Yankees kept charging and charging and overtook them.

Then the Red Sox wound up winning all these games at the end of the season to put it into a play-off game. So the season itself had these highs and lows that sort of brought you to this one play-off game. You've got this one game, and, of course, it had to be against the Yankees.

That particular game in '78 was sort of a microcosm of the whole season. Red Sox get ahead. Then the Yankees climb ahead of the Red Sox. Then the Red Sox come back and fall just short, just short, when Bucky Dent hits this home run. Books have been written about it, but some of this stuff gets exaggerated in the retelling. Some of the stuff—we just sort of wallow in it. It is fair to say that my heart broke a little. I'm not one to cry, but was I sad and impossible to be around for a while, you bet. I was not married at that time.

Now here it is twenty-five years later, and I can tell you every single aspect of this. The recall is total about that game. I was in a funk, and it was deep. It was as deep a funk as I can remember until 1986. Sixty-seven was not a funk. Even though they lost the World Series, I was disappointed, but I was old enough then to just appreciate the exhilaration of the pennant chase. All the years I had rooted for them, it was so bland and so uninspiring. Then came '67 when every single day, every day, was exciting to read about. There were some ups and downs. They lost some games, but just the sense of being in this race and having games that mattered in September and August was a totally unfamiliar experience to us and one that we had envied all these other cities—those of us who love baseball— envied all these other cities. Suddenly we were it. This was the "impossible dream." They had finished last place the year before so it became a national story as well. We were right in the center of it. The positives of that year almost balanced out the heartbreak of the succeeding years. That's how great that summer was.

So many of the people who live in the Boston area, and not that many people move in up there, so you have this region, of which I was a part for the first thirty years of my life, where it's just everything we do and we are and we care about just gets magnified because the other parts of the world and the country aren't as shared up there. It's not diluted.

One of the reasons is while they are all so different, even in 1967, in this all but segregated city back then and with all these ethnicities and this Jewish population where I grew up, as cliché as it sounds—it is absolutely true that amidst all these incredible differences, and the lines are so bright in many ways for all of us in this vulcanized place—the one thing that's absolutely in common is Red Sox. Everybody out there—everybody—no matter what group you pick from if you grew up there, you root for the Red Sox. That's just it. Nobody who grows up there doesn't do that.

You have people in New York, much more so than in Boston, who may have come from some other place or who left to go to some other place. In Boston, people just stay. Some people tend to be: "Okay, so when's it going to go bad?" In large part, it's because of '67. I know I keep coming back to that, but that was the experience that was vivid for people. So many of us were 16- to 20-years old and that's the time of life when you're just ready to sort of have that imprinted on your brain. Subconsciously, Red Sox fans don't want to admit that they think at the end of the day, the Yankees will always prevail. Some will admit it now, but it's a more recent phenomena. It was certainly not true in the 1940s and 1950s.

But in '67, the Yankees weren't part of that pennant race. They were terrible. They weren't one of the four teams going for the pennant. In '75, the Red Sox won, but they were much better than the Yankees then. The Cincinnati Reds were the team that beat them. Beginning with the 1980s and especially all those years—then the Red Sox got to be pretty good year in, year out, but the team that always seemed to prevail back then, and now, were the Yankees.

The Bucky Dent thing was important and pivotal because for my generation, it was the most vivid example of the Yankees' success and the Red Sox failure. Here they went through this pennant race. It looked like they were going to win. Then it looked like they were going to lose. Then they were tied. Here's this game. They look like they might win. Then up comes Bucky Dent. He hits the home run. And from that point forward, again it's twenty-five years ago, the Red Sox would get in the Series, but the Yankees always seemed to do better. Amidst the hatred and resentment that others have, myself included, I think there's a growing, almost admiration for how they do it. There is for me. It doesn't mean I like them any more. I don't.

HEAR ME NOW,
LISTEN TO ME LATER

RADIO

Ted Williams became my hero. My first great Red Sox memory in a game was while I was lying in bed—coming from Connecticut we couldn't get them much on TV. The Sox were on radio out of WTXC in Hartford. To get to a game was quite a chore. I was a radio fan first, before anything else. Then, on Sunday afternoon, they'd be on TV once a week. **Curt Gowdy** was the radio announcer. He was everything. He was very clear. He was kind of a thoughtful man. He wasn't overly excitable. He was homey. He was like a grandfather coming over the radio. He's not like New York broadcasters that were much more outgoing or garrulous. He was the "Voice of the Red Sox." My first great memory of the game was lying in bed in my father's bedroom apartment one weekend when I visited him in 1960, when I was twelve. It was late September, and I was lying there listening to the game and I heard Ted Williams' last home run, his last time up in baseball. That was probably the most exciting moment all through my childhood as far as the Red Sox go. He was like a god to me.

When my mom and stepfather would go to the beach club every Sunday afternoon—we were very close to the ocean—I would never go. I would stay home, and that would be my time to watch the Sunday games. I would dig out a bat and I would pitch, but mostly I would hit. I would time their pitches so I would actually be down there swinging during a game. I actually learned how to time pitches, and that's exactly the same thing I did when I played. I felt like I was in the game that way.

——**TY WATERMAN**, 55, Social worker, raised in southern CT

One of my happiest Red Sox times was living over in Somerville in 1978, the year the Red Sox were so hot. You could leave the house to

> Curt Gowdy was Mel Allen's radio partner with the
> New York Yankees in 1949 and 1950.

get a six-pack or go down to the corner to get some food. It would be a hot summer night, and you wouldn't miss a pitch. Every single radio or TV was on. You could walk around the city and hear the ball game. Everybody had it on. One night the Orioles were in town, and the Sox hit three dingers off Jim Palmer. They were all solo shots. He never gave up two-run or three-run homers. I think it was in one inning, he allowed three out of four batters to hit it out of Fenway. You could hear people yelling and screaming.

———JOHN LINCOLN WRIGHT, 55, Boston native

On October 2 or 3, 1990, the Red Sox have to win their final game to win the AL East. I'm at the game against the White Sox, and it comes down to one play. Ozzie Guillen hits a line drive down the right field line. Tom Brunansky runs to the ball, dives in the warning track dirt and comes up with the ball. A great catch! The Sox win the East, and it's a celebration at Fenway. But I'm a little down. I was so busy filming the play on my video camera—they do allow this at Fenway, though most people don't realize it—that I didn't really get to enjoy the game. Everyone is screaming and I'm just trying to keep the camera steady and watch through the little black and white lens. I felt that I had cheated myself out of a great moment in Red Sox history by detaching from it as a photographer. And for what?

About thirty-six hours later, a friend calls me and says, "Didn't you tell me that you filmed the Brunansky catch at the game?" I said, "yes." He said, "Well, it's all over the news. No one got it on film. Brunansky disappeared off camera as he caught it and every other camera was focused on the dugouts for reaction shots. No one even got it on replay!"

Sure enough, I turn on local sports news at six and Channel 4 sports anchor, Bob Lobel, is talking about how nobody got the shot. It was a big story all over town. Someone from a tiny TV station, Channel 68, got a long distance shot from a bad angle. Very bad and very distant. Useless. *Boston Globe* sports TV critic, Jack Craig, writes that no one will ever see the catch.

As a comedian, I have been poking fun at Channel 4 for years. They even hired me to do comedy at their Christmas party and encouraged me to hit 'em for all it's worth. I had a business card from one of their execs left over from the party. I called him up and told him I had a home video of the catch. A few calls later, I'm on the phone with Lobel and he tells me to drive down to Channel 4 and they'd take a look at it.

Next thing you know, I'm deep in the catacombs behind the scenes and my tape is cued up. Lobel and a bunch of support crew, probably fourteen people, watch the tape. When Brunansky makes the catch, they erupt into a huge cheer. They could not have cheered louder if they were at the game cheering the catch itself.

That night, my footage is the teaser for the night's eleven o'clock news. "Coming up at 11, a fan has the film of Brunansky's catch to win the AL East."

The tape was featured prominently at 11 and then again at six a.m. I never asked for any money. I got them to give me a plug for where I was working around town. Besides, I felt like I wanted to give something back to baseball for all it has given me. If I took $500 for it, it would have been spent in two days and I wouldn't have felt that I had given anything to anyone. It was like a dream. It was like an ABC After School Special. A person can live a hundred times and not have something like that happen.

My video got a little writeup in both the *Globe* and the *Herald*. Jack Craig's coverage came out with a later patchwork edition that made no sense. First, he repeated that no one will ever see the catch, then it's told how I filmed it. There was no time to edit the piece.

More than one local media person criticized me in print and on the air. Jerk killjoys. Their angle was, "Who are these people bringing cameras to the ballpark? They need to get a life."

First of all, they kiss ballplayers' butts FULL TIME FOR A LIVING! Who—or is it whom—are they to throw stones? Even if they are ripping ballplayers, they still are sycophantic leeches who would have to get a real job if the ballplayers went out of existence. I have a life outside of sports. Don't get me wrong. I think sports-leeching is a great profession, and I would love to be a full-time sportswriter. But to suggest that a fan needs to get a life because he brought a camera to the ball game?

Second of all, people have been bringing cameras to the ballpark since President Taft started the seventh-inning stretch. Just because mine was a video camera and not a ten-dollar Kodak Instamatic, I'm a chump? Thirteen years later, I'm still steamed.

——MIKE DONOVAN, 47, Brookine, MA

I have been noted for sitting at church meetings on Sunday afternoons with a blank stare on my face with everybody wondering what was wrong. They didn't know I was sitting there listening to the game.

I was a big Ned Martin fan. I loved Martin and Jim Woods when they did the radio. I grew up with Curt Gowdy. He was the first Red Sox announcer I remember. He was good, but I really loved Ned Martin. He had a great knowledge of the game, a kind of iconoclastic wit and the way he would say "mercy" whenever someone would hit a home run. That was his signature call. He would just say it in a flat way, but I thought it was great. They had Jon Miller—who does ESPN games—for one year and I can't believe they let him get away.

I have satellite radio. I scour what's happening in technology not because I have to have the latest thing, but just to enable me to stay in touch with the Red Sox.

Back in the days when I couldn't use this new technology, and there was a really big game, and I would be thinking, "I'm just not missing this." I would come up with some excuse that I wouldn't be at church that night.

I can remember in the fall of 1999 when the Red Sox and Yankees were in the ALCS, I had a wedding on a Saturday afternoon. I couldn't get out of the wedding, but I do remember having an earplug in my ear at the reception, which was kind of futile because receptions are so loud. I do maintain some sense of propriety—I've never had an earpiece in my ear while doing a church service. You believe me, don't you?

——REVEREND CARL HEICK, 51, Centerville, MA

In the early 1970s, my wife and I lived in a section of Williamstown that didn't get cable TV. I was listening to the games on the radio just like I did when I was eleven years old. I would lose the transmission, or the station would fade in and out late at night. Even on the old, beat-up little radio I'd had since 1960, I could turn the dial and tell, based on the quality of the silence, whether I'd found the game and was between pitches, or whether I was on the wrong frequency. I could just intuit the quality of the sound. Of course, I could tell instantly whether the Red Sox were ahead or behind from the tone of the announcer's voice.

We moved closer to the town of Williamstown in the summer of 1978. The reason we bought our house was so that my wife could have a yard big enough for a good garden, and I could be on the cable TV line. We renovated the house before we moved in September, and I used to come over to an empty house and sit alone up on the second floor because the cable TV company had forgotten to turn off the previous owner's connection. I bought a little, $79 black-and-white TV and hooked it up to the cable, and I'd sit in the dark on a wooden floor for two and a half hours and watch the Red Sox. That season, the Red Sox were something like fifteen or seventeen games ahead in first place.

When we finally moved in, the one thing I wanted was a big TV set so I could have the guys over to watch the World Series. I bought this great big Zenith TV that's about six feet wide. In those days, it was astonishingly big. I still have that TV.

———**ROBERT BELL**, 57, Williamstown, MA

Games have always gotten me into a lot of trouble. They are embarrassing. You know when your daughters are into dance like ballet. They have lots of recitals. I love my child more than anything in the world, and I'm a very good parent. I really am. I am just about the only parent that will sit there *ad nauseam* and go through every tech rehearsal and every dance rehearsal. But it's during baseball season. So what I do is I have this really tiny, tiny headset that you can tuck in your hair. For the longest time, I wore long hair because I could get away with my headset. It's tiny and you snake it through your clothing, and I sit there and I act very, very attentive. Well, your child is only in a couple of these acts, and my child is always in the first and the last one.

Well, I'm sitting there and Brian Daubach had an awesome, awesome grand slam, and I jumped up and said, "Yes, go Dauber!" In the middle of a recital. I was in deep dog doo. And I did that at a memorial service once; and I did that in the middle of work. I've done that several times, and finally, one of my family members killed my little headset. I promised not to buy another one. I think the memorial service was the last straw. They all conspired together. It just disappeared one day. Nobody will say where. My intentions are never, never bad.

I love the season! It's always there; it never leaves you. I'm miserable in off-season. I count down the days.

———JOCELYN SMITH, 33, Hampden, MA

The '67 season has such great memories. I still occasionally listen to the *Impossible Dream* album. Ken Coleman, the Red Sox announcer, wrote a poem and included clips from the whole season. From that allbum, they started playing this stupid Carl Yastrzemski song on the radio, and it just took off and later became part of the *Impossible Dream* album.

———JIM DECROTEAU, 43, Customer service representative

I was still in college in Washington, D.C. I cut class to watch a Red Sox-A's play-off game. I didn't care how much my education cost; there was no way I was going to miss a Red Sox play-off game. Who knew, if in my life, I'd get that chance again? My friends went out and partied as usual while I stayed home. I'd tell them, "No, I can't go. I have to listen to the Red Sox-Yankee game." I would cram myself into the bottom of a bunk bed in this weird place in the house that got good radio reception, turn to 77 WABC in New York or 1080 in Hartford and get this whiny Red Sox broadcast. No matter where you are in the country, I can tell you how to tune in Red Sox games on the radio.

The Internet's great, but it's taken the fun out of listening on the radio. I'll never forget the SportsPhone number in New York: 1-212-976-1313. They provided scores. I'd listen to the Baltimore game simply to get the Red Sox score, but when I'd get bored with that, I'd call up SportsPhone or *USA Today* sports phone, and let it ring repeatedly because every five minutes they updated the scores. It was the number one button on my speed dial. God, I had three hundred-dollar phone bills, but I had to know what was going on.

When the Red Sox clinched the American League East title, I was so happy that I put the phone down and forgot to hang up. The Brewers lost to the A's at one o'clock in the morning. Forty-five minutes later, my roommate tapped me on the shoulder. Ooops! Forty-five minutes of SportsPhone. It cost about seventeen dollars. I was so excited I was jumping up and down. I had bought a bottle of Dom Perignon champagne, which cost me my entire monthly allowance. It's amazing how fast champagne goes when a few people are drinking it.

———JOHN BENNETT, 34, high school math teacher

When I was twelve or thirteen years old, I had a paper route and one of my neighbors had one of those powerful antennas. She was a woman who had adult kids grown and out of the house, and her husband was deceased. She would watch the game, and I would watch with her. This went on for a couple of years until I was about fourteen years old. I thought this was so nice because I could go over there to her house and watch the game because she got Channel 38. All we got were the local Providence channels, and the only time they showed the Red Sox, was on the weekend. Channel 6 would pick up the games when the Red Sox played the Yankees.

——WAYNE TUMBLESON, 39, Rhode Island native

Carl Yastrzemski, Tony Conigliaro, guys like that, were my favorite players. That 1967 season was so unique about all of a sudden here's this sport, this pastime going on that I can remember staying up late or going to bed with the ear plug in my ear, listening to the radio, listening to Ned Martin, the Red Sox broadcaster for thirty-five years. He just recently passed away last summer—about the same time as Ted Williams. He was smooth and he got to the point. He was also well informed. There wasn't a lot of editorial comment. No one laughed at him the way he did it.

——BRUCE BOSLEY, 46, Vermont

I have a first cousin who was about to marry—I don't know what faith he was, because they had a minister. It wasn't a priest. It was a minister, so maybe like a Pentecostal or Episcopal or something. I don't really remember what religion it was, but it was my uncle's daughter. It was my father's only sibling's daughter. Weddings have ruined more Saturdays for more people in my lifetime than the Red Sox have in 100 years.

It was one of those unbelievable family obligations that everybody has. It was the weekend when the Red Sox were playing the Yankees, and I was livid. I tried to get out of this every which way. It was the really early 1980s. They were getting married in Maine of all places. So I said to my parents, "If you're going to force us to go, I'm bringing my radio." My mother said, "Oh no, you're not!" Well, I have one of these pencil thin transistor radios. It's like the size of a credit card, and it comes with those collapsible ear pads, where you can literally just stick the ear pad in your ear and dangle a wire like you were the FBI or the Secret Service. I had long hair back then, and it could literally hide the wire. So, we're listening to the game on the way up.

Of course it's way up in Maine. And fortunately around here, the Red Sox radio network has a very strong signal. Everybody in the family knows what a huge fan I am, what a sacrifice I made because everyone knows they're playing the Yankees. The Red Sox Nation goes way up to Vermont. Word had gotten out how disappointed I was that I wasn't able to go to the game, or watch it on TV. So the minister is performing the ceremony, and I'm sitting there in the pew with my family. Of course, I've got the ear pad in my ear, and I'm listening to the game very quietly, not trying to show any emotion at all. The Red Sox were way ahead. Right before "We now pronounce you man and wife" the minister, who happened to be the groom's brother, spoke up and said something about good times and bad times, and blah, blah, blah… And he says, "I have it on good authority that there is somebody in the congregation that could tell us what the score of the ball game is." Well, somebody must have either seen it, or just figured I would do it. I was mortified. Everybody turned around, and my face completely blew up. I could feel ten shades of red. I kind of put my head down, and everybody started to laugh. But then he went on and finished the ceremony.

Of course, right after that, I must have had 15 people say, "What's the score? What's the score? What's the score?"

———CHERI GIFFIN, 51, Randolph, MA

My parents were a little older than my friends' parents. They would go to bed early, and they would send us to bed earlier than my friends. I used to take my transistor radio to bed and be listening to the game. As far as I know, they did not know. I do remember in '75 when it was the World Series, and they had the famous Game 6. As the game got later, I was sent to bed. But I did sneak back out, and I was actually hiding behind the couch while my older brother and sister were watching the game. Of course, when Fisk homered, I jumped out and was caught. But at that point, I didn't care. That was unbelievable. Too bad it wasn't Game 7.

As a kid, I used to caddy at Woodland Golf Course. The Red Sox game would always be on TV in the little caddy shack. We were always watching the game, or you would at least see part of the game. I remember one Fourth of July, Ken Harrelson swearing on the air. It was a holiday, so maybe he had had a few drinks. Larry Hisle was up for the Twins, and Ken Harrelson was saying, "He's got quick power! Quick Power! Every once in awhile, he just gets up and hits the —— out of the ball!" Then there was just this long silence. No delay, or anything. The funny thing was he realized it immediately, and so did the other guy. They did not say a word. I remember all the caddies were just stunned. They threw four pitches, and neither announcer said a word. After the fourth pitch, the other guy just said, "Two and two."

Actually, it was said that Babe Ruth had played golf at Woodland. Legend has it that as a lefty golfer, he sliced one over the clubhouse, which if you know where the first hole is and where the clubhouse is, it's like hitting like a 500-foot foul ball. Jim Rice had somewhat of a **long ball** record for golfers. He wasn't that accurate, but he would just crush the ball.

—— BRIAN KILEY, 41, Newton Native

My mother loved the Red Sox and I would take her to Ladies' Day. That was the only time I ever missed school because Ladies' Day started at 12:30 Wednesday afternoons. My mother always wore a nice hat. In those days, all the women wore nice shoes and a dress; they never wore slacks. She liked to sit in Section 16 on the first-base side. I wanted to sit on the third-base side so I could look into the dugout and see Ted Williams rubbing his bat or going through his routines, and I finally convinced her that the third-base side was better.

Mother especially liked Bobby Doerr, and she loved Dom DiMaggio with his glasses and being referred to as "the Little Professor." She listened every night to the ball game until she passed away when she was ninety-five. She was hard of hearing and turned the radio up loud but the neighbors never complained. They always said they knew when the ball game was on because they could hear Helen's radio.

—— JIMMY HAIN, 71, Retired, living in Medfield, MA

Geoff Long, a St. Louis Cardinal in 1963-1964, once won golf's National Long-Drive Championship. Lon Hinkle is the only touring pro to win the same title.

We very seldom saw televised games in the 1960s. Only about one out of every seven or eight games was televised, so I'd listen to the radio. I'd stare at a picture of Fenway Park as I listened to the broadcast, and as I was staring, I'd imagine the ball game being played.

In the 1960s, when the Red Sox were really awful, I was pretty passionate about them. I was ten, eleven years old, and I'd get all upset about regular season games. I would sneak a transistor radio into bed at night when I was supposed to be asleep and listen to games. I remember one in particular. It was a meaningless game in the standings, but I was wrapped up in it. I was eleven years old. Al Worthington was a relief pitcher for the Minnesota Twins. I'll never forget it. The Red Sox were down by a run in the top of the ninth, and they had the bases loaded with nobody out. Then Worthington came in and struck out the side. I wept. I shut the radio off and wept. This was the game that broke my heart, this meaningless game, not Buckner. The game was played in Bloomington, and the crowd was going nuts. On every pitch, the crowd roared. "Strike three." Roar.

———MIKE DONOVAN, 47, raised in southeast Boston

I stopped a gig in 1975. I was playing in a place called "The Lazy River," in Northhampton, Mass. The Sox were in the play-offs. I pulled a radio out of my gig bag, and I said to the people, "We're not going back on until this game is over." I heard the club owner say, "What's going on?" I said, "Come on. Everyone else is down the block where they have televisions. We're gonna listen to the ball game." So I pulled the radio out and put it into the PA system. The people in the audience were happy that I did.

———JOHN LINCOLN WRIGHT, 55, Boston musician

If I had to analyze what it is that attracts me to the Red Sox, I would say it has to do with the part of the country they represent, the way they have lost, and the courage one needs to be a fan of that team. It's easy rooting for the team that wins every year. There's no challenge. The years become a blur. I remember details of almost every game of every World Series in my lifetime, including 1946. I've become friends with Johnny Pesky, who played in that game. He knew my father well. I see him every summer when we go up to Fenway. It's '46, '67, '75 and '86. Not many World Series to remember, but enough.

In 1985, Bill White, the former President of the National League, took us around Pennsylvania. We were looking for a weekend home. We saw a lot of beautiful homes. I said, "Wait, wait, Bill! You can't get Red Sox games here." So, our weekend house is at the northern tip of Eastern Long Island, where you get the games perfectly. During the games, I would sometimes call Joe Castiglione if they had a rock-n-roll trivia question or some baseball or archaic movie question, and the game was boring and I thought I would try to solve it. Now, with e-mail, I talk to Joe all the time during the games. Now that you can listen to the game on the computer, too, it's a lot easier to know what's going on.

——JEFFREY LYONS, 59, Film critic, New York City

I can remember the 1946 World Series against the Cardinals. Oh God, I can still see myself sitting on the arm of the couch in my living room all alone listening on the radio. My mother didn't have a clue or any interest in baseball. My brother wasn't that interested, and he wasn't home. I was in tears—in tears, inconsolable. My mother said, "Oh, for heaven's sake! It's only a game!" My dad was sympathetic. Pesky of all people! As an adult I look at it, and it wasn't his fault at all. He hesitated. Part of it was I think was the fact that he was facing the center fielder, Leon Culberson, to get the ball. Somebody should have yelled to him, "Turn left, turn right," whatever. They didn't, and we know the history. I was devastated. I got some consolation from my father.

The next day when I went to school, a lot of the other kids who were baseball fanatics, we talked about it, and I guess a few days later we got over it. But you don't really get over it.

Jim Britt was the announcer when Enos Slaughter made his dash home. I have this picture of Slaughter just running and not slowing down. And I remember Britt saying, "He has his head down. He's rounding second; he's rounding third!" That's really all I remember. And then, of course, the next thing is, he scores. God, I was devastated! I was young and impressionable and it was devastating. I went to my room, and I was in tears. I couldn't believe it. I was crying. It was just awful. I didn't eat dinner that night. I didn't want to live. It was a crushing blow. It really was because they were my heroes.

——GERRY MURPHY, 67, Wellesley, MA

Chapter 7

The ERA of the E.R.A. and the ERA

Earned Runs and Equal Rights in a Woman's World

ED JURAK CARDS ARE SELLIN' LIKE HOT CAKES—$2 A STACK

—AND WHAT DOES "BASICALLY" MEAN? ...AND DOES SHE KNOW ABOUT OLD UNCLE RICH?

ROBERTA MOCKENSTURM

Forty-six year old mother of three, Roberta Mockensturm grew up in Brookline, two miles from Fenway Park. She has lived in Clearwater, Florida since 1989.

The night Roger Clemens struck out twenty batters in one game, my husband, Dan, and I had incredible seats at the ballpark. We went to the game, and though Roger was striking out batters—maybe he had already struck out nine or ten—the Red Sox weren't doing that great. The Celtics were in the play-offs, and we really wanted to watch them. We thought, "It's no big deal for us to be here," so we left.

We weren't yet married, but were living together, and we went back to our apartment and watched the Celtics. When we woke up the next day, we picked up the *Globe* and saw that we missed an historic evening to go home to watch the Celtics *lose*. Here we had been sitting in incredible seats watching Clemens' performance unfold, so we felt like dummies.

They sometimes re-play classic games on television and whenever they play that Clemens game, the big joke is: "There we are, and there we aren't." To this day, whenever we see a ball player do something phenomenal on television, my husband, Dan and I will say, "Remember the time..."

When I was younger, I didn't have crushes on the ball players, but when I was older, about twenty, I had a crush on Ed Jurak. I used to flirt with him and throw notes to him over the dugout wall. I'd say things like, "What are you doing after the game?" "That was a great hit. How come they don't use you more?" He'd say to me, "What are you doing after the game?" but I'd get embarrassed and leave. We did go out for Chinese food once, but I was a virgin when no one else in the whole universe was still a virgin, but I was, basically, a virgin through college. I would get dates with famous people who were huge Red Sox fans like Chico Ryan, the bass player for the band Sha Na Na—I think Chico liked my seats better than he liked me—but I would clam up. I talked a big game. I'm sure he expected sex on the first date. A groupie is a groupie, and if someone's dropping you notes over the wall....

My family's seats being so close to the dugout, there would be a lot of interaction between the players and the people who sat around us. We knew every regular in the Park. This is going to sound ridiculous, but anyone who knows me knows that I adore "old men." I just have this thing for old men. The older, the more crippled up, the more drooly, the better. I just love listening to old people tell stories about the world and their lives and their experiences. My guys at Fenway, the guys I had crushes on, were these "old guy" **ushers**. Dominic and John the Postman were my guys.

I loved the fact that they knew who we were. My dad always tipped them. My father was a great guy. He was a real fun, Damon Runyon kind of guy, short, fat, bald, but really dynamic. He would sometimes bring a couple of roast chickens and hand them over the wall. He had gotten this rotisserie chicken contraption and went into a contract with Frank Perdue, the chicken purveyor. Dad and Uncle Harry sold zillions of Perdue chickens out of their store. They were great barbecue chickens. So Dad always brought food to people, and now I bring

> The most famous usher currently is Ed Hoffman, "The Singing Usher" at Edison Field in Anaheim, CA. His son, Glenn, managed the Dodgers and another son, Trevor, holds the record for most saves with one team. In 1990, Trevor Hoffman and Troy Percival were everyday players in the minors, not pitchers.

food to people, too. Before September 11, I'd get first-class seating in airports all the time by bringing food to the gate attendants. No one believed it until they flew with me. All it took was a couple of bagels and they put me right up there in first class. I got that from Dad. He would bring barbecue chicken, a pound of bologna—ball players eat anything. They love food. They're bored sitting there for inning after inning. Years ago, there was no such thing as security. We were a much more relaxed society. It was a different kind of world.

After my Uncle Harry retired, he got a job taking tickets in the bleachers at Fenway, so we would sit in the bleachers. We would all sneak in. He would let us all run under the turnstile. Sitting in the bleachers after having sat all those years in great seats by the dugout was a completely different experience.

I would dress up when we sat in the nice seats. We were never a jeans kind of family, and I would wear a dress or skirt and blouse and pull my hair back and sit quietly and not scream things out because it just wasn't acceptable. The owners' box had been to our left, and it didn't feel right to yell out. In the bleachers, we let it all hang out. I don't think Dad ever sat in the bleachers. He liked to sit behind home plate, although he never even liked our seats because he thought they were too close. He liked the anonymity of being back and being able to yell at someone who was being a bum.

When we sat close to the dugout, we'd watch the players talking to one another or arguing over something. I never saw a fistfight among them. The photographers were to the right and one time, a photographer said something to Carlton Fisk. As Fisk came in from the batter's box, he pulled off his equipment and went over the pit wall toward the photographer. Everyone had to come out and get him. That was kinda fun. Of course, the other photographers were snapping away like crazy. I'm pretty sure there was a full-blown picture the next day in the newspaper with a headline like, "Fisk Sizzles."

I went to Emerson College in Boston. I was still a big fan, but after Dad passed away in 1986, which was the last year that the Red Sox were in the World Series, it wasn't the same. The next year, Uncle Harry and Harry's wife, Ann, also passed away and they were the four who had owned the tickets. I actually believe Uncle Harry had owned the four tickets and gave two to Dad and never made him pay full price. When Dad died, Uncle Harry sold the tickets. I would get in with a regular ticket, but all my buddies, my usher guys, would still put me down into a good seat. Dominic and John were the old-time guys. They wore the red jackets with pride. They would tell stories about players like Babe Ruth when he played for the Sox or came to town. They were almost like flies on the wall because no one knew them, no one took them seriously, yet these guys had spent thirty, forty years in the ball park. They all had day jobs. John was a mailman, and I remember seeing him once in a post office. I said, "Oh, you're John." It's like when you see your teacher in a grocery store for the first time.

It just was so normal, or so much a part of my life to spend so much time at Fenway Park that it wasn't extraordinary in any way. It was just something I did. And it was so close to our house. When you were in our house and on our street, you felt like you were a million miles away from Kenmore Square and Fenway Park. It didn't seem anywhere near there when actually it was about ten minutes from our house. We would walk to Coolidge Corner and take the Beacon Street line down, drop a dime into the machine and take the trolley cable car to St. Mary's stop, which was the last outside stop before you went into the tunnel. The first stop in the tunnel was Kenmore Square, the Red Sox stop, the classic ballpark stop. Every one would take it to St. Mary's and walk the last quarter mile to the Park. Then leaving the Park, I'd say eighty percent of the time, depending on the weather, we would walk home. We'd walk up Beacon Street the same route the trolley car took, but the cars were so packed with people that we walked up Beacon Street to Coolidge Corner and arrived home faster.

In college, I knew a lot of Yankee fans, especially BU students. One of them was Diane Jaffe, who I grew up with, whose father owned Jaffe's pic-A-chick, a big, famous deli in Brookline. In 1975, our freshman year, the Red Sox were in the World Series. We couldn't get into the game, and we were in Kenmore Square with about 200,000 other people. The Red Sox won and Diane and I were jumping up and down. I'm five feet tall, and Diane is five feet, nine, and we were hugging and jumping up and down like maniacs along with all these thousands of other people jammed into Kenmore Square.

The reason that night is so memorable to me, not just because the Red Sox won the game, was that I had borrowed a necklace from my mother that she had not given me permission to wear. It was gorgeous, and it had been her mother's, and that night I lost it. It was a very, very expensive gold and pearl necklace. My mother, who didn't usually get mad about those kinds of things because she would say, "It's just material," was really mad. I don't know why I would have taken it to wear there for that event, but I distinctly remember wanting to wear that necklace to look beautiful. My mother was pretty upset. She was "disappointed" in me. It was worse punishment for her to say those words to me: "Extremely disappointed!" The only times I would get in trouble was when I did something stupid bad. When I did something really bad, I never got in trouble.

THESE TEN THINGS ARE THE SEVEN SIGNS THAT YOU ARE HOOKED ON THE RED SOX

CHERI GIFFIN

Cheryl Giffin, 51, is president of the Boston Red Sox Fan Club. She grew up in Dorchester and Brookline, Massachusetts and currently lives in Randolph, fifteen miles southeast of Fenway Park.

The happiest moment for me as a Red Sox fan has to be Game 6 of the '75 World Series. Until they win it all, nothing can ever top that. I was with Dave, my fiancé.

We were three months from being married. We had to walk back to Brookline, and I got up and went to work about four hours later. I was on pure adrenaline. I still see it like it was yesterday.

It was interesting how we came by the tickets. We did not have season tickets, and at that time we didn't really know any Bostonians who did. Back then, the Red Sox had a **lottery** system, whereby you could send in two envelopes, one for the play-offs and one for the World Series, with a check. They supposedly sorted out the envelopes at random, and they would choose fans who would either go to the play-offs or to the World Series.

My boss at the time also wanted to go to the play-offs and World Series, so I devised a brilliant plan. I was familiar with the post office box in Kenmore Square where the envelopes were supposed to be delivered. I told Dave, "I think we should post-date the envelopes and take them down to that post office on the day the envelopes are

> Former Red Sox lefty, Maury McDermott, won the Arizona Lottery in the late 1990s.

due. We should drop them in the mail slot so the next day when the postal worker turns the contents of the box upside down, ours is going to be on top." I thought that was a brilliant idea.

I'm a devious woman. About a week later, my play-off envelope came back and I said, "Oh, shoot! We're not going to get to go to the play-offs, and we'll probably get the World Series envelope back any minute." The next day, my boss got his World Series envelope back, which meant that he wasn't picked, but I didn't get mine back. I said, "Wow, ours is probably lost in the mail or something because there is no way we're going to get tickets to the World Series." The very next day the tickets arrived for Game 6 of the World Series! Of course, we had no idea of the importance the game would take on.

It rained for two straight days after Game 5. Game 6 finally came, and I devised a brilliant plan to park our car at my parents' house in Brookline, which is about five miles from Fenway Park. We parked and took the subway, the infamous Green Line.

At that time, the subway stopped running at 1:00 a.m. Game 6 ended up going 12 innings and didn't end until about 1:30 in the morning, so about 12:30 they made an announcement over the **P.A.** system that the subway was going to stop running. Of course, nobody left. Who's going to leave a World Series game like that? Also, the score was tied at the time.

When Fisk got a home run, I practically went into hysteria. We were sitting in the second to the last row at the tippy-top of the center bleachers—but who was going to quibble about such a thing—and in those days all the seats were bench seats. Thank God, I only weighed about eighty-five pounds then, because we were totally squished together. It was utterly ridiculous

After the game, all the cars were beeping their horns, and people were screaming and yelling in the streets. It was really unbelievable! Everybody either had to walk or take a taxi. You can imagine how

> The public address announcer for the Astros (Colt '45s) in 1962 was Dan Rather. John Forsythe, the actor, was the P.A. announcer for the Brooklyn Dodgers in 1937 and 1938.

easy it is to get a taxi at one-thirty, quarter-to-two in the morning, with so many people trying to get one. People have all sorts of horror stories about people hitchhiking and trying to jump on top of the backs of trucks as they drove through Kenmore Square. Of course, there were no buses either. Public transportation completely ground to a halt. You would think the city of Boston would run late that night, wouldn't you, but that's how insane the whole thing was. There was such a public outcry afterward, the city learned its lesson. Starting then, they add extra subway cars when they know the game is going to end.

We walked five miles. We got back to my mother's house at nearly three in the morning. We were walking with other people all the way down Beacon Street. In those days, people were allowed to bring those plastic horns into the stadium, so on the way home all we heard was, "Honk! Honk!" It was really wild because at that point we thought for sure we were going to win the World Series. When your team comes back and wins a game like that, you know you're going to win.

Of course, the Sox had a 3-1 lead in Game 7, and they lost the game at the top of the ninth. See here's the thing: They always have these fantastic games, and they always take it to the very, very end. They push you to the precipice and bowl you over. It doesn't matter who is on the team. It's always been this way.

Carl Yastrzemski was never one of my favorites. He did have that unbelievable year in 1967 when he won the Triple Crown. He was the last person to do it. But he's kind of a jerk. He's not kind. One of the most recent affronts to us fans was during the '99 All-Star game, which was held at Fenway, which was another great event. Dave and I were there for the Hallmark Hitting Contest. It was like a Hallmark moment. And that was the game when they had all the old time players that surrounded **Ted Williams**. All of the All-Stars from both leagues surrounded Ted Williams, who was in a wheelchair at the

> Ted Williams is in two different fishing Halls of Fame... In 1991, he was awarded the Medal of Freedom— America's highest civilian award—by President George Bush.

time, but riding in a golf cart that night. And it was an unbelievable, spontaneous event. That was also the night that major league baseball was honoring their all-century teams. Carl Yastrzemski was there. He was the only one to come out without a hat on of his team. They introduced him, and then he left.

Last summer when the Red Sox held a special night after Ted Williams passed away, what they did was they invited a bunch of former players to come back…former left fielders, of which Carl Yastrzemski was one. He came for the introduction, but then there was a point in the ceremony where the players were supposed to take their position in the field. He left. He never went to left field like he was supposed to. He was kind of a "——," to be honest with you. Pretty sad. He's not really a favorite. People don't really talk about him too much.

Actually, the time I met Ted Williams is a really funny story. He was quite a bit before my time. But he was always my father's idol, as he was for Dave's father. We were in Winter Haven, Florida in 1978. It's a godforsaken place smack dab in the middle of the Florida. There are two hotels and a restaurant. It's an absolute godforsaken place! By the way, our honeymoon was in Winter Haven. We did not go on a honeymoon when we got married because it was in January. Our honeymoon was delayed, and it was on Route 17 South, in the beautiful Holiday Inn in Winter Haven. We had planned it that way around Spring Training. We didn't want to go away in January, and we had to go away in March. If you've ever been there, you know how close the ballpark is to the two hotels that are there. We would get up in the morning, and in those days they would open the gates at nine. You could go over there, and you could watch the minor leaguers, and watch batting practice, and hang around until one in the afternoon and see the games. If you were to ask Dave, it is his least favorite thing to do. But it is my favorite thing to do involving the Red Sox, which is the obsession I have with batting practice. We get there the second they open the gate no matter where we go, and we've been all over the country to baseball stadiums. We're always standing there banging on the gate, waiting for them to open the doors. I just love to sit there. It's the whole symmetry and all that.

It was almost nine and we were walking in behind the Holiday Inn on the way to Chain-O-Lakes Park. You cross over a little street, and there's a small strip mall. There used to be Zayre's Department Store there. So we were cutting through an empty parking lot. It was a Sunday morning. All of a sudden Dave says to me, "Hey look! Look down there!" He's pointing maybe a hundred feet away towards a man walking near Zayre's. He goes, "Who's that?" And I said, "I don't know." He says, "Look closer." I said, "Oh, my God, it's Ted Williams. He's there all by himself." He must have been on his way to the park. He was the Red Sox hitting instructor. He was one of their roving instructors. I had never met him before, and he of course is twice my size. Dave started pushing me toward where Ted is. I'm going, "What are you doing?" He goes, "We're going to go and see if we can take his picture." So he starts pushing me, and I said, "I don't want to go near him," because I am totally intimidated. I was still young. Now, these days, of course, I would barge right in. So, he's pushing me, and pushing me. And Ted is walking closer, closer… the closer I get—that kind of thing. As he got maybe twenty-five feet away, Dave, the ———, ducks in behind a car and leaves me in the middle of the parking lot all by myself. He was being fresh, and he wanted to force me to meet with Ted. And I was totally shocked. The guy is walking toward me, and I'm going, "Bluh, bluh, bluh!" I went, "Hi, Mr. Williams." He looks at me. He looks at me and goes, "Hello, young lady!" because he's like eight feet tall. I was a BoSox Club member then, and I know that he knew the BoSox Club because of our work for the Jimmy Fund, which is a charity to find a cure for cancer in children. So the first thing I could think of was, "I'm down here with the BoSox Club." Well, with that he reached out and he took my hand, and he darn near broke it. He was shaking my hand, and he was going, "Well, you are wonderful people! You do so much work for the Jimmy Fund!"

At this point, Dave comes out of hiding after I've greased the skids. The little slime ball comes out from behind the car, and now we're introducing ourselves, and I said to Ted, "Would you mind taking a picture?" He said, "Oh sure!" and he backs up. Of course I have to back up to get his large frame in the viewfinder. I'm backing up, and I'm backing up and I'm pointing the camera, and I'm going, "I don't see you! I don't see you!" And Ted bellows, "Turn the camera around, honey!" I was so nervous! I had it backward. And I'm so short. I am not even five feet tall. He towered over me, so when the picture eventually was developed, and Dave made the scrapbook, he put under the picture, "Turn the camera around, honey!"

Bob Ryan, a columnist for *The Boston Globe*—one of the best writers around—has this acronym for Red Sox fans. He calls them PWNCC-ers—Provincial Whining Narcissistic Chronic Complainers. He's a very passionate Red Sox fan, but he doesn't believe that there's a curse or that there is some mythical being preventing them from winning. He just loves baseball. And he does not like the fact that people become so masochistic of the team. They just take it so personally. But you know, when you haven't won for eighty-five years, people do not know any other way to behave. They're so used to losing.

There are people who scream and say they'll never watch another game again. Stupid stuff! I don't know anybody personally who would lock themselves in a room and not come out for a month, but it would not surprise me at all. We have 24/7 sports talk radio here in Boston, WEEI, and it's the Red Sox Flagship Station. And I'm telling you, when the Red Sox lose, they have a thing called the "Whiner Line" where people call and leave voice mail messages. It's just nasty stuff! People really hate when the Red Sox lose. And the fact that even the best teams lose sixty-two games a year. It doesn't matter. When the Red Sox lose, it's like life and death.

I don't root for them because they win, or because they lose, or anything. I became a Red Sox fan because I happened to be born here. I mean, who else would you root for? I am a very loyal person by nature. I would *never* quit on them, not in a million years. I enjoy their history and tradition. I really just enjoy everything about them.

I wear special baseball sneakers to the games. **Keds** came out with a line of sneakers about ten years ago called "Lady's Champion." They

> In 1916, Keds produced the first mass marketed sneaker. In 1949, they unveiled it as a basketball shoe.

are leather and have red stitches like those on a baseball from behind the heel, which is a leather home plate, all the way around to the front. I actually bought a second pair on eBay last summer, because Keds doesn't make them anymore. I only wear them to baseball games. They might have had rawhide ties at one time, but I put in Red Sox shoelaces. They're gorgeous, and everywhere I go people say, "Where did you get those shoes?" I wouldn't tell people where I got them even when Keds was still making them. When I bought them originally they were $29. I paid $50 for them on eBay, which is a lot, but they're worth it. My God, they're so gorgeous!

I have tons of special Red Sox clothing. One other thing that I did—and people ask me where I bought it, but I won't tell anyone how I made it because it's so simple—I took a gold chain, and some oversized baby beads and spelled out "Red Sox." Then I bought a bead for the center that has a heart on it and added two baseball beads on either end. So there's a baseball bead; the word "Red" spelled out in white tiles; then there's a red heart in the middle; then "SOX" in white tiles, and a baseball bead on the end. I wear the necklace throughout spring training and to all the ball games. Everybody asks me where I got it but I won't say. I'm so greedy and selfish, I don't want anybody else to have it.

I found the beads and the tiles at a craft show. I usually don't make crafts, but I happened to go to a craft show because I was looking for a dried flower arrangement. There was a booth that was selling beads and I happened to look and see the two baseball beads. I said, "Oh, maybe someday I can use these." So I grabbed them and then I looked around and I saw the giant baby beads. I'm telling you, they're at least an inch square. They're heavy. I wear it around my neck everywhere I go.

I have a Red Sox mouse pad. I have a Red Sox screen saver. Microsoft Plus makes a desktop theme that's all baseball. "Da-da-da-da! Charge!" plays in the background of the screensaver. I change my baseball sounds so when the computer opens, it plays "Take Me Out to the Ball Game."

Dave wouldn't let me name our pets after the Red Sox. Our nephews wanted to name the dog "Nomar," but Dave said no, because he doesn't like naming pets after athletes because then if they get traded away, we're stuck.

I am the president of the BoSox Club, which is the Red Sox Booster club. It's the largest fan club in organized sports. There are 840 members. The dues are $65 a year. That entitles the member to a Red Sox Media Guide, which is about a $12 value right there. It also entitles them to one special night at Fenway every summer. It's called Family Night. The Red Sox open the doors at three in the afternoon. We hold a clinic given by three Red Sox players. There might be a pitcher, a hitter, and a catcher, instructing the children. We have 1,000 children, all family members of Club members. Every member is allowed to bring two additional people for a maximum of three clinic tickets. They put us in the stands right behind the Red Sox dugout. Then we have hot dogs and a soda, and the kids get to watch the Red Sox take private batting practice. The Red Sox, like most major leagues clubs, no longer give the public access to batting practice, because the home team always takes batting practice first. The clubs don't open their stadiums until ninety minutes before game time, so the fans only get to see the visiting team's batting practice. Teams used to hold practice hours earlier. I think they do it now, primarily, because of cost, because they need to have security in the bleachers, and they just don't want to pay for it.

The BoSox Club was founded in 1967. I became a member in 1978. Then I became a board member in 1994. It's an elected office. I did not campaign. When I was made second Vice-President, I knew I would eventually become president. I was inducted this past January. Dave likes to refer it to as my coronation. I was the first female officer, so I'm the first female president. It just goes to show you what you can do with hard work and determination. Where there is a will there is a way! And I only did it to impress a boy!

Last August, the Red Sox celebrated their 35th anniversary of the 1967 Impossible Dream Team, which was the same year that the BoSox Club began. Dom DiMaggio not only was the person who sponsored me—you have to be sponsored to be a BoSox Club

The King (Stephen) of Red Sox fans in the Sox
radio booth, August, 1995.

July, 2002

New seats being installed atop
left field wall—March, 2003.

Red Sox fan, Susan Johnson, on 2003 Sox Cruise. From left, Doug Mirabelli, Frank Castillo, Willie Banks, Luis Tiant and Manager, Grady Little.

Ted Williams with son,
John Henry, outside
Fenway, 1992.

Ramon Garciaparra,
Nomar's father, talks
baseball with
Johnny Pesky

member—but he was the first BoSox President and a founding member. So the Red Sox dedicated a plaque to the BoSox Club. It's this gorgeous blonde plaque. It says, "The BoSox Club: Community Service through Sports. Founded 1967. First President: Dominic DiMaggio."

The Red Sox held a ceremony outside Fenway before a game, and they hung the plaque right on the façade. It's one of only four plaques that are hung on Fenway Park, right next to where the media goes in and where the turnstiles are now located. They have this weird thing where they open up the street now, right where the turnstiles are, to turn it into Camden Yards. It's created a kind of carnival atmosphere.

Because I am a woman, my presidency has actually brought quite a bit of notoriety to me. Of course, it is a bit of sexism. But the fact is, it is a novelty. We make three minor league trips a year. We make two trips to major league cities a year. This year we will be going to Baltimore and Philadelphia. The most attended trip we took was two years ago when we went to Montreal, and we probably had sixty people. Now a lot of people go to spring training. We have over a hundred people go to spring training. We stay as a group. A lot of people do have places down there, but they come over to the hotel to stay with us for the three weeks.

In 1968, Bo Belinsky married 1965 *Playboy* Playmate of the Year, Jo Collins. In 1973 they divorced. Belinsky died in Las Vegas in 2002. Tennis ace, Jimmy Connors married the 1977 Playmate of the Year, Patti McGuire in 1978. They are still married.

CY YOUNG, CY OLD, CYBEX, CYANARA

JOCELYN SMITH

Thirty-three-year old Jocelyn Smith, known as Joce to her friends, grew up in the western part of Massachusetts, in Hampden, where she still lives. She is a physical therapist's assistant, treating mostly elderly clients in their homes.

I specialize in grumpy old men. Baseball is very big here. It is huge, and it's very healing. Old men become little boys. Baseball's a way of life.

Where I live is right along the Connecticut border. It's very interesting. It seems like most people are Red Sox fans, and then there's the odd Yankee fan, because somebody didn't like their father, or just to be contrary. People are very knowledgeable about both teams. I mean the rivalry is huge. And it's very genteel. It's very polite. This area is very different from Boston. I mean we pronounce our R's correctly. I refer to western Massachusetts as the civilized part of the state. We're very polite; we're very hard working. We don't take handouts. We take care of ourselves because we're very separate from Boston. We are not a part of Boston. Boston doesn't even acknowledge us. They take our tax money, and then say, "Go away."

The way I became a season ticket holder is that I had an old gentleman friend. I seem to collect these 80-year-old, 90-year-old gentlemen friends. I'm sent to these clients, who are at the end stage of their life. They happen to be baseball fans. It's just luck of the draw. Well, I would see this person three times a week. And I looked forward to his "visits" so much because his mind was wonderful even though his body and health were failing. He was a season ticket holder and he owned a business. People sometimes wouldn't go to games, and he owned a weekend package for three seats. He would leave tickets on his dryer for me. I was in shock, and I would try to pay him. He would say, "Don't you dare! Nobody will go to these games. Take them." I just didn't feel comfortable. It wasn't right. And he said, "I'm going to rip them up in front of you, or you go."

He also had this magazine called *Diehard Magazine*. When he was done reading it, he would leave it for me. I saw him off and on for about two and a half years. He died about a year ago. He had these season tickets for years, and his employees would go, but the whole fun had been going to the game with him. The employees lost interest in going when he couldn't go with them. He was fantastic. He was one of the most incredible human beings you would ever meet. He was in his late eighties.

Anyway, I was treating him. He says, "Why aren't you a season ticket holder?" I said, "Why, I don't know. I'll bring it up to my husband." My husband says, "We are not in that class. I'm a carpenter; you're a physical therapist assistant. This is a business owner. No." So I told the gentleman, "Well, my husband doesn't think this is right." I'm not going to argue with my husband. He works fourteen hours a day. He's a good man. He makes the financial decisions for our family. The old man would tell me, "If this is something you love, do it." And I would tell him, "Thank you very much." He never pushed. He was a good man.

So we would talk baseball, and I would do physical therapy, and as the years would go on, things would happen. Well, the 1999 season happened for the Red Sox, and it was a magical season. They were billing it as the Cy Young vs. Cy Old; The Red Sox against the Yankees; Pedro Martinez against Roger Clemens. Well, my client's business, which was a family business, was holding a huge outing at Fenway Park where everybody in his company was going. Everybody in his family was going, except for the son in Georgia. These tickets were going like hotcakes on eBay. They were going for like a couple thousand a seat. My gentleman friend made a promise to me. He said, "Listen, you're going to that game." I said, "I'll give you anything in the world!" He said, "I will sell them to you at face value. Nobody but a fan is sitting in those seats!" I'm jumping up and down like I hit the Lotto. I'm telling my husband. My husband says, "Until those tickets are in your hands, don't get so excited." I said, "I hit the Lottery!" I am walking on Cloud Nine. I can't work. I can't eat. I can't sleep. I'm going to this game. I mean I am so excited I can't function.

Then the man's wife calls up the son in Georgia. The son drives up from Georgia and goes to the game. My client didn't talk to his wife until nearly Christmas. Now I was disappointed, but I understand.

He was heartbroken. I was heartbroken, but hey, I'm an adult. I can handle it. But this is the best part of the story: My husband and I are watching the game in the living room. And I must have pouted like a child…like a child! Like you've never seen someone pout before! And I'm watching the game. Pedro Martinez is pitching the game of his life against Roger Clemens, who is my childhood idol. I never hated the man. I've always loved Roger Clemens. I watched him pitch in the minors. I still can't boo against him. I drive people nuts, because every once in a while, when he really strikes someone out, really good, even if it's a Red Sox, I forget because I'm a 14 year-old kid all over again. Oh, I go, "Oops, that's us he just struck out!" You know what I mean. It's hard. I'm still praying **Roger Clemens** is coming home. Some Boston people and some Boston sports writers are still bitter, but they can get over it. I want Roger to come home.

Anyway, I'm watching the game in my living room, and I'm pouting really bad. My husband says, "That's it! We're going to be season ticket holders!" So starting in the year 2000, my husband and I ended up with a weekend-season ticket holders package. And guess what? That was the last year they offered the weekend package. We're grandfathered in. I don't know what we spent. My husband takes care of finances.

This has made me beyond happy! We have a running joke. The funny thing is, now remember, I know nothing. So tickets go on sale in January. I'm standing in line. I am like a little kid. I'm in my thirties.

> In 2001, Roger Clemens won his sixth Cy Young award…
> without pitching a complete game.

Here I am, I'm standing in line, standing in line, standing in line like all the other people trying to get in on Opening Day, or a Yankee game, or something. I'm standing in line and we finally go. This is four and a half hours on the coldest day in January. I'm standing, I'm standing in line, I'm going to get my season tickets, right. I'm standing in line, standing in line, get to the window and I go, "I want my season tickets!" They say, "We don't treat season ticket holders like this. You call and schedule an appointment." I'm dead serious. And I go, "Really!" I almost started crying. My husband said, "I think we're going to order a couple extra games."

We called back and scheduled an appointment. We got to sit in every available seat to test them out. It was so much fun. When we came to the seats we ended up buying, I started crying. I started crying because they were the most beautiful seats in the world. They are great seats. I can call balls and strikes, and when Tim Wakefield pitches, I'm still trying to figure out this knuckleball. Oh my God, it's so beautiful! You sit there and it just flutters. And it looks like it almost stops halfway between the mound and home plate.

My clients have so many stories. I have a ninety-year old right now who saw Babe Ruth play. I can tell you about the story about the day Ted Williams died. The day Ted Williams died, I came in and I was a little bit sad. My client said, "What happened?" I said, "Ted Williams died." He started crying and crying and crying. And he's a Yankee fan. And his whole family is Red Sox fans. I said, "You loved **Ted Williams** too?" He goes, "No, I hated the ———! Every time you turned around, the guy was getting a hit. He made my life miserable. I hated the ———." He's crying. I'm crying. He cried because he was great! It's hard to see the great ones go.

I have this book about the great Red Sox-Yankees rivalry, but this man will tell me more about Williams and DiMaggio and about those magical seasons. You don't know baseball until you talk to people who have actually seen it played during those times, and he tells me all these stories. I do his physical therapy. I help him breathe. I want

> Joe DiMaggio once said of Ted Williams; "He throws like a broad and runs like a ruptured duck."

to have long baseball talks with him; the only problem is, I have to wait until he can breathe better so he can talk long enough.

I'll never turn a Red Sox game on during a physical therapy session, because I get too distracted. But you know, if someone's not feeling well, or someone's on their way out of this life, I'll just kind of sit with them. When old men are dying, and they are used to being in control of their lives, but no longer have control, sometimes they just cry. I just kind of wrap myself around them and hold them and rock with them. And just tell them that there is something that they are still in control of. That is that they were good men, and that they have put everything in order, and everything is okay, and that the season's over. That helps. And sometimes there isn't another visit. But what else do you do?

For both them and me, baseball is therapeutic. These people have devoted their whole lives to family. Maybe they never had a college education, but they made darn sure their sons did. They made sure their daughters did. Their daughters married well; their wives are taken care of. Maybe they never asked for one thing for themselves. The moment someone else walks in the room, their tears stop, they're fully in control, and they are suffering with un-Godly pain, but they will not let another human being know.

Things are changing this year.

Rogers Hornsby holds the single season batting average record for three teams: Boston Braves (.387), Cardinals (.424) and the Cubs (.380).

I ALMOST WENT ON A CRUISE IN COLLEGE. THE DEAN SAID I WAS #1 ON HIS SHIP LIST.

SUSAN JOHNSON

Susan Johnson grew up in Connecticut, lived around the world and now resides in Houston. She recently took her entire family on a Red Sox cruise.

Susan Johnson and Roger Clemens
(1986 photo)

When I heard about the Red Sox cruise, I thought, "Now that is something I would really like to do." I thought it would be a lot more fun if there were more people on the cruise, so for Christmas last year, I gave my siblings and their spouses tickets to go on the cruise with us. There were nine of us—no kids—off to the Caribbean.

None of my family people who went on the cruise actually live in the Boston or even in Massachusetts—one came from Philadelphia, two from Connecticut, one from New Hampshire and myself, from Texas. Players and officials there were: Grady Little, Luis Tiant, Frank Castillo, Willie Banks and Doug Mirabelli. Doug and Grady both had their wives with them. Luis had a son. Frank had a girlfriend.

We had a hundred percent interaction with them. We thought we'd be happy if we got an autograph and a picture. We ate dinner with them. Every night at dinner you had a different player sitting at your table. The first night they sat Luis Tiant at our table, and I almost started crying...from laughing so hard. It was just real incredible—we talked baseball and cigars. He sat with us two nights.

The third night we were going to have Willie Banks sit with us, and we were all thinking, "Oh, what are we going to talk to Willie about? We don't really know him." We thought we wouldn't have anything in common. From the minute he sat down, we laughed through the whole dinner. We just adopted him. That was just wonderful. And now he's gone over to the Yankees.

They were all just the nicest people you could ever imagine. They were having drinks with us. Grady and his wife went on some of the day tours with us. There were times when they would do "question and answer" sessions, and do photographs. After dinner, when they sat with us, we took pictures of them having dinner with us. They had a Jeopardy tournament where the players were the head of the team and you were on their team. There was a "Win, Lose, or Draw." You just had total access to the players. They were just around. When we would go to the casino at night, they would be in there, and you would be playing blackjack with them or craps or whatever.

We had sixty-two passengers with the Red Sox, but there were groups with the Padres and with the Orioles. Earl Weaver, who is just the nicest guy, was on the cruise. He came over to meet our group one day in the bar. The first thing he said was, "Is there anybody in the group that is my age?" I said, "Well, there's my brother-in-law." They spent the entire week where Earl Weaver would give the name of a player from the forties or fifties, and my brother-in-law would answer with the team and the position, and he didn't miss a one the whole week.

The Orioles and Padres had much smaller groups—around thirty people each. Some of the things we did, we would do together as a group of all three teams, and other times there were things we were doing just as a Red Sox group. Most of it was intermingled. You still had a chance to meet Randy Jones, the ex-pitcher, and Bruce Bochy, the manager of the Padres. They were all there.

I went to bingo one night, and I won the upgrade to the penthouse suite—it was the "Royal Suite" actually—for the rest of the week, so we decided to have the players up for cocktails in our suite. I have pictures of Grady Little serving hors d'oeuvres around the room, and all of us chatting with Luis Tiant.

Grady Little almost killed us on the cruise. We were on this jeep ride where Grady was in the middle jeep. Grady likes NASCAR, and he drives like NASCAR. He was going like a bat out of hell, almost killing all of us. Grady Little was absolutely the nicest guy. First time I meet him, we're going through the little line where we can get an autograph, and he stands up and gives me a kiss on the check—for bringing nine people. "Oh, this is a fun cruise! I'm having fun already." You don't want to bother them so you just kind of walk by and give a wave. Well, they wanted to talk to people. It's like you think you should leave them alone, but they were interested in talking to people. He and his wife are just the most charming, fun, really down-to-earth people. What's really nice, is that you get to see a different side of all of them. All nine of us said it was THE most fun vacation we'd ever had in our lives.

At the spring training camp this year, 2003, I loved going to the park and watching the guys come out and do their stretching and their running. My favorite part is when all the regulars, after the seventh inning, go home so they can beat the traffic. That's when you stay and you watch all the young guys coming up to bat for the very first time, seeing how excited they are, seeing them play with the big league players, that's the most fun. Those are the ones you remember, when you see them finally make it in the big leagues, you remember when they were first playing in their first game.

We are actually moving next year to Ft. Myers to be close to the Red Sox. We're building a house, which will be ready in October. With both my parents dead, the Boston Red Sox are the one thing that keeps my whole family together. It's our one common bond that really keeps us going.

Johnathan Schwartz wrote a book, *A Day of Light and Shadows,* about the 1978 play-off game. At the end of the book it says, "The team that represents you, your choice at an early age, will, guided by your honor, remain a lifelong partner. It is you. You are it—an emotional business together. There is no other way, so then, no regrets." As a Red Sox fan, you have to have a lot of "no regrets."

EQUAL RITES

During a tour of Fenway, we saw that on the Green Monster, on either side of the scoreboard going horizontally, were the Yawkeys' initials in Morse code. If you look at old pictures of the scoreboard, you can probably see the dots and dashes. Since they were the owners, they put their initials there in a subtle way. That was one of those cool little things that you learned on a walk through the park.

When you stand at the foot, at the bottom, of the Green Monster, you can see all the places the balls ever hit the wall. Standing at the foot of that wall, the Green Monster is really huge. On TV, and even when you're sitting in almost every seat except the bleacher seats that are right next to it, it's just so much smaller looking than it is when you see it up close.

We have a real home plate for a doormat. You can't wipe your feet on it, but it's "home." You go away on a long trip and you come and you jump on it and you say, "I'm home."

——JANE WOYCIK, 38, living in Westwood, MA

My wife, Linda, is a huge Red Sox fan. She's a big believer in the Curse of the Bambino mythology. A couple of years ago, she set up a Babe Ruth shrine in our kitchen. It consisted of a photograph of Babe as a pitcher in a Red Sox uniform. Underneath, she set a little candle and every Friday she would light the candle. Every Friday, she would also go buy the Babe a cigar. These weren't cheap cigars either. After about six months, I told her that the man had been dead for over half a century, and I really didn't feel like spending five bucks a week on cigars for him anymore.

I never worried about my wife's sanity. All Red Sox fans are mentally ill. They can't help it. They're tormented. They're tortured. They're self-pitying. They're angry. I totally respect her for her feelings. She hates the Yankees as much as I hate the Red Sox. I would be less impressed with her if there were any equivocation in her hatred of the Yankees.

——MARK JURKOWITZ, 48, Boston, Yankees fan

Chapter 8

Heartbreak Pill— The Real Boston Marathon of 1986

That's the First Time That Ever Happened…Again

LARRY BARNETT WAS ONE OF THE BEST UMPIRES IN THE COUNTRY. THE COUNTRY WAS MONGOLIA

JOE DURKIN JR.

Joe Durkin Jr., 41, was raised in Acton, Massachusetts and now lives in Scituate.

Joe Durkin dancing with his mother.

I remember Game 3 of the 1975 World Series like it was yesterday. I was thirteen and absolutely livid! I hate umpire Larry Barnett to death. I hate him! My God, he made such a wrong call, saying Ed Armbrister didn't interfere with Fisk. After that, Barnett would show up at Fenway Park, and the crowd would boo him. Some of my friends ragged on me, though, because my favorite player of all time was and is Carlton Fisk. I started to follow his career in 1972, the year he won Rookie of the Year. The kids said, "Fisk threw the ball into the center field. That wasn't interference." I said, "Uh-uh! That was complete interference. If Armbrister hadn't been blocking Fisk's throw to second, the ball never would have sailed off Burleson's glove. He gripped the ball too tight, and he was forced to make a fast throw to try and nail the runner, Cesar Geronimo." Oooh, I was filled with such anger.

Nineteen eighty-six was the very best, because I was on the grounds crew at Fenway Park during my last year at Northeastern University. The campus is only a couple of blocks away from Fenway, and I got the job through the longtime head grounds-crew keeper, Joe Mooney. He and my parents were very close friends way back from Scranton.

I don't remember what I made, but it was a paying job. It was so great. I could be at the park prior to the game, and I could watch some of the guys come out really early for batting or fielding practice. Of course, I'd be there for the game. I was there for Roger Clemens' twenty strike-out game against Seattle on a very cold spring night. He was absolutely dominating. It was a very electric environment!

One game really stands out for me. The Red Sox had just acquired Don Baylor in a trade. Baylor used to play for the Yankees, and my brother, Billy, the Yankee fan, loved him. There was a rain delay, and after we had pulled out the tarp, I waited in the dugout.

I was sitting there by myself when Don Baylor came out, his bat in his hand. He was putting **pine tar** on it. He sat down next to me, and I gave him that, "Welcome to Boston. How are you enjoying everything?" He said, "Oh, I love the atmosphere! This is great!" In the meantime, I reached for his bat. It was all sticky, but heavy. I remember the big barrel. I said, "With you coming here, it's kind of bittersweet for my family. My brother is a Yankee fan. You were his favorite and he hated to see you go." He said, "I'll either hit a dinger, or I'll hit a big hit for you, not your brother, tonight." I said, "Oh, that would be great!" never thinking that was going to happen.

When the game resumed, I watched it down in Canvas Alley. Baylor came up in the bottom of the ninth with two runners on. Baylor hit a big shot off the left field wall. The Red Sox won the game 4–3. Baylor rounded first and headed to second. When the winning run scored, he was at second base. The team came out celebrating.

I had to run out to the field with the crew to clean up. We were all out there clapping, and Baylor came off the field. I said, "Nice hit!" He gave me a wink and said, "See, I told you!" I thought, "Oh, my God!

I called my brother that night and said, "You'll never believe what happened!" I told him the whole nine yards. Then *Sports Illustrated* published an article called, "Holding Court!" It showed Don Baylor in a center spread, dressed in a judge's robe. At the time, Baylor was involved with something called the Kangaroo Court, which tried to command leadership in the locker room. They would do things like fine players for doing something wrong. I had Baylor autograph the magazine article to my brother. It was awesome! I couldn't believe that I had really met him and that he'd said he'd get a hit for us.

> For the finish of the famous George Brett "Pine Tar" Game in the early 1980s, Ron Guidry was in center field for the Yankees and Don Mattingly was at second base.

THIS GUY'S FROM SAN FRANCISCO. NOT THAT THERE IS ANYTHING WRONG WITH THAT.

MARTY NOLAN

World-famous columnist, Marty Nolan, is semi-retired and living the good life in the San Francisco Bay area. The former Globe mainstay is credited with a famous Red Sox saying, paraphrased many times to: The "Red Sox killed my father, and now the ————— are comin' after me!"

My father, Neil, gets out of the United States Army after World War I, and instead of moving back to his little town in Maine, he said, "To heck with that. I'm going to go to Boston and make my fortune." He gets to Boston. He's a ball fan, and who does he see the year he gets there—this great team—the 1918 World Champion Red Sox.

Time goes on, and he's waiting for them to repeat the event. He's has four sons and a daughter, and I'm the youngest, and he took me to games. We'd go to games when you really could afford to. I caught a **foul ball** off the bat of Hall-of-Famer, Luke Appling.

Years go on, and about '75, he says, "You know, Martin, my boy, I think the Red Sox aren't going to make it again in my lifetime, and I'm not too sure of yours." I'm about twenty-something. Dad cashed in his chips and went to his reward before the 1986 Series. Thank God, he didn't see it. It was post-Buckner that I wrote that quote. I heard it coming back to me, and people would say, "Did you say

> A major league game uses 80 balls…Each one lasts an average of five pitches…Major League Baseball uses 29 tons of balls each year.

that?" I'd say, "Oh yeah." And it was no exaggeration. The exact quote was "The Red Sox killed my father, and now they're coming after me." That has been referred to as one of the great phrases in Boston Red Sox history. It's only because it's true. You can't make that —— up. It's true.

I lived in Washington D. C. from 1965 to 1981. For the first six years there, we had the Senators. Then the Senators left, and we had to go to Baltimore. Even though Baltimore had a good club, they didn't sell out. One time, a bunch of Bostonians was at a bar in Washington. We're talking about Fenway and the Red Sox, and we say, "Let's get a group and go up to Baltimore to watch the Sox when they come to town. Let's hire a bus, get some beer aboard, and have a good time." Chris Reedy, the bartender, goes right to the phone, calls the Orioles and orders fifty tickets. "Wow! Fifty tickets. Yes sir. And, what's the name of your group?" I said, "Tell him we'll call him right back."

So I called Peter Gammons, who was then working for *The Globe*. I said, "Peter, we've got to come up with a name of somebody who played for the Orioles and Red Sox—we've got to come up with the name for our group—not like the Catonsville Abbots or the Glen Burnie Knights of Columbus." Gammons said, "Hey, Willie Tasby has a life-time average of .250, played for the Orioles, Red Sox and Senators, a six-year career that ended in Cleveland. He was most remarkable for this reason—whenever thunder and lightning threatened, he would take off his metal spikes and play barefoot. He thought he would attract lightning if he wore spikes."

With that, we made up fifty T-shirts from his old baseball card, and formed the Willie Tasby Fan Club. On the back, we had his statistics, everything, his minor league play, Moose Jaw and York, Pennsylvania, all this stuff, and we had a lightning bolt going through it. The Orioles in those days were desperate for fans. They were happy to have us. They'd put our name on the P.A. system. "We'll welcome the Willie Tasby Fan Club, yes sir. When can you come back?" We used to go up a couple of times a year. It just kept on growing. The Baltimore Sun newspaper would write it up. One of my happy times was when I was brought up into the booth to be interviewed by Jon Miller about the Willie Tasby Fan Club. And I had to put out a newsletter, which was a pain in the neck—it's hard to find scraps of information about Willie Tasby. I had to go to *The Boston Globe* library to look up information and there was a headline that says, "Tasby reminds me a lot of Mays," says Casey Stengel. *Yeah! They're both named Willie, and that's about all.*

Then years go by, and I've been a corporate officer of *The Globe* and so I'm doomed to going to this police athletic club dinner in Boston. The publisher says, "I can't go. You've got to go. We have to be represented at this fundraiser." I go downtown and here are the big guys from Gillette and John Hancock there. The organizer gets up and says, "Thank you for coming. I know it's an effort, but we have a surprise guest speaker for you, Ted Williams. And Ted is going to autograph a bat for every one of you." There were only about thirty-five people there. Isn't America a great country? So I stand in line behind several of these businessmen. Ted Williams looks at me and says, "Marty Nolan, the Knight of the Keyboard, huh?" He asked if I knew Clif Keane. I said, "Yeah." He said, "Tell that son of a —— I said hello. What would you like me to write on your bat?" I said, "How about, 'Good Luck to the Willie Tasby Fan Club.'" He throws the bat down and stands up and says, "I played with Willie Tasby. You know, he used to take his shoes off in a storm. He wasn't a bad fielder, as a hitter, not so great, slow. The Red Sox were the last team to integrate, the last team to hire blacks, and we get a guy who can't run." Willie was the second black player after Pumpsie Green.

Tip O'Neill had a little reception of congressmen and senators for Carl Yastrzemski one time when the Sox were in Baltimore because Yaz had his three thousandth base hit. He invited me, and Yaz brings in Dewey Evans with him and Don Zimmer. Somebody told me that Don Zimmer knew Willie Tasby because he was a neighbor of his in Florida. I went to Zimmer and took one of the shirts, and I said to him, "Zimmer, I want you to bring this down to your friend Willie Tasby." He looked it, and he said, "Look at this. What the hell is this Willie Tasby Fan Club? I played with Willie." I said, "I know you did. You played with Marv Throneberry, too." He said, "Yeah, I know I did." So I said, "Well, it's the same thing. People made a deal out of Marv Throneberry with the Mets. Willie's the same thing. What does he do down there in Florida?" He said, "Well, he's a steward at a dog track." I once met Willie Mays when the Giants were building their new ball park. He was looking at the model of Pac Bell, and he said he could hit a lot of home runs in this new park. I said, "The paper says they should name this the 'Three Willie Park' after you, Mayor Willie Brown and Willie McCovey.'" He said, "No, none of us got enough money for that." Then I said, "How about Willie Tasby?" He looks at me and says, "Willie Tasby? You're an old dude, ain't you?"

Our membership included the fifty from the bus and various people at different times because it went on for quite a few years. We never did meet Willie Tasby.

The knowledge of the Sox fans is really something. When they needle a guy, it's a very well-informed needle. One day, Tommy John was pitching and there was a little rain delay. John had just come back from his surgery, and he was throwing from the mound while they were talking about whether or not to call the game. A guy shouts, "Hey, Ump, you better call it off, or Tommy John's arm is gonna rust." They are really creative. Some of them are stupid and vulgar, and all that, but some of them are very creative.

I remember when the Florida Marlins won a World Series and I'm listening to the radio and this woman said, "I waited *five long years* for this." A great Red Sox fan is the one guy who carries a sign around the grandstand every opening day. This year it said, "Every Eighty-Five Years. Just like Clockwork." He really does the sign, and I've seen it many Opening Days. He just changes the number. "Every Seventy-Nine Years. Just like Clockwork." "Every Eighty-Five Years. Just like Clockwork."

When Jim Bunning, currently the U.S. Senator from Kentucky, retired in 1971, Walter Johnson was the only pitcher in baseball's history with more strikeouts.

1986 POSTMORTEMS

MANAGER MCNAMARA: OXYMORON OR JUST MORON?

I was watching the game with my friend, Al, who is from Lexington. He's a psychology professor. As the Red Sox had the lead in the final inning, and they were down to the last out, I remember Al saying to me, "I can't believe the Red Sox are going to win the ——— World Series!" I said, "Never underestimate the power of the malevolent gods." Twenty years later, Al still quotes me. I was superstitious. The Sox had the champagne on ice. At Shea Stadium, the sign had actually lit up, reading: "Congratulations to the Red Sox, 1986 World Champions.
———ROBERT BELL, 57, English professor, Williams College

I don't know think many Red Sox fans will admit this, but the team had no business beating the Mets in 1986. That would have been one of the greatest World Series upsets in history. In fact, going into that World Series, they were the biggest underdog in Las Vegas history; the odds were something like 3 to 1, which is incredible for a World Series. I remember saying, "They are in way over their heads with this team, and if they win, they'll be the luckiest team in the world."

I was in college at Georgetown University. I had a class during one of the play-off games, and I brought a Sony with me and sat in the last row of the lecture hall. I watched by myself on a small black and white TV with the sound turned off. The only time I turned the sound up was during the ALCS when Dave Henderson hit the home run in Game 5, which I still consider one of those weird miracles of sport. If you're a fan long enough, you'll see your team do one miraculous thing, and the Red Sox coming back and beating the Angels in Game 5 was it. But it was a "false dawn," as they say, because that win set them up for the big collapse later.

People who think that the Red Sox were locked into winning the '86 World Series don't understand how good that Mets team was. They were one of the great teams of all time. They had won 108 games. I don't complain about Buckner like other Red Sox fans. As soon as Bob Stanley came in to pitch and the game became tied, it was over. I remember saying, "I don't care what happens now, they are going to lose this game." You can only play with the devil so many times before he beats you.

——JOHN BENNETT, 34, Shelburne, VT

In 1986, my dad died of a sudden heart attack. But thank God, he died in January of that year. If not, the 1986 World Series would have killed him anyway.

He would have seen the rookie Calvin Schiraldi on the mound in the tenth inning of Game 6 and not Bob Stanley. My father wouldn't have understood John McNamara's managing. That game made me the maddest I've ever been at the Red Sox. You have to have a veteran reliever on the mound to start the tenth inning when you're trying to win a World Series. You don't throw in a kid who's only been up for two months, and hope that the dice will roll the right way. If McNamara had managed properly, the Red Sox would have won the championship. Every other Red Sox mistake pales in comparison because we were never that close. Even in Game 7 of the 1975 World Series, the score was 3–3 going into the ninth.

At the time, I was teaching at a private boarding school in West Newton, Massachusetts. I was watching the game with a group of friends, some of whom were lifelong Red Sox fans; others had just started following the team since moving to Boston. During Game 6, with one out in the tenth inning, the Red Sox were up by two runs, and I remember my friend, who is from Spokane, Washington, saying to me, "I have to go to my apartment and bring something back!" I said, "Okay fine, go!"

When he returned, there were two outs and he began snapping photographs of me. I said, "What the heck are you doing? You're going to jinx them." He said, "I want documentation when the Red Sox win that I actually see your reaction." I said, "Put the ———— thing away, please, now!" And then, of course, the world fell away, and we entered the abyss. My friend couldn't believe that I had no visible reaction. I quietly walked to the TV and turned it off.

We lived in an old building at the school and in the middle of the living room, there was a pesky metal support pole about as wide around as a baseball bat. My friend from Washington hit it as hard as he could, and the pole vibrated for about five minutes. It went ba-ba-ba-bum! I remember just watching the pole vibrate. He wanted the Red Sox to win, and because he's from outside the area, he doesn't understand that all of us were sitting there trying to figure out how the team was going to break our hearts beyond our wildest imagination. Sure enough, it happened.

I told my wife, "I'm going out for a long walk." My wife isn't a baseball fan, but she had been watching the game in the bedroom. She didn't want to be in the same room with us. Oh no. I pace back and forth. I shut my ears. In very big games, I can barely watch.

I started walking around the city of Newton. I felt I needed the solitude to process what had happened, but I never took into consideration that there would be hundreds of Bostonians doing the same thing. Not one single person I ran across had had a drop of alcohol, but we were all wicked ——! We were crazed! Women *and* men!

I ran across one elderly couple about two or three miles from my house. Of course, we were all wearing Red Sox hats. The woman was comforting her husband, who wasn't crying, but was upset to the nth degree. She looked at me and said, "You know what? We're both in our seventies and we just wanted to see them win it once in our lifetimes." I said, "I'm sorry!" and I walked on.

I ran across another guy who looked at me and said, "I'm free! I'm free! I'm finally free! That's it! I'll never follow them again! I'm free! I'm done with those ——! That's it. I'm free!"

I cut across Commonwealth Avenue to go home. It was probably three o'clock in the morning. People were passing me left and right, all saying, "—— ——!" I would see a silhouette a hundred yards away from me, stomping and then I'd hear, "——! ——!" Oh God! I ran across a guy walking his dog. He was elderly. He noticed my Red Sox hat tilting aimlessly on my head. He looked at me and said, "Son, this is the darkest day in this town since Jack Kennedy was shot!" Then I went home.

I thought to myself, "Thank God my father died. This would have killed him." I talked to my mother the next day and said, "This would have killed dad." She said, "God, it's killing us all!"

About six or seven weeks after the end of the Series, I go to my doctor, who is then head of Internal Medicine at Mass General. I said, "Doctor, I have a problem because I've gained thirty pounds since the Red Sox lost the World Series." And he said, "You know what. I have never seen more grieving people and people that have developed eating disorders in all my life." He was laughing about it; joking about it. He said, "Well, Shaun, I want you to eat right, blah, blah, blah…" and he goes through everything. I said, "I'll think about the whole experience and I'll go down and order three mocha frappes." I really gained thirty pounds. I never really lost it. My line is I actually want them to win it one year, so I can start losing weight. By that time, I was thirty-one years old, and I had been a Red Sox fan for twenty-five years. So I really felt like I had paid my dues here.

——SHAUN KELLY, 48, Teacher, Greenwich, CT

My father, Samuel Jacobs, passed away in January of 1986. When the Red Sox made the play-offs that year, our family was very sad because my father had been an enormous Red Sox fan who went to many, many games. Many summer days of my youth were spent in Fenway Park with my father and his brothers and my cousins. My father had waited at least since 1975 to see them make the play-offs.

During the summer of '86, my mother was devastated and didn't want to go to any games because she wished Dad had held on so they could have gone to games together.

On the night when we thought the Red Sox were going to win it all, we called my mother and she was crying and upset and thought it was so unfair that Dad couldn't live to see it. After Buckner's error, Dan, my husband-to-be, said, "You have to call your mother because she's probably freaking out that they lost." I called her and she was laughing hysterically and in a great mood. I said, "What's up?" She said, "I am so glad your father's not alive to have to see this." The Red Sox losing brought her out of her funk. It was the first time she had laughed, and it set her on the road to recovery to learning how to be widow. You can't imagine how often our family has talked about this and laughed over it.

——ROBERTA MOCKENSTURM, 46, now living in Clearwater, FL

Right when they got to two outs, two strikes, my father had said, "Oh, I want to stand up for this moment. I've been waiting for this moment for forty-three years." Of course, the Mets get a couple of hits and errors, and the next thing you know, the Sox lost the game. I'm like,

"Oh well, there's still Game 7 and they can come back and win it." He said something like, he swore—he never swore—but he said, "It's over. They lost. There's no way they can win Game 7." I was still hopeful and optimistic that they could come back. The next day on Sunday it was rained out so they had it on Monday. We had to go to church for a weekly class that day. Everyone was so glum and depressed.

I was in sixth grade then and usually went to bed pretty early for someone who was eleven or twelve, so I knew I wasn't going to be able to stay up for Game 7. My mom said she would wake me up if they won. At six or seven in the morning, I rushed to the paper, thinking against all odds—maybe they won and they just didn't want to wake me because I had school. It didn't happen.

—————PAUL MALONEY, 27, Arlington, VA

A lot of people probably say the same thing as me—that the angriest the Red Sox ever made them was at the end of Game 6 of the 1986 World Series. I never blamed Bill Buckner; I always hated Calvin Schiraldi for the fact that he gave up three straight singles with two outs and two strikes. I was at home. I had watched the game down in our family room by myself, and I was just devastated. I sat in the same chair just watching TV through all the post-game. I don't recall if I cried; I probably did. I just sat there for three or four hours after the game.

My mom came down several hours later and I'm still sitting there, not saying a word and she's saying, "It's only a game, you really should go to sleep, you have school early in the morning." I will always remember, I said, "It's not just a game." I was upset for a long time after that.

—————SCOTT GREENE, 31, Marketing consultant

I'm not really superstitious about games or players, but I do have about two dreams a year with game results, and I've never missed. I'm afraid if I used a dream for gambling, I'd bet the house on it, and that would be the one time I missed. It would be like the Twilight Zone.

I had a dream that the Patriots ran this weird Statue of Liberty play, where the snap came to Brady and he did a reach-around hand-off, where he's not really handing off, he's pretending that the back is blocking for him, but instead he reaches around and stuffs the ball in his breadbasket and he takes off. But then instead of taking off, the runner ran to the right and threw an option pass back to the quarterback. That actual play went down in the ball game four days after I dreamed it. As I watched the game, I said to myself, "I dreamed that play down to the finest detail four nights ago."

Another time, the **Patriots** were in a play-off game against Denver, and I woke up at 12:30 p.m. and said, "The Patriots lost. It was a bad game. It wasn't even close." And then I looked at the clock and I realized, "Oh my God, the game hasn't started yet! They're done. They're going to lose!" And they got killed. But I knew it was hopeless before the game started.

One game where I did feel superstitious was Game 7 of the 1975 World Series. In the sixth inning, the Red Sox had a 3-0 lead. I was thinking, "Don't anybody yell out anything stupid, because that's going to jinx it, you know." In the middle of the silence, this clown yelled out, "Just nine more outs and the Red Sox are World Champions." I sat there thinking, "You bum! You had to say that didn't you?" Suddenly, Tony Perez hit a two-run homer, and then in the ninth inning Joe Morgan got a single. Of course, the Sox lost.

I actually had a chilling episode watching the Buckner game. The Sox were down 3-2, and there was one out to go. Gary Carter was at the plate. The count on him was 1-2. There was nobody on base. They're down to one last batter. I was holding a bottle of champagne in my right hand. It was angled toward my thigh. I remember exactly how I was holding it because what I had forgotten was that the heat of the human hand will eventually make the cork pop on a bottle of champagne. So as Carter was at the plate, the cork popped and the champagne went flying all over the rug. Then I knew. I said, "That's a bad omen. That's it, man. The Mets are going to come back." About five seconds later, Gary Carter hit a single to center, and I thought, "Oh man, that's it!" It wasn't my fault, but it was a symbol. It was a message. A lot of people were like me—holding champagne in your

In the history of the Patriots, they have played home games at Harvard Stadium, Boston University Field, Fenway Park, Boston College and in 1971 they made their debut at Schaefer Stadium in Foxboro. Schaefer was the one stadium to have when you're having more than one.

hand one minute; five minutes later drinking Jonestown Kool-Aid with no ice.

——MIKE DONOVAN, 47, Brookline, MA

In the 1986 ALCS, when Dave Henderson homered—before the Sox won the game—I was literally dancing in the room with my friend, Victor, and his mother. His mother is not even a fan. We went crazy after Henderson hit that home run. Victor and I drove to Providence to a Bob Seger concert that night. Right after the concert, we drove into Boston, and we greeted the Red Sox at Fenway. The thing was, they were still down 3-2 games, but we just knew—you ask any Red Sox fan.

I guess I'd have to say I'm a fatalist regarding the Red Sox. After '86, I do not think I will live to see them win the World Series. I think they're jinxed. Just from that one game! Just look at their history. The Yankees have won twenty-six championships and the Red Sox have won zero in the last hundred years or whatever. I cannot switch allegiances so I'm doomed. I don't see the Red Sox winning in my lifetime.

——WAYNE TUMBLESON, 39, Customer service supervisor

My most intense memory is certainly that of many others, which is the debacle at the 1986 World Series. At the time, I was serving a church in North Adams, Massachusetts. In anticipation of a Red Sox victory, on that Saturday evening, I had instructed our custodian to be in the belfry of our church. The church had a huge steeple and some beautiful bells. I told him to take a radio up there and as soon as the Red Sox win the Series, start ringing the church bells. I told him, "I don't care what time of night it is." I had gone to New York that day to go to the opera, and was rushing back up the Taconic State Parkway, trying to catch the beginning of the game on the radio. I finally got home to see the second half. I had chilled champagne in the refrigerator ready to go. It was one of the lowest moments of my life when they lost the game. I quickly called the custodian and said, "Go home." The next day was Sunday, October 27. I could barely get out of bed to lead worship the next day. It was the last thing I wanted to do.

Believe it or not, there's always a good fifty percent of even a New England congregation that doesn't care about baseball, but for enough people, there certainly was a sense of depression for many, and they understood where I was coming from. I did my best to get through the service. I did acknowledge what had happened and tried to frame it in some kind of humorous vein for those that might have thought it was beneath the dignity of the occasion. It certainly was the thing that was most affecting me at the time.

I don't think I got heavy enough with it to blame God. I don't believe that God has disappeared when the Red Sox lose.

——REVEREND CARL HEICK, 51, Centerville, Cape Cod

My best moment in all my years rooting for the Sox came on my wife's birthday in 1986, when Dave Henderson hit the home run to beat the Angels. That was the most exciting, even more so than Fisk's home run. It was a victory from the jaws of defeat. They were about to lose the game, and these were the play-offs. Henderson hit a home run, a bomb to left field. He was a mid-season acquisition from Seattle—he and Spike Owen, the only player whose name is Spike. It says it on his birth certificate.

The closest that I have come to crying was the Bill Buckner incident. My then-little son, had twenty-seven of these rubber ninja warrior little figures. I had them all lined up while I was watching the game. With each out, I flipped one down. The last one was there. There were twenty-six outs, and then that horrible thing happened, and I swear that one is still up on a table in that hotel in Disney World. I can remember I just had to take a shower. I stayed in there a long time. I was almost afraid to come out. I must have lost seven pounds watching the aftermath of that. That was the most shocking thing I've ever seen. Up to then, it was a family vacation. We came back the next day.

——JEFFREY LYONS, 59, Film critic, New York City

God is good, because She hasn't allowed us to win that World Series. If we win the World Series, what the heck are we going to do? We won't start a dynasty. We'll say it's a fluke! How are we going to handle it? What are we going to complain about?

There is some essence to the Red Sox fans, that he wants the pain of losing and the pleasure of complaining. But in my case, I just want to change one little word here. Yes, there is that out there in Red Sox Nation—but in my case, it's the natural order of things. And I've accepted it. That's the difference. It's the natural order of things; it's not meant to be! My fantasy about the World Series is the next World Series ought to feature the Red Sox and the **Cubs**. It goes to a seventh game. As the ball is hit to the outfield for the final out, a meteorite hits the earth and we'll never know! Really, that's the way it should be! That's the way the world should end! A fly ball has to be hit, and it's in the air, then a meteorite hits and none of us will ever know! That's the way it ought to be! God in Her justice will do that!

—— GERRY MURPHY, 67, Supervisor of student teachers, Boston University

The Bill Buckner year, I was watching the Series with a boyfriend, who was a musician, a drummer, from Belfast, Ireland. At that last game, he was saying, "You're going to win. Why don't you relax? You're going to win." I was like, "Oh, no, no, no. You can't say that. You jinxed them, you ———." I got really ——— at him. "You can't do that." "Well, what are you talking about? It seems obvious they're gonna win." He had no idea. He didn't know anything about the Curse. When the ball went through Buckner's legs, he said, "I don't believe it." I screamed at him, "How dare you. That's why you don't say anything." He didn't get it. He didn't understand. I dumped him!

—— LAUREN DOMBROWSKI, 46, now living in Los Angeles

The worst moment I've ever had as a Red Sox fan would have to have been the whole Buckner thing in 1986. That was a really bad one. I was not at the game. We were at home. We had a finished basement in that house, and it had quite a bit of memorabilia. My friends used to refer to it as "The Shrine."

The Red Sox were ahead, and there are two outs in the top of the tenth, one strike away from winning. It was 0 and 2 on the batter. My husband, Dave, went up to the kitchen to the refrigerator. When we

When the Cubs won their last World Series in 1908, there was no radio coverage…because radio had not yet been invented.

Wrigley Field opened in 1914, built at a cost of $250,000. Fenway Park, costing $300,000 debuted in 1912.

got married, friends of ours gave us an expensive bottle of champagne, which we were going to use when the Red Sox won it all. It had already been over ten years later. He brought it down, and he put it on the coffee table in front of me. He never took the foil off. He brought down the champagne glasses from our wedding reception. He just placed them there. He had been keeping score, and I was just sitting on the sofa in a yoga position. I get very superstitious when something important like that is going to happen. A friend of ours, Dan Riley, wrote a book, called *Red Sox Reader*. He referred to it as the power center position, that when your team is ahead, and you're sitting in a particular position, you can't move. So if you're in a yoga position, you stay there. If your hands are on your side, they stay there. If your hands are under your chin, they stay there. Just don't move, because it's superstitious. So, I was basically sitting in a yoga position. I was so nervous, my fingernails were digging into the palms of my hands. And I ended up when the whole thing was over I had not cuts, but ridges in my palms from my long nails basically digging into my palms. I really didn't think the Red Sox were in jeopardy. I really didn't, even after the Mets got a couple of runners on.

I was yelling at the manager, because the manager is a buffoon, and he ended up costing us the World Series. Not Bill Buckner! There was so much that went on in that game, that you can't really pin it on Bill Buckner. I can't blame him. He shouldn't have been in that position in the first place. The manager was John McNamara. He was a drunk. He really was a drunk. The thing is he was what we called a "veterans manager." He loved to keep his veterans in the game, except that for every other World Series game that preceded Game 6, when the Red Sox had a lead, he took Buckner out of the game and put Dave Stapleton in at first base for defensive purposes. Well, when the Red Sox had the two run lead, he wanted Bill Buckner to be on the field, to jump on the pile when they won it all. So for the first time, he left Buckner in the game, instead of Dave Stapleton. And as they say, the rest is history. And besides, even if Buckner had fielded the ball, he never would have made it to first in time to get the runner. So the game was tied either way. The game was already tied.

Plus that wussy-faced Roger Clemens took himself out of the game. He claimed he had an "owie" on his finger. Who takes himself out of a World Series game in the seventh inning? What was that all about? He said he had a blister.

The champagne is out. I'm in my position. Then it happened. My husband threw his scorebook across the room, and shouted an obscenity that he doesn't usually repeat. I usually do. It's the word that rhymes with "puck." I use it all the time. Then, basically, without saying anything, I ran up two flights of steps to the bedroom and threw myself face down on the bed, and started crying uncontrollably. That was it!

They played Game 7 on Monday. The Red Sox got off to a 3-0 lead in that game. They ultimately blew that, too. I didn't want to go to work because I didn't want to face anybody. Because what happens is when you are as close to the Red Sox scene as I am, people tend to think that it's your fault. People tend to identify you with the team. They think like you're actually part of the team. They don't say it's your fault, but people take it out on you. The group is like an arm of the Red Sox. And we're so closely identified with them, that people take it more seriously. I'm talking about people who are Red Sox fans. They beat up on themselves. That's part of being a Red Sox fan. They say, "We blew it! We suck! We're never going to win it!" Absolutely, it's like masochism.

——CHERI GIFFIN, 51, President of the BoSox Club

I'm not at all sure that I'm going to live to see a World Series championship. Seriously, I do remember the one moment watching Game 6 of the 1986 World Series that I really knew I made a mistake. I had said to myself, "This is it! I can't believe it! We're one strike away! I can't believe it, but it's really going to happen. We're really going to win it." I just knew the moment I said that, that I killed it. The ball went through Bill Buckner's legs, and that was that.

I am a little more pessimistic than I used to be. It's sort of like Charlie Brown and the football from the old *Peanuts* strip. How many times is the ball going to be pulled away from me before I finally figure out that that's what's going to happen every year.

——JOHN GORDON, 57, Mystic, CT

Over 1,700 of the *Peanuts* comic strips had a baseball theme.

Chapter 9

Damn Yankees

The Evil Empire Strikes Back

EVERY OCTOBER, HE PAINTS THE TOWN BEIGE

BRUCE BOSLEY

Bruce Bosley, 46, was in sales for Sherwin Williams for seventeen years before becoming the Assistant Sports Information Director at the University of Vermont in 1998.

New England is pretty much Red Sox country, and the fandom is taken for granted. I'm one of these people who has a big resentment for New Yorkers. They come to this area and they love to live here—the whole Bob Newhart thing—"We've made our money on Madison Avenue and now we're going to relocate to Vermont because it's a better way of life." But when they get here, all you hear about is *their* way of life. There are enough of them who are loud enough and a lot of them are Yankee fans—their pizza is better, their bagels are better, their restaurants are better—everything's lousy up here in Vermont because in New York it's so much better. They don't mention about the crime and the racism, the taxes, the cost of living, or the swill of the city. They're real loud about everything. It's a loud, yappy group. This is my take, but it's shared by others, too.

They ruin a lot of things. A lot of them came up here to college in the 1970s. If you were to take a hundred baseball fans that live in Burlington, Vermont, or just American League fans, you'd probably have to say eighty percent of them are Red Sox fans and maybe seven or eight percent are Yankee fans. Who makes the most noise? Who are the bullies? They're the ones who create the tension. They chirp about the success of their team. They make fun of Red Sox fans.

I can be both kinds of Red Sox fan—the intellectual quiet fan or the noisy fan. You're either a fan or you're not. I take the offense with the Yankee fans. I don't care about their four hundred and seventy five straight championships or anything like that. One thing about New

Yorkers, too, they are they are the biggest hypocrites in America. **Darryl Strawberry** is a hero to them. Darryl Strawberry is the scum of the earth. He's about a nine-time felon. They were the only team who he could play for. They pushed the rules so he could play. One of the biggest scum bags in America that the Yankee fans tend to overlook, two of the biggest, are Joe DiMaggio and Mickey Mantle. The reason Mickey's exploits were never revealed at the time was because they hid them. Guys like Mickey Mantle, Joe DiMaggio, Whitey Ford, Paul O'Neill, Darryl Strawberry, Steve Howe—horrible role models. Yet Carl Everett, because he bumps an umpire, is run out of town, and is vilified nationwide. Yet, Joe DiMaggio is the biggest hero ever. Joe DiMaggio beat his kid up.

Of all the games I've been to at Fenway, which is probably over three hundred, the 1999 ALCS when Martinez pitched against Clemens, had to be the best in terms of having the most unbelievable atmosphere. It was almost like a college football bowl game the way the people were acting outside Fenway. Everybody was there early, all excited—instead of just walking into the game at the last second. There was tailgating going on in the parking lot, and things like that. The restaurants around Fenway were all packed. The Dominicans, who normally would go when Pedro pitches, most didn't have tickets. They were all out dancing and playing their drums in the streets. You came out of Fenway, and it was dark when the game was over, and the Prudential Building was all lit up. That stuff was neat. I love Fenway Park, but I think it's time to go. These tree-huggers that want to save it are.... The consensus should be either a new one or rebuild it. It's horrible. It's going to be condemned sooner or later or fall apart.

The Red Sox fans are there every game, not just in the play-offs. You can watch the Red Sox games on TV in your own city. You don't have an owner who's an idiot. Take George Steinbrenner—he has a pattern not only of success but self-destructing success. The Yankee cycle is up now—the Yankee cycle is about to go down.

Who is the most famous person to pinch-hit for Darryl Strawberry? Homer Simpson on an episode of "The Simpsons."

I HATE PEOPLE THAT ARE LATE...
LIKE THE LATE MICKEY MANTLE

JOHN GORDON

Professor John Gordon, 57, spent his youth in the western United States before moving east for college and graduate school. He teaches English Literature at Connecticut College in Mystic, Connecticut. John bought his first color TV just so he could watch the 1986 World Series.

I teach James Joyce. The endless postponement, the cyclical futility and frustration, the almost, "almost, but never quite" in Red Sox history has parallels to Irish history, and Jewish history, too—the idea of always waiting for the Messiah to come. In James Joyce, the Irish waited 800 years for their Messiah to come, and according to Joyce, when he finally came in the form of Charles Stewart Parnell, they didn't recognize him.

In my classes at Connecticut College, I sometimes draw the analogy. Here, we're in an evenly divided part of the East Coast. Half the students are Yankees fans, and half are Red Sox fans, so they empathize. But I do think that Red Sox fans can understand the literature of failure better. To be a Red Sox fan is to always be the sort of Sad Sack in the group. That's the role you're playfully resigned to. I don't think Red Sox fans could understand anything particularly triumphal.

A lot of people say this has to do with the New England temperament—the feeling of flintiness, that we are not put on this earth for pleasure, but are meant to suffer. Red Sox fans are definitely more romantic fans than others. We're like people in the South who mourn the old Confederacy. It's a romance of a lost cause.

Yankee fans, on the other hand, would find James Bond more identifiable than James Joyce. They'd understand any sort of sequence

The view from the new seats
atop the Green Monster

Old ball players never die...

Gary Bell
2002

Dick "The Monster"
Radatz
2001

Luis "El Tiante" Tiant
2003

Rico Petrocelli
1999

...they just go to Fantasy Camps!

Bill "Spaceman" Lee
2003

Bernie Carbo
1996

Bobby Doerr
1988

Frank Malzone
1994

Boston Fantasy Camp

Ed Schaffer   Walt Macone   Lefty   Al Fountain
Gillette

Kim Fletcher   Wayne   Tony Basile   Kevin Marden
Brockney

Dave Mulvey   Mark Haugile   Stan   Ed McGuire
Lichtman

Bill Sullivan   Curt Pollitt

Fans Hall of Fame

Dale Clarke   **Harold Vosko**   **Steve Durkin**   **Bill Hofmann**

John Torniero   **Rob Watkins**   **Joel Weinstein**   **Joe Diamond**

Bill Donovan   **Lee Gregory**   **Laura LaPalme**   **Scott Boyer**

Joe Saloman   **Bill Grogan**

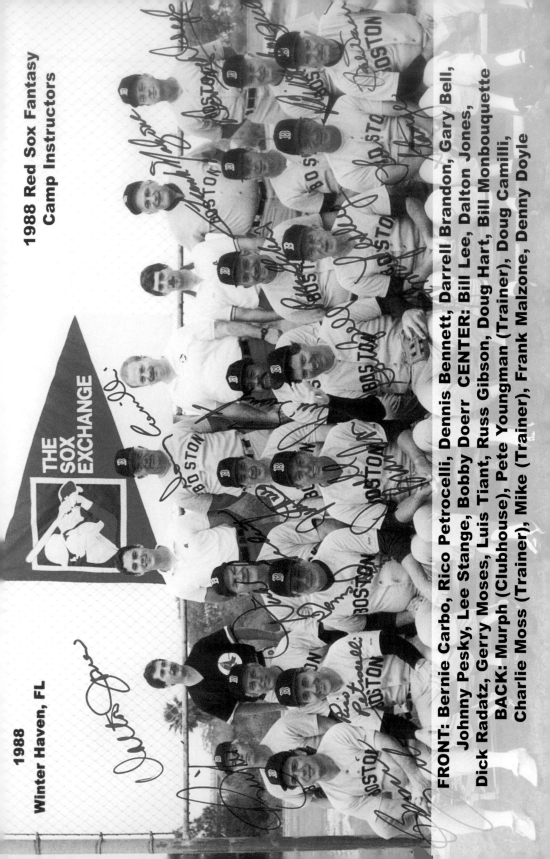

1988
Winter Haven, FL

1988 Red Sox Fantasy
Camp Instructors

THE SOX EXCHANGE

FRONT: Bernie Carbo, Rico Petrocelli, Dennis Bennett, Darrell Brandon, Gary Bell, Johnny Pesky, Lee Stange, Bobby Doerr CENTER: Bill Lee, Dalton Jones, Dick Radatz, Gerry Moses, Luis Tiant, Russ Gibson, Doug Hart, Bill Monbouquette BACK: Murph (Clubhouse), Pete Youngman (Trainer), Doug Camilli, Charlie Moss (Trainer), Mike (Trainer), Frank Malzone, Denny Doyle

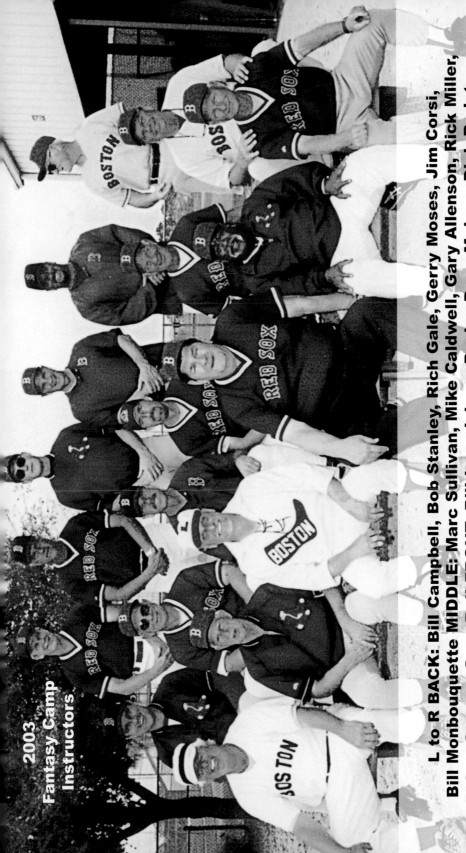

2003
Fantasy Camp
Instructors

L to R BACK: Bill Campbell, Bob Stanley, Rich Gale, Gerry Moses, Jim Corsi,
Bill Monbouquette MIDDLE: Marc Sullivan, Mike Caldwell, Gary Allenson, Rick Miller,
Lee Stange, Gary Bell FRONT: Bill Lee, Johnny Pesky, Dave Mulvey, Dick Radatz,
Luis Tiant, Denny Doyle

AMERICAN LEAGUE

P	1234567890	R	H	E	P	INR	P	INR
22	NY 0000000000	0	0	0	27 SEA	2	6 KC	1
	45 BOSTON 0001 1001	3	7	0	21 OAK	1	11 CLEV	2
					14 ANA	1	12 MINN	1
					31 TEX	3	17 TOR	2
					23 CHI	1	21 BALT	1
					17 DET	1	7 TAM	1

AT BAT   BALL   STRIKE   OUT ℍ   Ⓔ

315

George O'Donnell of suburban Portland, Oregon won the 2002 Radio Shack Extreme Fan Contest by recreating part of Fenway Park in his backyard.

where the most powerful guy winds up winning. We used to say rooting for the Yankees was like rooting for General Motors. A lot of popular literature and entertainment is like that. It reconfirms that notion of "Might makes right," and that the winner is the good guy. I'm reminded of the beginning of the movie *Patton,* when George C. Scott says, "All Americans love a winner," or a "wiener," as Luis Tiant would say.

There's an episode of the TV show ***Cheers*** that shows the Bostonian's idea of a Yankee fan. It's one of their best. There's this big, fat, obnoxious guy that comes to the bar and starts tearing Sam down for getting drunk and blowing games. Sam's saying, "No, no, no." At one point, Carla, who's been simmering, jumps on this fat guy's back, grabs him by the ears, and starts pounding his head on the counter. There it is, what Red Sox think of Yankee fans. It's a great moment!

Tom Yawkey spent a lot of money, but he never spent quite enough. To this day, we're always outspent. Anyway, that's just my rationale. My favorite TV show of all time was *The Phil Silvers Show* with Sergeant Bilko. There was a character named Ritzik, who was always Bilko's patsy. He'd always get into some kind of scheme and at the end Bilko would say, "I've outfoxed him again!" And Ritzik would always be saying, "I knew it! I knew it!" Well, that's kind of the Red Sox refrain. Whether it's a ball going through Bill Buckner's legs or whatever, something is going to happen. Other teams have won the World Series. Why haven't the Red Sox ever won? You would think the law of averages would eventually give us one break. I don't know. It makes you philosophical in a doomy kind of way.

The Sam Malone character in *Cheers* was patterned after former Red Sox pitcher, Bill Lee. Bill Lee once demanded number 337 from the Boston Red Sox because 337, upside down, spells Lee's last name.

SOME PEOPLE FEEL STEINBRENNER IS THE BACKBONE OF THE YANKEES. I WOULDN'T PLACE HIM QUITE THAT HIGH.

ROBERT BELL

Bob Bell, 57, lives in Williamstown, where he is a professor of English at prestigious Williams College—George Steinbrenner's alma mater.

Baseball is one thing that most males have in common. Sometimes I use it as a way of being a more typical guy. For example, I might go into my class after the Red Sox have beaten the Yankees 4-2 in a big series, and I'll write the score on the board. Or, I might develop a friendship with a student that would be, in part, based on sports, as I would with one of my friends. I might talk about the American pastoral and baseball's mythic and ritual elements and the ways in which, for instance, it's kind of like the Forest of Arden. It's a green world. There are very clear boundaries. Things are either in play or out of play. It's very territorial, very special, and there is no clock. That's one of the great points about baseball. It's not just the timeless tradition of baseball. It's a game that's very interesting, but it's much more interesting when you're sitting there with your friend talking about previous games and people's batting averages, which pitches would have stymied which batter in what year, or who got voted for the MVP and so on.

We haven't been as been as deprived as many other sports franchises. It's only that we haven't won the bloody World Series. The rivalry with the Yankees is a kind of neurotic aggravation. But there are many other teams that have been nowhere nearly as successful. In fact, the Red Sox have a very successful franchise. Even I, in 1975, wasn't depressed about losing that seventh game because Game 6 was such a high.

A VASECTOMY IS NEVER HAVING TO SAY YOU'RE SORRY... SO IS BEING A NEW YORKER.

JEFFREY LYONS

Famed film and theater critic, Jeffrey Lyons was born and raised in New York City where he still lives. Jeffrey, 59. is a self-professed trivia addict, and appears regularly on national television.

Some of my dearest friends are Yankee fans. I talk to a Yankee season ticket holder every day. I send him stuff; he sends me stuff. He's played left field on my team for twenty seasons. A very big real estate family named Resnick. We talk baseball all the time, and we don't get into fights. No, not at all! I don't like the guys who wear "Boston sucks!" shirts, and I don't like the Red Sox who wear "Yankee sucks!" shirts. That's vulgar and disgusting! I don't like that Red Sox fans are too preoccupied with the Yankees.

During the season, the Red Sox really obsess me day to day. The news anchors kid me about it on the air when the Red Sox are losing. It gets you through one day after the other. I have a few Red Sox fans. My son's high school college advisor makes me looks ambivalent about the Red Sox. He goes down every day and gets *The Boston Globe* in his hand, rather than reading it online. The Red Sox have typically beguiled, enticed and mesmerized me all my life. I've suffered years of horror and heartbreak, ever since the heyday of Lu (Lou) Clinton, Jim Pagliaroni, and Norm Zauchin. Even in the 1961 baseball year-book photo from Fieldston, my high school, I'm wearing a Red Sox hat. To be a Red Sox fan, especially living in New York, is to be a slightly eccentric cliché, an exercise in annual self-examination when April brings hope and October brings the inevitable heartache.

After all, Fenway Park was Ray Kinsella's destination in *Field of Dreams*.

I grew up admiring Ted Williams' bat, Jimmy Piersall's glove, and Ike Delock's ability to hang on averaging about eight victories a year for more than a decade. When I was growing up in the 1950s and 1960s, the Red Sox always seemed to finish around fourth, a dozen games behind, but with an ability to give the Yankees a run for their money. Back then, they were managed by someone whose first name was Pinky, who was fated a few years later to die while on parole from a prison term for vehicular homicide. How could they win? Year after year, the Red Sox would trudge into the stadium, stocked with players like Don Buddin. Ted Lepcio, Eddie Bressoud, and others.

Now this condition of mine might be understandable if I'd grown up in Boston. But I was born in the Upper West Side of Manhattan. I didn't even see my first game at Fenway until 1978. Central Park West isn't exactly a gathering spot for wizened fans swapping Frank Malzone or Pete Runnels stories.

My father, the Broadway columnist Leonard Lyons, the quintessential New Yorker of his day, tried to nip my wandering affections in the bud. He introduced my three brothers and me to all the Yankee greats of the 1940s and 1950s, when we accompanied him to Toot Shor's restaurant on his daily news gathering rounds. But it didn't help. My heart was headed to Fenway Park.

Part of the beauty of baseball is that it is a wonderful escape from the trials and tribulations of daily life. It is order, logic and symmetry between the lines usually absent from the real world. But try rooting for the Red Sox for a season! That's when life itself is the only escape from chaos and catastrophe on the diamond!

That fateful season of 1978, a colleague at WPIX took me to Yankee Stadium and into the visitors' dressing room the first night the Red Sox came in to New York. And there they were, leading the Yankees by 14½ games. Joe DiMaggio was my boyhood idol because he had the greatest natural skills of anyone who donned a uniform. But Yaz became the hero of my later years because he did more with ordinary skills than almost any other player.

During the game there was an extended rain delay, and Phil Rizzuto asked me to fill the time on the telecast. I was explaining on the air what a thrill I had just meeting the Red Sox. How it even eclipsed being Ernest Hemingway's houseguest in Cuba, and Truman's guest in the White House. I noticed a frantic signal from the assistant director. Suddenly the interview was over. George Steinbrenner had been watching from his box, and ordered Al Rosen, the Yankee president, to get that Red Sox fan off the air.

Being a Red Sox fan in New York has always been a challenge. From April to October on game nights, I often wear my Red Sox hat around town, usually on the way to a movie screening. I feel I'm sporting a green beret on a main thoroughfare in Tehran. At home, working the dial of my radio with a delicate touch of an experienced diamond cutter, I'll search for my station like some resistance fighter behind German lines trying to reach Radio London. I spent years suffering the good-natured taunts from the Yankee fans in the local deli, from doormen as I pass by them regularly, from ushers or theatre managers, almost anyone whom I come into daily contact.

The worst day of my life was the day my father died. Next to that, was the dark October afternoon in 1978 when a light hitting Yankee shortstop with a child's nickname and a career .247 batting **average**, fouled the pitch off his foot, borrowed a bat that might have been corked, and off of a former Yankee pitcher who took no warm ups while Dent was hopping around, blasted my hopes into a nearby screen! None of the other thirty-nine home runs this otherwise ordinary player would ever hit in his entire career would have any meaning.

Eight seasons later came the third worst day of my life, that awful autumn night when a usually reliable first baseman on creaky ankles, who should have been in the dugout anyway, let a routine ground ball and along with it my hopes and dreams, dribble through his legs. Like people who recall hearing the attack on Pearl Harbor, every Red Sox fan remembers where he or she was that night. Perhaps appropriately, I watched that disaster on TV from Disney World.

> The difference between a .250 and a .300 batting average is one hit per week.

I am constantly asked two questions by friends and people who stop me on the street. They'll either want to know about a new movie in town or why I root for this team that has broken my heart every year of my life? The answer to the first question changes every week. But to answer the second, I always quote Blaise Pascal, the 17th century philosopher, who said, "The heart has reasons that reason itself knows nothing about." He was history's first Red Sox fan.

I have a standing promise with James Earl Jones that I can take him to his first baseball game. He hates baseball. I revere *Field of Dreams.* To me, it's the best film of the 1980s. I can't see it without crying.

Johnny Pesky is the only man to have something named after him inside a stadium, The Pesky Pole. One of my favorite bits of baseball trivia is the record that is held by a Red Sox that, in all probability, will never be broken. That is the most hits in one inning—three. It was Glen Eugene Stevens, otherwise known as Gene Stevens. He got three hits in one inning. It was a seventeen-run inning in 1953.

I have a Red Sox gold watch that the team gave me. Instead of numbers, it says, "B O S T O N R E D S O X," and it's got a Red Sox emblem in the middle of it. I've never seen another one like it. It's a Bulova watch. I knew Artie Bulova. He gave me a watch, which he inscribed for my bar mitzvah, but I never used it.

I've worn my Red Sox hat up the Nile. I've carried it with me at the Academy Awards. I carry it with me to the Tony Awards. It's my yarmulke; Linus had a security blanket. It's showing the colors. I've worn it in Chile; I've worn it in Uruguay. I wore it running with the bulls in Pamplona six different years. It didn't falloff. The first time I went to Pamplona was in 1956. I went with my father and Richard Condon, later to write *The Manchurian Candidate* and *Prizzi's Honor.* In 1961, I ran with the bulls for the first time, and I wore my Red Sox hat. Ernest Hemingway would stand right outside the arena with a long stick and keep the bulls running all the way through because the bulls are not the major danger. The major danger is the drunks and the crowds. I don't like it at all. It ruins the bulls' afternoon.

I have a lot of autographed baseballs. Steve Lyons gave me his road uniform that says "Lyons" on the back of it. I have a game-worn Yastrzemski jersey. For my fifteenth wedding anniversary, my wife gave me a Yastrzemski game-worn 1973 uniform. She got it through my brother, George. It's in a closet at home hanging on a hanger. It's not in an air-cooled room, but I do want to be buried in that, or in my Steve Lyons road uniform that says "Lyons" on the back. He's the only man who played for the Red Sox four times, and he's a friend of mine. He's also seen "Phantom of the Opera" twelve times. DiMaggio gave me a game-worn hat of his. His name is sewn into it. He autographed it, so I have his signature.

I take one or the other of my children, and we go to Fenway and they see these vendors outside with the sizzling hot franks and their tank tops. I say, "Look at this now. This won't be here in a few years. You will never see this again. This is the old way it was."

DAMN YANKEES

YANKEE DOO-DOOS

I go to Yankee Stadium about two or three times a year to watch the Red Sox/Yankees. I always go with my friend who grew up in upstate New York. He is a Yankees fan, but is the son of a Bostonian and a Red Sox fan, so he knows the Red Sox history. He's great to go with because he wears his Yankee apparatus and I pretend not to root for any team. I would root for the North Koreans before I would root for the Yankees.

One time, though, I happened to be carrying a hat that I had bought for my son. A Yankee fan walked up to me during a rain delay and said, "Hey Boston, what does 1918 mean to you?" I looked at him and said, "On November 11, the Armistice officially ended the Great War, and a few weeks later President Wilson proposed a 14-Point Plan." He said, "You Red Sox fans think you're so smart, but we Yankee fans have all the championships!" "Alas," I replied, "then we Red Sox fans must have all the brains!" Several Yankee fans actually applauded me. They said, "Good for you!"

——SHAUN KELLY, 48, raised in Wellesley, MA

One of the worst moments of my life wasn't just a moment, but the whole 1978 season. That was the absolute worst disaster in Red Sox history. I will never get over it. They could win twenty World Series' in a row, and they could never absolve that loss.

I was in sixth grade and had just moved to Vermont a couple of years before. In Vermont, Red Sox fans who yell, "Yankees suck," are so safe. They can run their mouth because they don't know what having to deal with Yankee fans is really like. I believe—and I will take this to my grave—that in the heart of every Yankee fan beats the heart of a bully, someone who wants to bully a Red Sox fan who's less fortunate. These people may be perfectly kind and nice but when the Yankees are playing the Red Sox, this bullying side of them

> St. Mary's Industrial School for Boys in Baltimore —now called Cardinal Gibbons High School—was known as "the House that Built Ruth."

comes out. I don't know why they worry about us. We're never going to beat them.

——JOHN BENNETT, 34, Burlington, VT

To me, George Steinbrenner is a highly objectionable human being. I think he's arrogant, domineering. I think he ruined baseball. He's as responsible as anybody for the commercialization of baseball, for the salaries that are on the other side of the moon.

I get most annoyed by the arrogance of the Yankees and the Yankee fans sense of entitlement; also by their ignorance or willful blindness to how important money has been to the success of the Yankees. This goes back to before Steinbrenner, but the Yankees were millionaires in **pinstripes**, and they always buy the aging star who's on waivers from the National League, or they sign that free agent. It was very, very painful losing Roger Clemens to the Yankees. I loved him so much that even after he went to the Yankees, I still wished him well. I don't know how people can imagine that baseball is just a sport and that the competition is fair. Rooting for the Yankees is like rooting for General Motors.

——ROBERT BELL, 57, Williams College English professor

I have no problem with Yankee fans who are Yankee fans the way I'm a Red Sox fan. I have a lot of friends who are Yankee fans and I have no problems talking about the Yankees. I have a big problem with the Yankee fans who frequent Yankee Stadium, and they're throwing things at the other team, and at fans who are wearing the other team's hats. To me, there are a lot of Yankee fans who are just sort of young, arrogant morons.

——BUD POLLAK, 56, Retired high school English department chairman

The old Hotel Kenmore in Kenmore Square, was about a block and a half from the ballpark, and the ballplayers used to come out a back door and take a back street and would walk up to the ballpark. Us kids who would be after autographs would tag along after them to get them to sign the book. This was long before it was thought to be

> The Yankees' pinstriped uniforms were designed by owner Colonel Jacob Ruppert to make Babe Ruth look skinnier. Ruppert once held the mortgage on Fenway Park as part of the Babe Ruth purchase.

commercially wise to do those things. I had these books full of them, and I think I just threw them away when I got to be older.

I remember when Mantle first came up, he was walking with Casey Stengel to the ballpark, and the kids were trailing along after him. Casey was telling Mantle, "Don't sign for these kids. They don't wish you well. They're all rooting against you. They wish bad things would happen to you." Mantle was just a kid, I can remember the pimples on his face. As Casey was telling him not to sign anything for these kids, "they're no good," he's signing his autograph and handing the books to Mantle for him to sign them so we all got a little bit of Casey's jargon, plus we all got autographs from Mickey Mantle and Casey Stengel.

———DICK FLAVIN, on growing up in Quincy

When I was at the University of Massachusetts, there were a lot of Yankee fans. There were a lot of New York residents who went there. I didn't have Yankees fans for friends—you couldn't have friends that were Yankee fans. It's like when you're were a kid, if there was a divorced kid in the neighborhood, you couldn't play with him. Well, if it's a Yankee fan, you can't be his friend. I would *never* have dated a Yankee fan. That would be excommunicatable. I wouldn't have to ask if a girl were a Yankee fan, I think Yankee fans generally reveal themselves pretty easily—that swagger, and that blind adding up the wins and not thinking about the integrity of the game, things like that. You can always tell Yankee fans, you just can't tell them much.

———DON SHEA, native, Springfield, MA

Here in Greenwich, Connecticut, I'm in Yankee territory. I keep almost twenty Red Sox books on my front desk right next the blackboard and two or three Red Sox hats arranged around the room. The kids love to poke fun at me. In their own short lives, they already know that the Yankees embody success. They're also the children of very successful parents, so they expect that things will work out in the end and that they'll win. Most of them are conservative Republicans, too. I don't mind being one of the liberal Democrat Red Sox representing the other voice. I'm used to it. In terms of my Red Sox favoritism, they pity me more than anything. They say things to me all the time, like, "Look what you've gone through all these years and never won." Or someone might open a door for me and smiling away say, "Hey, did you see the ball game last night?" of course, referring to a game the

Yankees won. Mostly, they're sarcastic reminders when the Red Sox are not doing well, that this is the team I've hitched my wagon to.

On the other hand, when the Red Sox do well, the parents and kids are still in your face, saying things like, "When are they going to screw up?" Of course, there is no precedent for me to say, "This is going to be the year!" I'd have to go all the way back to 1918. So, I just nod my head. I take the teasing and my standard line, after which they usually shut up, is: "You know what, you don't deserve the Red Sox because you wouldn't know how to handle them!" They just look at me.

In a way, I'm making them a backhanded compliment, but it's true. If the Yankees were screwing up, they'd all be Mets' fans. There were plenty of Mets' fans up here in the 1980s, and now, all of a sudden, they're Yankee fans. Of course, not *true* Mets' fans and not *true* Yankee fans, but there is a fluidity between the fandom of those two New York teams because they're not as passionate as we are. Red Sox fans stick with their team no matter how they play.

In a way, when a person deals with loss and disappointment, they appreciate the notion that you never really, truly, get what you want in life. Maybe that is heroic. It's a little more sophisticated and advanced a notion than I can teach most ninth graders but a couple of the sagacious ones pick up on it and they shake their heads.

I've been known to incorporate the Red Sox into my teaching when my students and I discuss the subject of disappointment and the fall of man. Stephen Crane's short story, "The Open Boat," particularly lends itself to the reference. The story is about four men shipwrecked, trying to land their little rowboat that has been washed away from their freighter. The story deals with existential motifs as the reader wonders whether the men will succeed in their journey or not. Red Sox fans can understand the view of a cruel indifferent fate the story expresses. Red Sox fans do not live in a Darwinian world, à la Jack London, where "By God, you take that hill, and you'll get that crown!" In the other world, the world with which we Red Sox fans are familiar, the hero tends to take the hill, get the crown, but in the meantime, some other factor has emerged to throw off the whole outcome. Red Sox fans are more existential. I think the most apt scenario to a Red Sox fan would probably be the myth of Sisyphus, the Greek tragedy where Sisyphus is condemned to roll a large rock up a hill only to watch it fall back down it again.

——SHAUN KELLY, 48, High school teacher, Greenwich, CT

THE EVIL EMPIRE STRIKES BACK

WELCOME TO BOSTON, WHERE THE LOCAL TIME IS ALWAYS 1918

One time, Ted Williams came to Torrington to do a fundraiser for the charity called the Jimmy Fund. It was a big deal. My dad was involved in something like the Rotary Club, so we got to go. He might have been involved in the planning, too. I was eight or nine-years old, and it seemed like the biggest gathering I'd ever been to. There were two or three hundred people there.

Somehow, my dad arranged for me to shake hands with Ted Williams. I was very sensitive to poison ivy, and during the summer we'd go play in the woods. I had poison ivy at that time, and I still remember going and shaking hands with Ted Williams—his big callused paw around my hand, and it was quite exciting. He was not wearing a tie—I do remember that. He wore a checkered sports jacket with flyaway collar. He was like John Wayne. I do remember that big hand and the strength he had.

Anyhow, on the way back in the car, I became very anxious and concerned that I may have given Ted Williams poison ivy, and even though I was a Yankee fan, I had a lot of respect for Ted Williams. I said, "What if he gets poison ivy and can't hold a bat? Can they trace it back to me?" I thought I'd be in trouble. I remember looking at the box score of the next game Ted played, and he went three for four with a home run.

——JIM COPACINO, 55, grew up in Connecticut

I live in New England where everyone just assumes you're a Red Sox fan. If you walk into my office, one whole wall is all Yankee pictures, but if I my radio is on, people will ask, "How are the Red Sox doing?" I'll say, "I don't know. I'm listening to the Yankees."

I don't hate the Red Sox team, but it's the fans who have antagonized me all my life. My friend, Robert Petrucelli, was a Yankee fan but then he became a Red Sox fan because of Rico Petrocelli, who came to the Red Sox in 1963. Robert made some kind of derogatory comment about the Yankees before school. I can still picture where we were standing—right outside the entrance to our school, Bain Junior High. He said something, and I said something back quickly, and then I said, "…and the Yankees are going to win ten games straight." He was dumbfounded. He didn't have a word of response. The Yankees won that night, and they won ten straight. It was like I was a prophet. We're still friends, but he became an Orioles fan after he gave up on the Red Sox.

I used to sit in the Fenway Park bleachers and I was very vocal as a Yankee fan. I remember Red Sox fans throwing things at me, and I went to the usher to complain, and he just said, "Shut up and sit down."

—**VINNY NATALE**, 52, raised in Cranston, RI

I didn't go to any games at Fenway last year partly because they jacked the prices up so high and you have to get tickets so early. I knew I was going to be traveling a lot to these different conferences, and as it turned out, every time the Yankees were in town last year, I was out of town. It was like a conspiracy—I was just never going to see the Yankees play Boston last year. I though, "All right, that's fine. I don't want to pay Manny Ramirez's salary anyway." Twenty million dollars? My God, he's not worth that much. And why are the Yanks paying Jason Giambi that much?

In 2000, my boyfriend, Corwin, and I went to a bunch of games. We went to some with friends who are Red Sox fans. We have a friendly rivalry and that was fine. We didn't get picked on too badly because we were obviously with Red Sox fans. We went to some games just with Yankees fans. For one game, I had five tickets—one for myself, one for my boyfriend, and three for friends. At the last minute, the three friends pooped out so I sold them to other Yankee fans I knew through the Internet. A couple of guys came up from Rhode Island, these really,

really die-hard fans that I've been corresponding with for years. This was actually the first time we had met in person.

The five of us were having a grand old time at Fenway. We were sitting in the right field boxes, not in the bleachers, good expensive seats so you're not expecting the people around you to be total idiots. There was a woman behind us, a nice looking young woman, maybe in her mid-thirties, nicely dressed, tasteful jewelry. Not like some boozy, wino kind of fan. A very nice looking woman. She had had a couple too many and throughout the game, she was threatening us. She'd say things like, "If Derek Jeter gets a hit, I'm pouring my beer on you."

There were other people who must have been with her, but by the fifth inning they pretended not to know her. Some of them had switched seats. She was getting more and more abusive and telling us to shut up. Meanwhile, Roger Clemens was pitching a shutout. So, of course, the frustration level of the Red Sox fans around us was getting worse and worse because it was also late in the season. This was a season when the Red Sox actually still had a chance.

In the seventh inning, the Red Sox were at bat, and she was getting worse and worse. Finally somebody hit the ball, and Derek Jeter made an amazing, diving grab, and she poured her beer on Corwin. It wasn't even like she tried to pretend it was an accident. She said, "That's it," poured the beer on him, and then was in his face, "Ha. Ha. You smell like beer." We each said, "I can't believe you just did that." Meanwhile, she had already tried to use her lipstick to write something on the back of his Bernie Williams T-shirt. We know that if you're a Yankee fan in Fenway Park and you complain to security you get thrown out. I said to Corwin, "You know what, I'm not willing to get thrown out before the seventh inning."

So here it was the seventh inning, she poured the beer on him, so now he was wearing this blue Bernie Williams shirt that's soaking wet. Well, it was Boston in September. It gets cold at night, so he had brought other clothing to wear. He took off the wet shirt, put it in his backpack and put on a blue Yankees turtleneck. The woman was so frustrated now. She said, "What is it with you Yankees fans?" Here she was thinking she's got him, making him soaking wet so he'll be miserable for the rest of the game, and he takes off his shirt and puts on a clean, dry, New York Yankee shirt. The look on her face was really precious at that point.

I turned to the guy next to me who was one of the fans I know through the Internet bulletin boards, and I said, "As soon as this inning is over—because the game was still very close—I'm turning around, and I'm punching that woman in the face." I have never actually hit someone in the face. I've never been in a fight. I've studied the martial arts, but I'm not an aggressive type of person. I said, "That's it. I'm not willing to get thrown out before the seventh inning's over, but as soon as this inning is over…"

We started to ignore her. We turned our attention strictly to the game. Roger Clemens got two more strikeouts, and when we turned around, she was gone. I think she knew she had crossed the line and that as soon as we got real quiet and serious, it was trouble. So she left and never came back. Either that or she went to get another beer, and they finally threw her out because she couldn't walk straight.

That's the kind of abuse a Yankee fan puts up with at Fenway Park. I've had my cap pushed down over my eyes, my ponytail pulled. I'm five foot four, this little harmless looking woman, and they don't know I'm a black belt so they don't know that they shouldn't be picking on me! Normally I just think, "Oh, the ignorant fools!" There's no way that I would even consider hitting somebody, but this time I felt, "Oh my God. This one's really asking for it."

———CECILIA TAN, 35, Cambridge, MA, Yankee fan

Toward the end of the 2001 baseball season, a writer at *The Providence Journal* called me. He was interviewing Red Sox fans about why the Red Sox are so important to people, and he mistakenly assumed that because I went to college in Rhode Island years ago, that I was a Red Sox fan.

I told him, "Man, you've got it wrong. I'm not a Red Sox fan. I'm a Yankee fan. I hate Red Sox fans. Well, I don't actually hate the Red Sox because they have good players and you have to admire them. It's just the fans. It's been a great pleasure of mine to watch them get their hopes up year after year and have them dashed unceremoniously. It's so predictable and so pathetic. It's one of the perverse pleasures of my life." I was the only Yankee fan quoted in his column.

Yankee haters see us Yankee fans as arrogant, which is probably true. They see us as thinking that we're entitled, which we are. Some day, the Red Sox will win a world championship, and I hope they do because no one should suffer forever. But when they get in my face, I know what to say to them: "'23, '27, '28, '32, '36, '37, '38, '39, '41, '43, '47, '49, '50, '51, '52, '53, '56, '58, '61, '62, '77, '78, '96, '98, '99, 2000."

——ROY PETER CLARK, 54, St. Petersburg, FL

Please don't mention the Red Sox—I didn't have breakfast yet. I hate the Red Sox. The Red Sox are just Red Sox. They're adrift in the sea. They're really nothing. I have no use for any Red Sox fan. I've never been to a game in Fenway. I'd be afraid to.

——STAN STARMAN, 71, Tamarac, FL

Don't even tell me you're a Red Sox fan, please. Red Sox fans do not have a chance.

In 1996, I was at the clincher when the Yankees won the ALCS. Jeff Nelson was the last pitcher on the mound. The next day, my Little League team bought me several tickets to Fenway Park to see Boston and the Yankees play the following day. My wife and I drove to Boston, and we found a little hotel. I had never been to Fenway Park, another stadium where you walk up the runway and see the field and you're totally impressed. It's different from Yankee Stadium, though, smaller, but the history is unbelievable. The smaller size makes it very accessible to the players. The players, guys like Graeme Lloyd and David Wells, who was with the Yankees then, were in a very casual mood. We were taking pictures and getting autographs.

Just before we walked into the ballpark, we went into a little store across the street and bought a little white and red flag that says, "1918, Boston Red Sox World Champions." I was wearing my

Number 7 shirt, which I always wear to games. My son was wearing his Yankee shirt. My brother-in-law was wearing his Yankee shirt. The guy who got us the tickets was wearing his Yankee shirt. We were waving this flag around and attracting all kinds of abuse. Beer was being thrown. We were having the time of our lives. How arrogant could we be? We'd just won the pennant the night before. This game meant absolutely nothing, and we were barely watching. I thought the Boston crowd was rougher on Yankee fans than the New York crowd is on Boston fans. It just seemed that way to me, but I may be a little prejudiced.

——JOE SANTOIEMMA, 50, New Rochelle, NY

I fell in love with the Yankees in 1977, when I was twelve. Being an obsessed Yankee fan has affected everything in my life, even my choice of college. I wanted to study journalism. I was trying to decide between two schools, Syracuse and Boston University, both of which have really great communications programs. When push came to shove, I said to myself, "Would I really want to be in a place where when I pick up the sports page and the Red Sox are the top story?" So Syracuse got the nod. And now we're NCAA Basketball Champions, too!

——LISA DUNLEAVY, 37, Sales director, ESPN

My brother, Bill, and I used to stand in our little yard and throw fly balls to each other. I'd be Mickey Mantle and he'd be Ted Williams. We'd keep throwing until one of us missed ten and had ten errors. We were convinced that as a result of whoever made the most errors that day, his team would win or lose the next day. It wasn't reliable, but we used to think we could will the outcome. If Ted Williams made the ten errors, dropped the ten balls, before Mickey Mantle did, surely the Yankees would win the next day. We weren't right very often because the Red Sox never won back in those days, and the Yankees always won. I think it was my brother's way to try to change fate.

——JIM COPACINO, 55, grew up in Connecticut

My best friend is the only reason I felt good that the Mets won the Series in 1986. Of course, I couldn't root for the Boston Red Sox. How could you? You can't. I would be excommunicated from the Yankees if I were to ever root for the Red Sox under any circumstances. It's like Yogi Berra said to Bernie Williams three years ago in the play-offs. Bernie said, "You know, Yogi, I'm kinda worried about these guys. They're good." Yogi said, "Don't worry kid. We always beat them."

———**MARK ROLLINSON,** 50, Yonkers, NY

Chapter 10

Hot Dates, Cool Mates

The Promise of a Lover,
The Performance of a Husband

OUR SEATS HAD A "FOR SALE BY NEIGHBOR" SIGN

JUDY ROBINSON

Judy Robinson, 33, grew up in Belmont, MA, and now lives in Boston. She is a director with the non-profit environmental agency, the Environmental Health Fund, which tries to reduce the impact of toxic chemicals.

My family, for as long as I can remember, has had season tickets to the Red Sox. As the epitome of the Red Sox fan, we gave up the season tickets at the end of the 1985 season because they were so expensive and there was just no chance the team was going to go all the way the following year. You know, typical Red Sox style, the ticket price has just gone up, and up, and up and of course, now they are the most expensive ticket in baseball.

We had what was, truly, a friendly Fenway package. We had Sunday games—all Sunday home games and holiday games. So you didn't have to buy 80 games a year; you could buy just the Sunday games. It was really friendly. They no longer have that. Now you have to buy the big, whole package and spend lots of money on it.

My dad and my mom were big fans, and they had four seats, right at the third base bag. Slim was the attendant who worked that area there. He was at least 300 pounds, constantly sweating. He became very familiar. There were six of us in our family, so we didn't all go at the same time. I used to go with a girlfriend of mine, and get dropped off right at the McDonalds right outside Yawkey Way. My friend's name was Kristin Doyle, a red-headed Irish-American.

My husband and I met through a mutual friend, and it was a true bonding experience. A friend kept saying to me, "You should come over. There's this guy who is staying with me for the summer before he goes off to graduate school in Buffalo. And he loves the Red Sox, and he loves books and writing. You guys would get along great." I sort of blew it off. But, eventually, I did go over and he was there at the same time. I was struck by him right away. We started talking about the cups, the "boil in the bag" hot dogs. You get the hot dog, including the bun. They boil the whole thing in a plastic bag. If you tried to separate the hot dog from the bun, it would sort of tear away from the bun. You could never really take out a naked hot dog. It would always be coated in the bun it was constricted to now. And then, we talked about the spicy mustard that you would get. What really quite fond memories we had!

And the soda cups in particular, back in the days when I would go with the season tickets, they would have cups of Coca Cola, and on top of the cup was a sealed plastic cover. Not sort of something that you would just put on and take off, and put on and take off. But it was actually sealed with some kind of heat around the edges. You would have to tear off the cover. It was like cellophane. The cup itself would deteriorate into the soda as time wore on. It would become grainier and grainier as the wax that comes with that really cheap cup started to come apart. So this was the bonding that began. Then, of course, we started talking about our favorite players, and our favorite plays, and it became clear. People would say to me later, "He must be so glad that he found a woman that loved baseball!" And I would say, "No, I'm so glad that I found a man who loves baseball."

I'll tell you a good story. It was 1992. I was working with kids and it was Opening Day. This gym teacher and I took off work. I was a school teacher, but not within the public schools. We took a vacation day, and we bought scalped tickets. This was back before bleacher seats were $30. They were something like $10. Fortunately, those aren't terrible, terrible seats. There are better seats in the bleachers sometimes than in right field.

So anyway, on Opening Day of the year, I'm there with my friend, Jody Johnson, and I paid $35 for a bleacher seat. It was most ridiculous. I mean it was crazy! It was more than triple. I was so embarrassed that I had paid all that money. We're walking around because we were there well before the game. Then, we go to Gate C to get into the bleachers, and there isn't a line-up at the turnstiles, but there are two turnstiles, and a big, huge gated fence that blocks you off from actually walking in. So there are two guys, one of whom is like 150 years old, and has, obviously, been there forever. The guys I love have been there forever. And then, there's another guy who's probably in his thirties. So, my friend Jody goes up, and I'm right behind her. We're both going to the guy in his thirties and we go up. She walks right through, and I start feeling around, and I go, "Where's my ticket?" I keep looking; I'm searching. I don't have my ticket. I just paid $35 for a ticket I don't have. I go over to Jody and through the chain link fence, I said, "Jody, I don't have my ticket." She gives me one piece of advice. She says, "Go to the old guy." So I walk over to the old guy, and I look at him, and I say very softly, "I cannot find my ticket." And he puts his hands up in front of both of our faces, right at sort of eye level and he mocks as if he ripping a ticket, and then he lets me through.

To top it all off, I go to the seat that I'm supposed to have because that's the $35 seat I paid for. It's Opening Day. There are not open seats anywhere. There's a guy sitting in my seat. I say, "Hey, man, you found that ticket. What are you doing? What do you think you're trying to pull? I know you found that ticket." He goes, "I paid $35 for this ticket." Who knows? The scalpers must have sold it twice. It was either I lost it; they picked it up; they resold it. Or they never gave it to me. I don't know. Who knows? So I started walking around. I spent the entire game walking around, and having the ultra-humiliating experience of having people go, "You're sitting in my seat." That was in '92.

The ushers are certainly one great thing about Fenway. The 350-pound usher that everybody knew as "Slim" when I was a kid, he had folding jowls. And he had very small arms in comparison to the rest of his body. And he could reach to his belt where he had a white handkerchief. He would spread it across his forehead and over the rim of his nose, and repeatedly try to get the sweat off the back of his neck. He was never particularly friendly—he was all business.

WHERE DID THOSE PEOPLE IN SECTION 35 GO? TRY SECTION EIGHT

DIANE LOMBARDO

Diane Lombardo of West Hartford, Connecticut, has been a Red Sox die-hard her whole life. She is an executive in the printing industry.

I got engaged on my birthday in April of '99. When we first heard that the All-Star game was going to be in Fenway in 1999, my husband-to-be and I decided we would get a hotel room in Boston so that if we ever scored a ticket, we would go to the All-Star game and stay over—dreaming! You don't score a ticket for the All-Star game. We just said, "It doesn't matter. We have to be in Boston. We have to walk around the park and go to Fan Forum. It's at Fenway. This is gonna be incredible."

A month before, I got transferred to a different branch in my work, and they told me that I was to be in Florida during the All-Star game. My husband came home—I wanted to cry. "Honey, this isn't fair. This isn't right. I can't do this." He goes, "Of course you can't." I said, "But how do you tell them that 'I didn't realize it was the branch kickoff, but....' What am I gonna do?" I'm beside myself.

Then I said, "I've got an idea." He said, "What?" I said, "Well, we weren't gonna get married until 2000, but what if we just get married the Sunday before the All-Star game. It would be just a business arrangement—we always would joke that it was a business arrangement—and then I'd tell them that I'm getting married, and I'm sorry I didn't realize that was the branch kick-off date. I can't possibly go." He said, "That's a great idea."

So we planned the whole thing. I said, "When we go to Boston for the All-Star game, it'll be like our honeymoon, which we don't have anyway, and we'll just go down there and stay overnight." I remember I told my boss that I was getting married—how can they tell you you can't go get married? I said, "I'm sorry. I'm getting married." So, I didn't have to go to the branch kickoff, and we ended up going to Boston for the All-Star game.

It was like, "Oh, this is cool." On our wedding day, Pedro was pitching. It was Sunday, July 11, 1999. We had the wedding at twelve, a Justice of the Peace, with a few people over, so that at one when the game started, we could see the beginning of the game.

Then on Tuesday, we went down to the All-Star game, and it was exactly what I thought it would be. It was just wild—the energy just like in a play-off game, so different. We went to a bar 'cause none of the "real" fans could get into the park because all the tickets went to corporate people. So right behind the Green Monster on Lansdowne Street, there's a bar called The Atlas Bar and Grill. You had to get there really early just to get a seat. When the game started, they had it on the big TV, and we were right in front of it. It was louder I think in that bar than it actually was in the Park. There would have been all these corporate-types in the Park, and they're not cheering. The people at the bars were just going absolutely nuts. It was so great when Pedro pitched and when Ted Williams came out, it was just wonderful—just great.

The first game I ever went to, I was in junior high school, and I just loved the Red Sox so much. My sister, who was eight years older than me, was working at John Hancock in Boston at the time. She had graduated from college, and so for my spring break in April, 1968, I talked to my mother and said, "Look, can I go stay at her apartment in Boston, and I'll go to the Red Sox games." I would have been fourteen years old at the time. She goes, "Okay. That sounds all right." She would let me do anything I wanted. So I went to Boston and stayed with my sister who is working at John Hancock, and she would go to work every day. She left me directions how to get on the subway, which was above-ground, the MTA, and I would get on it. If you got off before it went underground at Kenmore Square, where

Fenway is, you only had to pay ten cents. It was the third week in April, and I went to the ball park, and back then, I remember my mother would say we had to get dressed up. So I remember going to the ball game and I had this little mini dress, navy blue with little white polka dots and a little white Nehru collar. I had great big hoops in my ears and a little red pixie haircut. I go to the park. My sister has let me borrow her box score book. I go all myself, I get off at the park 'cause she had given me directions and I walk up to Fenway Park all by myself. You go out by the Cask & Flagon, and there was always this nun who would collect change as you went by. She was there for years and years and years. Then you go up to the bleachers, and it only cost one dollar for a ticket, and I sat down. I didn't realize it was the Boston vacation, too, so all those kids from Boston and Southie— I'm from Hartford so I'm not a Boston person. I can remember sitting there watching the game, and I could hear little snickers and things around me. I took out my scorebook, and I'm keeping score. I can remember in the middle of the game, they missed one of the plays. They go, "What happened there?" I go, "You didn't get that? That was like 3–5." I gave them the whole score and the play.

Then every day I would go there, and they were there. I started to get to know the people in the bleachers. They would talk to me. I stayed the whole week and went by myself every day. There were all these kids around me watching the baseball games—no parents. The bleachers back then were just benches, not seats like now. At the end of the week my mother came back up, and the whole family went. I remember seeing a grand slam the week I was there. I remember thinking, "Oh, my God, this is the best thing I've ever seen."

I never even thought about hanging around after the game was over to try to get autographs. I knew I was supposed to go home now so I would do that. I don't think they ever stuck around to give autographs back then. At Fenway Park, you didn't get autographs. It's "Friendly Fenway" now, but back then it was really hard to get autographs. The kids that would hang around the bullpen would throw little notes that they would fold all up and throw into the bullpen and the pitchers would have conversations with the fans. I remember seeing that and thinking that was so cool.

One of the best parts about the bleachers, after I did that, I became a real "bleacher bum" and would always go to the bleachers 'cause in college, it ended up costing about two-fifty. One of the cool things about the bleachers is that my sister had season tickets out there. It was Section 35, right next to where the cameras are at Fenway Park. If you sit there, you can look out into home plate and you can see the ball go from the pitcher's hand go straight over the plate, and you know if it's a ball or strike and see anything that happens. People who would sit in Sections 34 and 35 were very knowledgeable about the game. You used to just be able to sit there because when you got a bleacher ticket, you could sit anywhere you wanted to. Then when they actually put seats up there and sold them for season tickets, all the people that used to sit there just all bought the season tickets, and they would sit in those seats. They hated the wave. They thought if you did the "wave," you would take away from the ball game. Here's your pitcher out there trying to get through the inning, and you've got the people behind the batter getting up and waving so the whole section would go nuts when people got up and waved. It became like this big deal. That section would never wave. They used to have T-shirts that said the "no-wave section." The whole stadium would get angry because sections 34 and 35 wouldn't stand up. It was like "yeah, well, you're supposed to watch the game, you're not supposed to be waving." Or, wave during the other team's being in the field. But people would get so excited, and the kids would get so excited they'd do it without realizing the play of the game, and the fans at Fenway know the difference.

They cover up those stands where the TV cameras are, and you can't sit there during the day. You used to always be able to sit there, and all the season ticket holders were just notified that "sorry, you can't have your tickets anymore unless it's a night game." Some people only had weekends and day games so they lost all the season tickets. This was done in the early to mid-1990s.

Wil Cordero, who beat his wife up with the phone, was my least favorite player. The fans gave him a hard time. When we were sitting in the bleachers, after that story came out, we'd yell at him, "Maybe you'd do better if you had swung a phone receiver instead of a bat."

In 1986, when Darryl Strawberry was out in the field. I'll never forget this. The bleachers were just merciless to every center fielder, right fielder—the left fielder couldn't hear us, but the center fielder and right fielder heard everything we said. I remember they started by softly saying D-a-rrrr-y-l. One person started, and it just became a chant. It got louder and louder. He'd stand out there and put his hands in his back pocket, then he would change his position, and the whole bleachers knew we were getting to him. The whole place would do it. Now you can't go a park where you don't hear the thing. But I remember they started "Darryl," and he got so upset, and it went on and on. I remember afterward seeing him and hearing him say, "Well, that's not very nice."

Afterward I remember when I went to the Pedro and the Clemens game, everyone started going "Roooo-g-er." I remember thinking, "Oh my gosh. The chant's being used against an ex-Red Sox hero." It was like, "Wow, this is weird. It's come full circle, hasn't it?"

David Justice was in right field, and we were at one of the games, and they started going "Hal—le Be—rr—y." They had just broken up, and she had gotten a restraining order. The fans would just do the worst things you can possibly imagine.

Then in '99, the Indians came, it was a play-off game, they started doing, "Man—nee, hit—less" 'cause he didn't hit in that whole series, and now it's like he's our hero.

The people at Fenway clap sincerely. They don't clap because they put it up on the scoreboard. There's a certain etiquette at Fenway. You've got to watch the music you play. Don't cross the line too much. It used to be like the organ music was all that you heard, and that's what you wanted to hear. The same with Sherm Feller and the voice of the Red Sox. Now they're looking for a new one, and it's because the guy that was there before, he was classic, like a Johnny Most. You listened to him, and it was like, "Ladies, and gentlemen, boys and girls, welcome to Fenway Park." Sherm Feller...He was it. Everyone "loved" him—it wasn't "like" him—and they still do. The other day on a message board, people were going, "Anyone know how to get a sound bite of Sherm Feller going, "Ladies and gentlemen, boys and girls, welcome to Fenway Park." He was the best.

Charlie Moss was the trainer of the Red Sox. Everybody out in the bleachers started to like Charlie Moss 'cause he would trot out in his red pants and white shirt and they started to cheer for him. On Charlie Moss Day, they made great big life-size pictures of his head and put them on sticks and they all went out in the bleachers. The fans would all wear red pants and white shirts that day and they would hold the "printed" face up over their faces so the whole bleacher section out by the TV cameras all dressed and looked like Charlie Moss. They would give him flowers and have a cake delivered to the locker room. They would all sign him a different card, and they would have a cake up at the bleachers, as well. They would deliver a cigar to him, and they gave a donation to the Jimmy Fund in his name. They did this for three years straight. I think the last time they did it, the third year, they had "Happy Third Anniversary—Charlie Moss Day." They had a plane with the trailing banner go over the ballpark. On the cake, they put the little plastic plane with the banner on the back of it. I don't know where Charlie Moss went. He hasn't been with the Red Sox for a while.

Charlie Moss is surrounded by his bleacher fans.

They used to have "Psycho Night" for Steve Lyons, and I was there for one of them. What they would do for Psycho Night 'cause they all loved Psycho, they went out and bought a shower curtain and the rest of them all would have plastic knives from Jack's Joke Shop, a big joke shop in Boston. They would have someone play Janet Leigh and go behind the curtain, and then they would all take out their knives and do the whole scene thing. It was supposed to be Psycho Night.

One night when I was there, Steve Lyons came out to the bleachers to say "hi" to them all 'cause he knew they used to do Psycho Night. I had an old painters hat from 1975, and he signed it. I still have his signature, "Steve Lyons, Psycho Night." The crowd just thought Psycho was great—remember the time he went to first base, he slid in, and he ended up getting all this dirt down his pants. Psycho was just in another world, sort of like a Bill Lee. He's on first base, and it was on TV. He undid his pants and he dumped out the dirt and then realized he was on TV and put his pants back on. He was just crazy. He was a great guy, and he was really fun when he went out there to the bleachers. I watch him on TV now and it's like, "Wow, look what happened to Psycho." When they did the things on Psycho Night, they always did them during the seventh-inning stretch.

Now the Charlie Moss Night and Psycho Night were not sponsored by the Red Sox. This was all from Sections 34 and 35. They just did all these things themselves. Then they had the "ugly T-shirt night." People would wear holey T-shirts or this or that. My sister is very artistic. She came with a T-shirt and on it she had different pictures and things on it—different sayings. Her ugly T-shirt said "domed stadiums," "artificial grass," "No-No Nannette," "Bucky Dent"—all these different things, so she won the ugly T-shirt contest that night 'cause most people would always just do raggedy old T-shirts.

One of the times there was a guy, Paul, an MIT professor, out in the bleachers sitting in Section 34. Every time Wade Boggs came up, Paul would get up. Of course, nobody knew he was an MIT professor. We just thought he was some drunk—we had no clue that this guy was somebody, but that was the fun thing about Sections 34 and 35—when you got to the ball park, we were just bleacher bums. He'd get up and do this thing, "W-a-a-a-a-ade." He'd yell it as long as he could. I was a singer, and I could really hold things for a long time. I remember one time, I got up, and I did the "Wade" thing when he did it. Mine was longer, and I was like, "Oh, I don't think I should do that again."

This is how people found out he was an MIT professor: He determined that the balls were bouncing differently and the home runs were different and that the wind currents had changed when the 600 Club went up in Fenway. He was a physics professor. He had his students do a whole paper on what happened to the wind tunnels and the aerodynamics of the park when the 600 Club went up. It changed the wind coming off in that direction, and it changed all the home runs going over the wall. They had a whole thing in *Yankee Magazine* about Section 34.

They used to sell beer, but they never had it in the bleachers. At Fenway, you always went downstairs to get your beer. They didn't have beer vendors. You could bring it back up, and could bring as many as you wanted. You could get sixteen-ounce beers. You'd take turns 'cause nobody wanted to miss the ball game so you'd get six beers at a time. "I'll buy this round," and you'd get all the big sixteen-ounce beers that you could carry. One time when we were there, it was in September, and the Red Sox were completely out of any race. We're watching the game, and we're winning by four runs or something, but we're all having a really good time in the bleachers. We've got these big beers. We're out there and we said, "Gee, we're not going to win anything. Let them tie it up, and we can stay here and drink." Well, they tied it up, and we went fourteen innings. The whole bleacher section stayed there.

I was supposed to move that night. My roommate at the time had gotten a truck for the evening for us to move, and I told her, "Well, the game should only be three hours. I'll be home at that time." It went fourteen-fifteen innings. I lived on Beacon Hill, and I had to stagger up to my apartment and she was like, "Where have you been? I said, "Well, it went extra innings. What am I supposed to do?" Back then, you could drink whatever you wanted to. There weren't as many people in the bleachers back then and we always just had a good time. The next thing you knew, when fights would break out, they decided they're not going to let you drink any more than two beers. No one can bring back more than two beers so you can't bring beer back for your whole group. And, you have to show your license every time at Fenway. I've seen them tell a seventy-five year old man he couldn't buy beer 'cause he didn't have a license. They're not as bad anymore but at one point, it was just like, "Come on. This guy's at the ball game. Give him a beer." Also, then, they wouldn't sell you anything but a twelve-ounce beer. All that changed because—a lot of Irish people and beer did not mix well. It's one of the only parks that you cannot buy beer in the stands. You can only buy two at a time.

I don't live in Boston anymore so I never run into any of the bleacher friends outside the park. When I used to live nearby, you could pay two-fifty and go. But when I was further away and had a car, it cost you a lot of money to park a car, and I didn't know if I was going to be able to get a ticket 'cause all of a sudden the games started to get popular. There's a taxi place down there, and I got to know the guys, and they would let me park my little VW Rabbit inside. If I was able to get a ticket to go inside the park, they'd charge me five bucks. If I couldn't get a ticket to go in, I could come back and get the car and leave and they wouldn't charge me any money for keeping it there. I had this little running thing where I could go there and just leave my car. This was '76 to '79. When they traded Carlton Fisk, I got mad at them so I didn't go to see the Red Sox for a while.

My husband doesn't believe in presents—birthdays, Valentine's Day, nothing. On my birthday in April, 1997, he said, "I've got something for you. I go, "You do?" He gives me something, and I open it up, and it's a baseball card. He says, "That baseball card I just gave you—he's gonna be the Rookie of the Year." It was Nomar. Just hold onto that card and someday you'll get it signed."

Last year my sisters decided at the last minute that they were going to go down to spring training for about four days. I happened to be in Boca Raton at a business meeting when they were going to be at spring training. I went, "You've got to be kidding. If I drive over there, can I come to spring training with you?" They said, "Well, sure." So I drive over there and go to two games with them. I said, "Look, on this day, they're going to be playing up in Port Charlotte." They've since closed that stadium, the old Texas Rangers Stadium. I said, "You know what? I know how to get autographs there." We go there and we're watching the game, and it's really hot. I asked them if they wanted to get autographs and told them I was going, "If you want to follow me that's fine, but you're not going to see the rest of the game. We're going to get autographs." "That's fine."

I had my rookie card of Nomar. I go over to where the players come off the field to go into the locker room, and then after the locker room, they go to the bus. We go over there. Johnny Damon comes out, and he'd just joined the team so he's signing autographs. My sister's very excited. I'm taking pictures of the players coming in and out. Nomar comes out. When he comes out to sign, nobody breathes. You don't want to get him angry. I took out my card—I'd been waiting so long to get this signed—and I gave it to him, and he signed it. I was just shaking, thinking, "This is just a kid signing my baseball card. Why am I getting all weak in the knees?" It was like seeing somebody that was really famous and important to you in your life. I thought, "Wow, that was weird." Now I've got the birthday card my husband gave me in 1997, Nomar's rookie card, and Nomar signed it last March. People ask me, "What are you going to sell it for," and I say, "What am I going to sell it for? The experience is what you go for, not to make money."

Hitting for the cycle is rarer than a no-hitter.

SILENCE MY SWEET, MY LOVE HATH NO LOGIC

HOT DATES, COOL MATES

On our first date, my now husband, Dave, took me to a big, bad Bruins-Broad Street Bullies/Philadelphia Flyers hockey game at the Boston Garden. This was in 1974, and in those days their rivalry was like the Yankees/Red Sox. Oh my God, the fighting and the blood and the guts! It was disgusting, but it was fun! Dave really liked me because he knew that I was a big Red Sox fan, and, to be honest, if a guy really likes sports, it's difficult for him to find a girl that likes sports as much.

Two months later, we were still dating. Now it was baseball spring training. A lot of the Red Sox exhibition games are televised in the Boston area, because the team is so huge. One Sunday afternoon, Dave turned the Celtics game on the TV. I said, "What are you doing?" He said, "The Celtics are in the play-offs." I said, "But the Red Sox are on TV." He said, "They are playing the Detroit Tigers in Lakeland. It's an exhibition game." I said, "I've been waiting all winter to watch a baseball game. I want to watch the exhibition game." Dave said, "But you don't understand. You need to get your priorities straight. The Celtics are in the play-offs. This is a meaningless exhibition game." "But I want to watch the Sox. I want to watch the Sox," I said.

This could have ruined our whole relationship, but Dave's always been a very flexible, compromising person. We kept switching back and forth between the Red Sox and the Celtics. We compromised.

Of course, he got madder and madder every time I flipped the TV channel. It was a 13-inch color TV. In those days, there was no remote. I was bopping up and down. And, of course, in basketball there's a friggin' time out every couple of minutes, so every time they stopped the clock I would bounce off the sofa and change the channel. I knew then and there that this was the person I was to marry, because he tolerated my boorish behavior.

——CHERI GIFFIN, 51, Randolph, MA

When I first took my wife to see the Red Sox, she knew nothing about baseball at all. This was in the 1950s. She came down from New Hampshire. We sat in a third-base box. The Newberry people got the tickets for us. The seventh inning came along, and they cleaned the field with the nets. She asked what they were doing. I said, "They're smoothing the field so they can play ball again." She said, "Well, why are they leaving those little white things on the race tracks?" Those were the bases. That's how much she knew about baseball. She became a Red Sox fan over the years.

————KEN HERMES, 95, Yarmouth Port, MA

I attended Dartmouth College. During college, I started going out with, Ilona, the girl I later married. Nineteen sixty-six happened to be a real middling year for the Red Sox and I had not been paying nearly as much attention as I had throughout my youth. Especially, when Ted Williams was still active. So when I was courting my wife, she knew me as a literary and a political person and I don't think she even knew I was a rabid Red Sox and Celtics fan.

In 1967, we got married after I graduated. She went to Radcliffe. She is really intellectual and aesthetic and she did gardens and poetry and politics and art and theatre, and was not at all interested in baseball and basketball. We went on our honeymoon. As we were nearing the end of it in August, we were in Zermatt, up in the Swiss Alps and we climbed the mountains every day. One day I came down from the mountain and I picked up a two or three day-old *International Herald Tribune* and the headline on the sports page was "Red Sox win tenth in a row—move into first place."

I thought this might be some kind of time gap because I had no idea that the Red Sox were in first place. I'd been totally out of touch in Europe for ten or twelve weeks. So when I saw this headline and I realized that it was only three days earlier, I said, "We're going home!" We were on our honeymoon. Also, we had a charter flight that didn't come back until several weeks later.

I went down to Geneva and tried to change the charter flight tickets. I couldn't get home and I was really antsy. I remember we still had at least two or three weeks to go and we went to Italy. I felt as though I was marooned in Venice. I was desperately waiting to get newspaper clippings from my parents back in Boston. You know, week-old *Boston Traveler* and *Boston Globe* box scores and things.

I remember coming home, and it was one of the most exhilarating experiences I have ever had. The entire town had become electric with excitement. There was a kind of, not just exuberance, but community spirit and openness that, I think, only a city that's in the middle of a pennant race can feel. I got home September 6th. So I still had three weeks. I remember Yastrzemski was on the cover of *Time* magazine and he was going for his Triple Crown. Every day, besides the obvious things like staying up late to listen to the scores and staying up to catch the Detroit score or the Chicago score because it was a famous four team race—the Minnesota Twins were the fourth team. But you would talk about it and not just with your friends and your fellow Red Sox fans, but with anybody, everybody. Everybody was tuned in.

I was twenty-one years old. I didn't think about explaining anything to my new bride. She was just taken aback and amazed. She wasn't angry at me. It took me out of the house a lot, though I remember when we were first married she didn't like being left home alone when I would go off to Fenway Park or the Boston Garden with the guys. But she also had an extremely busy and active life of her own. She's an avid gardener and, fortunately, the baseball and growing seasons coincide.

———ROBERT BELL, 57, raised in Belmont, MA

It never occurred to me not to date a Yankee fan. I always went for, "Was she gorgeous?"

———JEFFREY LYONS, 59, Sox fan living in NY

I met Alex, my husband, by answering his ad in *The Globe* for a roommate. This was 1989. At point Alex had season tickets to

> Who is the only major league manager to later become *Time* magazine's Man of the Year? Braves owner, Ted Turner managed Atlanta for one game in 1977 before being removed by Commissioner Bowie Kuhn. Kuhn's high school basketball coach was Red Auerbach.

the Red Sox and that's when I really started going to Sox games on a very regular basis. He had the night game package, back in the mid-1980s, when the seats were actually cheap. He has always split that with three friends. So we get tickets for twelve games a year.

The tickets were split up by pairs, and I would always go with Alex. Our relationship really blossomed from the beginning.

I had never dated a non-Red Sox fan until I met my husband—he's a Yankee fan. It has been funny. Before Alex and I were married, one year at the end of the baseball season, at the end of August, the Yankees and Red Sox were in first and second place. The Red Sox beat the Yankees. Alex and I are walking out of the park together and Dan Hausle, one of the local news people, was standing outside Fenway Park with a camera. It was a great game because the race was so tight and the Red Sox had won, and the crowd was pumped coming out of the park. The camera lights come on, and he started interviewing Alex and me. He asked us how we liked the game, and we told him I was a Red Sox fan and Alex was a Yankee fan. He asked us if this ever caused any problems in our life. Alex said, "Only at dinner when we start throwing food across the table at each other." That had never happened, but it was on the news that night.

——JANE WOYCIK, 38, Nurse

Back in the late 1950s, maybe 1956, my wife, who was my girlfriend at the time, called me and said she won tickets from where she was working to the Red Sox game. "Do you want to go?" I said, "Yeah!" So we went, and it also happened to be the night just by coincidence where they were filming background shots for the Jimmy Piersall movie, *Fear Strikes Out*. She paid no attention to the game, wasn't interested in it; still isn't interested in it. She was more interested in the movie people.

——GERRY MURPHY, 67, Textbook consultant

In late July of the 1966 season, I proposed to my wife Nancy. She lived in Woburn, Massachusetts. Her older brother was a great Red Sox fan, and her dad was a Red Sox fan so she grew up being a Red Sox fan.

We'd been going out for seven or eight months and I wanted to propose to her in a nice way. I bought a diamond ring and drove to her house to pick her up for a dinner date. I was already listening to a game on the radio. Luis Tiant was pitching for Cleveland. She got in the car, and as we drove away, I was so enthralled listening to the ball game, I handed her a little blue box containing the ring and said, "Here, will you marry me?" Nancy said, "What?" Here I was about to change my life, ask this woman to marry me, and all I wanted to do was listen to the ball game. I turned up the sound on the radio. She looked at me and said, "My God, I can't believe it." I said, "Yes or no?" Later, she told me she was thinking to herself, "Wow, my life has just changed forever, and I wonder when the inning is going to be over so I can say yes."

———RAY FOSTER, 62, raised in Hamilton, MA

One time, my friends and I were watching some games in a bar, and I mentioned Pedro Martinez. Someone asked, "How did the Sox get Pedro?" This gal pipes up from the other side of the table and quoted exactly who was traded in exchange for Martinez. That told me right there. For months, I was thinking, "Okay, this is someone, because she's a Red Sox fan—that means more than anything else." But I soon found out that's not the case.

For several years I had the view that I would only date Red Sox fans. Through a friend, I met someone who was a real die-hard Red Sox fan, and I was more concerned with that than with other things. She's pretty, she's nice, but what was really attracting me to her was that she's a Red Sox fan. I was still down here in DC and she was up in Boston traveling on business, so I only saw her a few times and we communicated by e-mail. The nature of our communications were mostly about the Red Sox.

I don't know if I could date a Yankee fan. That would be a major blemish. Everything else would have to be really, really good.

———PAUL MALONEY, 27, raised in Westwood, MA

I became a Red Sox fan because history's first Red Sox fan, the great 17th century French philosopher, Blaise Pascal, said, "The heart has reasons that reason itself knows nothing about." There's no explaining it. Why do you love the people you love? My wife's from Chicago. Isn't there any woman I could love in the city of eight million people? Maybe because my older brother liked the Red Sox. George worshipped the Cardinals, but he also liked, to a lesser extent, the Red Sox.

My thirtieth wedding anniversary, unfortunately, falls this year on the day the Red Sox are in town. I have two choices. Either convince my wife we were really married a week earlier, or just miss the game that night. I'm prepared to miss the game that night. But I gave up tickets to *A Chorus Line's* record-breaking performance when they had all the old members of the cast there. I gave it to my sister, because Yaz was in town for the last time. I wasn't going to miss that.

I have three different types of earphones. When I'm sitting around a pool, if I'm using earphones, I'll wear two so I don't subject other people. The other one is if I have guests over for dinner, and Judy, my wife, makes me turn the game off, if it's a crucial game late in the season I will have one earphone. I'll tell anybody that asks that I'm working security. I did have to go to a family wedding during a very crucial game in 1978. Both sides of the wedding family were Red Sox fans, so I was the designated listener. I gave updates every half inning. Everybody loved that, except my wife, of course.

———JEFFREY LYONS, 59, Film critic, author

During one of those falls when the Red Sox were in it, and then collapsed, and something else was going on, I was in a bad mood. My wife, Mindy, said, "What's the matter with you?" I said, "Nothing." Her first response was exactly what I thought it would be, "It's not those ——— Red Sox, is it?" That just summed it up perfectly. She doesn't quite understand my fanaticism and the devotion.

———ANDY CORNBLATT, 53, Washington, D.C.

In 1942, the Cleveland Indians paid Lou Boudreau $25,000... $5,000 for playing and $20,000 for managing. That ruse allowed the Indians to adequately compensate their best everyday player without upsetting the other players.

Boudreau's daughter, Sharon, was married to Denny McLain for over 30 years.

Chapter 11

Fandemonium

We're Declarin' Shenanigans

OUTSIDE OF A DOG, A BOOK IS MAN'S BEST FRIEND. INSIDE OF A DOG, IT'S TOO DARK TO READ

TY WATERMAN

Ty Waterman, 55, is a social worker, supervising foster homes in Boston. He grew up in southern Connecticut, and has been living in the Boston area for more than fifteen years. He now lives in Attleboro, Mass.

I only go six or seven times a year. I watch or listen to probably eighty percent of their games. The price has been jacked up so much in Fenway Park. My salary hasn't been jacked up anywhere near as quickly, so I buy their half-price, discount-day tickets in the spring. I buy up all the ones I can possibly get and those are the games I go to. My wife and I also go to Pawtucket to see the Red Sox AAA team.

I have one great memory of the '71 season—best game I ever saw in my life. It was the most hyped game, maybe I should put it that way. It was around Memorial Day and the Red Sox had not really done much since '67. They had been mediocre—they hadn't competed for first place, that's for sure. Baltimore was the top team in the league at that point. They had a hot start and they were running in first place in late May. Oakland came in to Fenway and I said, "I've got to see this." Oakland was in first place. Vida Blue was gonna pitch a Friday night game. He was a rookie, and he was 10-0. Sonny Seibert was pitching for the Red Sox. He was 9 and 0. I saw this game with thirty-five thousand people. They were hanging from the rafters in this place. I don't think they'd allow that many in there now. I did standing room only behind the first-base area and watched every single pitch, and they beat Vida Blue. Rico Petrocelli hit two, two-run homers. Dave Duncan hit a foul-ball home run in the top of the ninth that just missed that would have tied the game. That's the clearest memory I ever have in my life of an individual game. A lot of people point to that game as one of the better games they'd ever seen.

My book about the Red Sox, *The Year the Red Sox Won the Series,* about the 1918 World champions, was published in 1999 by the Northeastern University Press. I started writing about the Red Sox in 1994. I got the idea about five years before the book was published. For more years than I care to remember, I had been hearing how long it had been since they last won. Nineteen-eighteen is almost like a code word around Boston. It's also a code word in New York but they use it for different reasons in New York.

But around Boston, if you say "1918," most people know what you're talking about. That's all you have to say. It's not even nostalgic because nobody remembers it. Maybe it means sadness, a kind of ineptitude. As much as I don't actually believe there was a curse, people feel cursed. I kept hearing it and I asked myself, "Who knows anything about it?" I've never read anything about the 1918 team. I don't know anything about that. There had been no books printed about it. Other than looking it up in the baseball encyclopedia where I can see the games and the line scores, I didn't know anything.

So, I decided to be the person who would bring hope to the Red Sox Nation, to make them feel like once upon a time, Boston was the center of the baseball universe, and we were on top of it, and to make people feel good. Because all I had been hearing was about failure—all my life. We'd get this close, particularly after Buckner's error in the '86 World Series, it got worse and worse and worse. At least in '75 we weren't expected to beat the Reds. In '67 we were lucky to make the World Series. No one thought we were going to get any farther. I wanted Boston to feel good about itself, so I got this idea. I had never written a book before and people kind of laughed at me. Nobody took me seriously, but it's sold over four thousand copies now and hopefully we're going to have PBS special next summer, at least we're trying to get one.

I had about ninety cartoons, many of them actually depicting specific games and action in games that were in my book. I got big black and white glossies of those, plus about forty photographs that went into the book. Of course, I didn't find anyone who had actually played on that team, but I found children of people who played on the team, particularly Harry Hooper's son, John, who lives in Texas. I found Harry Frazee's grandson in the state of Washington. Harry was the owner of the team.

It's been difficult to maintain a sense of humor. The Red Sox need to have more of a sense of humor. The Red Sox players that have brought levity, brought a sense of humor, into Boston have generally left kicking and screaming. Take Bill Lee, for example. He was the best fresh breeze Boston ever had prior to Pedro, in my opinion. He couldn't have been driven out on a rail faster. Management didn't respond to him—intentionally didn't respond to him. He wasn't into drugs; he was just into having fun. It was hard for Boston to understand him, unfortunately. If you've never read *The Wrong Stuff,* by Bill Lee, you've got to read it. It's almost like baseball isn't fun anymore. It's like a very, very serious religion, but it's not fun anymore around Fenway Park.

Certain things are still great. Ted Williams being worshipped at the time of his death was a wonderful release for fans. It made people just realize how much they actually loved the player, and it was pure. It was wonderful. But most of the time, the seasons just get blacker and blacker and blacker—just "let's get it over with."

Almost every player here who goes down as being worshipped now at one point was booed and hissed. Williams wasn't always the most popular player. Yaz, as great as he was, there was a whole period there where he got booed. I'd say the most perfect player for the Boston area was Luis Tiant. It's not a black-white thing, it's a character thing. Luis Tiant chomping on a cigar, wheeling and dealing, his crazy wind-up in his hesitation pitches—the fans just absolutely took to that guy. I never heard him get booed, and that's pretty good. I enjoyed him immensely.

My best story is about the song, "Tessie." Tessie was written in the 1890s for a musical called, "The Silver Slipper." It was "found" by Boston fans in 1903 during the World Series in a Pittsburgh music store. The Royal Rooters, two-three hundred men strong, sang it in the second half of the 1903 Series every time the **Pirates** came to bat. It was sung constantly until about 1918. The Sox won the World Series five times with these men just singing this over and over and over. Every time the word "Tessie" came up, they would insert the name of an opposing player like Honus Wagner, for example. I was once asked on public radio what I thought it would take for the Red Sox to win again. I said, "The fans have to remember the song "Tessie," and they have to start singing it again." The radio guy thought it was a joke. I was half serious. We have to bring some joy, and music is part of it.

The summer of '99 when my book came out, I was interviewed on NESN on a pre-game show before the Yankees-Red Sox. Later in the year, NESN brought back me and Mel Springer, my co-writer, who is a pianist and composer. He had composed a four-part barbershop quartet to the song, "Tessie." He's a big Red Sox fan, originally a Brooklyn Dodger fan. Mel did this adaptive, four-part version. We recruited some really good singers and I was one of them—I was the baritone. We got to sing this song at Fenway Park as the opening of a one-hour, pre-All-Star-Game special which aired in '99. Then, the Sox had it on before the game from about six to seven o'clock for the rest of that summer. So I got to watch myself sing up on the big screen.

The Pittsburgh Pirates was also the name of an NHL team for five seasons in the 1920s.

ROOTIN' FOR THE RED SOX IS LIKE GETTIN' MARRIED AGAIN... HOPE WINS OUT OVER EXPERIENCE.

Richie Hebner and Bruce Hop

BRUCE HOP

Bruce Hop, 51, is big, loud, likeable and the biggest Red Sox fan in the Midwest. Married four times, he once was on a national TV talk show with all his former wives....The topic was "My Ex—Meet My Ex" and they all still liked him. He is an insurance tycoon in Cedar Rapids, Iowa.

L iving out here in the Midwest, you don't run into too many Red Sox fans, but you will find a cadre. All you have to do is put on that neat hat with the red "B," and, they come out of the woodwork, or, in our case, the cornfields. The real Field of Dreams is not far from here.

I've been married about four times, and each time I've gotten the wives interested into baseball. They took to the friendliness of the Red Sox players because it's easy to meet them. They all became baseball fans and enjoyed the day games, loved the night games, but didn't like the dome games.

When you travel to see the Red Sox, the key is to stay in the hotel where they stay. The Pfister, in Milwaukee, was a great place. That's where I took one of the wives for her first game there, and we got in the elevator, and Dwight Evans was in there along with Mike Green-well. I whispered to my wife, "Honey, do you know who that is riding down the elevator with us? That's Dwight Evans." She said, "If that's

Dwight Evans, I'm the Queen of Sheba." Evans said, "How you doing, Queenie?"

The players were always very, very helpful in giving you tickets. Where they wouldn't talk to the Sunday fans, the people who go out there just to get an autograph, they could easily identify a Red Sox fan, especially if you stayed in their hotel and met them for drinks. We spent many, many good, late evenings with five, six, seven, eight Red Sox players, all at the same time. Of course, it helps to have a good-looking wife, too.

In Kansas City, there was an extra-inning game in late September—about the fourteenth inning, Mo Vaughn was in the on-deck circle. If you had a yardstick, you could lean over and touch him. I yelled, "Hey, Mo. I got corn to get in. Send me home." He looked over at me, and for some reason, he dropped his bat and leaned forward on his hands, and he was there laughing on all fours.

I was in Milwaukee with Cheryl, my current wife. She had a nine-year old, a seven-year old and a five-year old. Their last name was "Brewer" so she bought them all Brewer T-shirts to wear. But in the meantime, they had put on their Boston hats. There they were sitting in the stands wearing the Boston hats and the Brewer shirts. A lady leans over and said, "I don't understand this. You've got Brewer shirts, but Boston hats." Cheryl goes, "Well, my last name is Brewer. These are Brewers, but when I married him, he made me sign a pre-nup agreement they had to be raised Red Sox fans, so that's why they've got the Red Sox hats on."

In 1984, the Kansas City Royals lost their Group Director of Sales after a five-year stint. He left to go into the radio business in Sacramento. His name was Rush Limbaugh.

SO SAY YOU ONE, SO SAY YOU ALL

FANDEMONIUM

There's a story I love. It ran in *Sports Illustrated*. I forget who wrote it. The writer was in a bar in Boston after the '86 Series, and there was some guy who was sitting there in his cups for about an hour without saying anything. Finally, he muttered through his beer, "The ———— Red Sox! The sons of ———— killed my father, and now they're coming after me!"

———ROBERT BELL, 57, Williamstown, MA

I have a Red Sox tattoo on my shoulder. It's the Red Sox hat with the letter "B." I brought the actual hat to the tattoo parlor, and they were able to Xerox it. I had one tattoo already and was thinking, "Okay, I'll get two, and that's it." But the first one, an Irish figure kind of like a leprechaun, was made in haste. I figured the Red Sox were more in my blood and, now, it literally is in my blood. My father didn't say anything negative and my mom is not really thrilled with it, but I think my dad can kind of understand that. I was thinking I'd want to have it if they won the World Series. It just seemed like a natural thing to do.

———PAUL MALONEY, 27, Financial analyst

In 1983, I pitched in the British Baseball League, an amateur league with Brits, Canadians, and Americans. One day, I was pitching and a guy came up wearing a New York Yankee uniform and a mustache. I said to myself, "That guy looks familiar!" I called time out and looked at the roster, and next to his number it said, "American" and his name was John Munson. I called time out. I went over and asked my coach about him. "Yep, it's Thurman's brother," my coach told me, "He's in the Air Force."

The guy looked like Thurman and he was digging away just like his brother always did. The first pitch I threw to him, I hit him right on the hip, but it was such a soft pitch that he looked at me funny. I called time out. I said, "I'm sorry there John. I'm an old time Red Sox fan." He laughed and said, "That's all right!" I told him, "When I was a bat boy for the Orleans Cardinals for the Cape League back in '66, I saw your brother play a lot." He said, "No kidding! Let's have a beer at the end of the game." So at the end of the game, Johnny Munson and I got together for awhile.

——SHAUN KELLY, 48, raised in Wellesley, MA

This is something I'm frankly not prepared to acknowledge to too many people, but in 1975 my brother and I were at the Carlton Fisk game and we left before he hit his home run. I've got to decide whether I'm going to give you permission to print that or not. The Sox were behind by three runs going into the ninth inning. The place was jammed and we just didn't want to watch Cincinnati celebrate at Fenway Park. We did not think the Red Sox were going to win. It's nothing I'm proud of. When I tell my son this story, it could be that I "may decide to stay this time!" I'm not sure. I haven't decided that yet. Between the time we left the ballpark and the time we got to our car and turned on the radio, it was tied. Bernie Carbo had hit that home run to tie the game. So we listened to Fisk's home run on the radio, went home and watched it seventy times on TV. We were mad at ourselves for doing it, but at the same time we decided—you know what, as mad as we are, that was so trumped by the joy of going from the darkest time to the brightest time. It was sort of that piece of it, that particular moment—being at that game and watching Luis Tiant pitch and all that kind of stuff. It was terrific.

——ANDY CORNBLATT, 53, now living in Washington, D.C.

The most ashamed I've ever been to be a Red Sox fan was the Jim Eisenreich incident. He had some problem where he was having these spasms, and the team didn't know what it was. He had been removed from a game because he was having like a seizure. It turned out to be Tourrette's Syndrome. But they didn't know what it was at the time. About a week later, he's playing center field for the Royals.

The fans in the bleachers started chanting, "Shake!" at him, which was so low. I wasn't there. But I remember the announcer talking about it. But that was below us. I was angry at the fans. Our losing Fisk was another really low point.

——BRIAN KILEY, 41, Irvington, NY

In the early 1990s, four of us—two French Canadians and two Irishmen—went down to Winter Haven for spring training. We were all fortyish at the time. We drove straight through in a Peugeot sedan. By the time we were moving through Georgia, it was time to get the case of beer so by the time we got to Winter Haven, everyone was drunk. By the time we got to this little cheap motel in Winter Haven, *Street Fighting Man* was on the radio at about a hundred and thirty decibels with the sunroof off.

One of our guys was still so drunk from the night before—he had gotten out of bed and had a few more—that we didn't sit by him because he was embarrassing. We're sitting in the bleachers and we hear some loudmouth up where the beer stalls are, and he's yelling at everybody. We said, "Oh God, there he is. He's in the room." Jerry Remy—because it's spring training—bails out on a double-play ball. He doesn't get spiked or banged around. We hear this voice bellowing from up in the beer stalls that says, "Remy, you bleed between the legs." The whole stadium heard him. It was just horrible.

——JOHN LINCOLN WRIGHT, 55, Boston native

Carl Yastrzemski had a great year in 1967. And he deserved to have a bread named after him, "Yaz Bread." "Yaz Bread" lasted about a year. The Wonder Bread people made it, and it was only distributed in New England. I didn't buy the bread. One of my former students, who's probably in his forties now, a few years ago still had a wrapper. He was a great Yastrzemski fan.

Yastrzemski had two things going against him. He was an above average ballplayer who got in to the Hall of Fame on longevity, in my view, for that great year. Then, he was a chowder head. He would say some dumb things.

He would say impolitic things; he was inarticulate; he was one cliché and one bland statement after another. He was not terribly insightful; not terribly interesting; not terribly articulate; not too well informed about much of anything. Toward the end of his career, he became venerable because of his age, and reminisced about that. He seemed to warm up to people just a bit more, but he never captured the heart and imagination of the fans. He never came off as Mr. Red Sox; he never caught their fantasy like that.

———GERRY MURPHY, 67, Supervisor, student teachers, Boston University

I'm only superstitious about sports. For example, I think sometimes the Red Sox lose when I turn them on. Sometimes, I know when one moment has turned the entire season around. For an example, I knew in 1978 when they were playing .750 ball and were so far ahead of the Yankees that they still weren't going to win. At one point, around June, they had a ten-game winning streak. The bases were loaded in a game in which they were down a run or two, and Jim Rice hit a sinking line drive with the bases loaded. He just clocked it. The fielders were playing in because the bases were loaded; Rice hit it to left field, and somebody made a shoestring catch on the grass and just barely caught the ball—an ice cream cone-catch. If Rice's ball had been two inches lower it would have gone for a triple and three runs. I remember throwing something and swearing. We were around twelve games ahead with a ten-game win streak, but I just knew. The point is that I was fuming; I was angry and upset because I knew that whatever the lead was, against the Yankees, it wasn't enough. We were going to need a twenty-game lead to hold them off.

I have a friend who was an Orioles fan as a kid and he tells a story about how the Orioles were losing a game that he, his dad, and brother were watching on television. He left the room and was on his way upstairs when he slipped and fell. He was okay, and when he returned, his father and his brother told him that his Orioles had scored three runs. After that, my friend got it into his head that if he fell down the stairs his team would win, so he started falling down the stairs to encourage the Orioles to rally.

———ROBERT BELL, 57, raised in Belmont, MA

I didn't like the casting of the late Tony Perkins in *Fear Strikes Out.* He was good in the *Psycho* part, but that was three years earlier. In the movie, *Fear Strikes Out,* at one point, he hits an inside-the-park home run. They go to a long shot and you see the third-base coach shaking hands with him as he's going around third base. That doesn't happen. I hate baseball movies that are inaccurate. That's why I love *Field of Dreams* and I love *The Natural.*

My godmother was in a baseball movie. The movie was *Death on a Diamond,* with Robert Young. She was the co-star, Madge Evans. It appeared in 1935. It was about the St. Louis Cardinals. Somebody was trying to poison the team by poisoning the mustard on their pretzels.

——JEFFREY LYONS, 59, New York City

I took some photographs of my batting cage with the Red Sox scoreboard with little kids hitting in it, wrote a brief summary about the whole situation and took it up to the Red Sox office the day I was there in 1997. I said, "I'd like to show you this stuff and you might want to do a human interest story about a fan!"

I told that lady, "I don't want any money and you could put down your name on this if you want to." I said, "I don't even really care but you know what you guys need is a human interest story and this would be great to put in your yearbook to show something about a fan." They just totally rejected the idea.

They looked at it and said, "We're not interested!" I said to myself, "That was the typical Red Sox organization! I knew they were going to do that because that's just how they react to everything!"

——GEORGE O'DONNELL, 51, Clackamas, Oregon

In 1988, I went to visit my brother. He had graduated from law school, and our whole family went to Arizona for some ceremony. The World Series was on, between the Dodgers and the A's. I was at this bar with my brother and his friends. His friend was saying, "I'm the biggest Dodger fan in the world." And I said, "Mike Sciosa just got hurt. I think he's out for the Series." He said, "I don't know the names of any of the players." It was one thing if he wasn't a fan, but to say that you're the biggest Dodger fan in the world....It just really made me laugh. Typical California phoniness.

——BRIAN KILEY, 41, grew up in Newton, MA

The Red Sox make me very angry almost on a daily basis. I am one of these people who analyzes baseball. The way to play baseball is to have patience at the plate; to wait the pitcher out; to get the pitcher's pitch count high; and to do all this kind of stuff. And the Red Sox have always had the exact opposite philosophy, where they are very aggressive at the plate. Nomar was second in the league at swinging at first pitches, which drives a lot of Red Sox fans absolutely crazy. Mike Greenwell was like that, also. Unlike

Bud Pollak

the Yankees, who have remarkable patience, Red Sox players are constantly making outs on pitches that are a foot out of the strike zone, because they up there aggressively swinging in these crucial situations. It just drives me nuts.

To some degree it comes from the manager. But I remember when the Yankees got Wade Boggs, he was hitting lead off and he had remarkable patience. All the other players used to watch it. They used to say they sort of realized watching it that that was a decent approach, and then it became the manager's philosophy. Well, the Red Sox star player and best hitter, Nomar, has exactly the opposite philosophy, and it rubs off on the other players. The manager doesn't tell them to swing at the first pitch. The manager tells them to swing at the pitch they can hit. In fact, their management now is even talking about trying to develop more patience in these hitters. But the manager isn't demanding that they do that.

It gets me remarkably angry when they have bad "at bats." I used to get really angry at Mo Vaughn for his horrible "at bats." I'll scream at the television. It depends on whether I'm watching with somebody or not. I like to watch alone. My wife is not a Red Sox fan. She has no interest in baseball. That has been an issue. She just thinks I watch too much. She doesn't go to games. She basically doesn't mind not being involved in that.

I don't get as angry as a lot of fans do at ownership and managerial decisions. I don't think they are as important as most people do. People on the "Son of Sam Horn" Web site are screaming all the time about how stupid Grady Little is. I don't really see it. To me, Tony LaRussa and Dusty Baker were making equally bad decisions in the

World Series and the play-offs, but their players were performing better, so it didn't result in as many lost games. All managers make decisions that when they don't work they are going to look bad. And if you're watching a manager 162 games a year, versus seven or eight games a year, you're going to notice a lot of these decisions. So it's impossible for a manager to satisfy you.

——BUD POLLAK, 56, grew up in Fairlawn, NJ

I was doing research on the epidemiology of tuberculosis in Lima, Peru. Toward the end of my time there, in April of 2002, I went to some ruins with my father. When we were doing some day hikes in that vicinity I would specifically wear my Red Sox cap as my headgear, because it was the only hat I brought down with me. I liked wearing it and knowing most people in Peru had no idea what that meant. But there was an occasional Peruvian or occasional other traveler or tourist from the States who would take notice of it. I do specifically remember meeting somebody, who also was from Boston, walking up while I was walking down the trail from the top of a hill next to Machu Picchu. He said, "Oh you must be from Boston. You're wearing a Red Sox hat." It was a conversation starter on rare occasions when I was in South America because Red Sox fans can identify each other by their paraphernalia. There were some other comments, usually along the lines of, "Are you from Boston," because no one else, other than someone from Boston, would actually wear a Red Sox hat that far from home."

I know there's that story from a few years ago that somebody left a Red Sox cap on the top of Mt. Everest. Maybe two or three years ago there was a story reported on the Internet or in the newspapers that a mountain climber, professional **mountain climber**, from Boston had summitted Everest and left a Red Sox cap there, an offering, in an attempt to reverse the "Curse of the Bambino." That was in my mind when I wore my hat on Machu Picchu. I did like the fact that

Mountain climbers "pass gas" violently at high altitudes. At 11,000 feet, the stomach's resistance to the expansion of gas is greatly reduced. Always try to be the lead climber. That's a free tip from your Uncle Rich.

I was kind of carrying this emblem of my team. I didn't make an offering of it anywhere.

———ROSS BLANK, 27, raised in New York City

My mom reminds me that I was a track star in high school and "now you smoke?" She can't understand that. But it's hard for me to watch a Red Sox game and not be that stressed out. I think my smoking habit—once the Red Sox win the World Series—is definitely going to go down and maybe even extinguish at that point. I know people who have addictions always say that if they can just get through this….But I've mentioned it on a message board and other people have said the same thing, that there's no way you can quit during the baseball season. I wouldn't be surprised to learn that Red Sox fans smoke more than other people. I've found in my experience that people from New England, for whatever reason, smoke more than people who live elsewhere.

———PAUL MALONEY, 27, Arlington, VA

I had a letter published in the *New York Times* Book Review in responding to George Will. Will was reviewing some baseball book, and he criticized Ted Williams for taking too many pitches. And that just seemed to me, even by George Will's standards, colossally stupid! Ted Williams had explained very precisely in the best book ever written on hitting, that you wait for the pitch in the center.

———ROBERT BELL, 57, English professor, Williams College

Shortly before he died, Ray Goulding of the great Bob and Ray comedy team, told his wife if he were to leave her, the Boston Red Sox, the team he loved all his life, would surely win the pennant. When the team was in town one time to play the Yankees, I told that story to Joe Morgan, the Sox manager at the time. On the pre-game show that night Morgan said, "Well, he kept his part of the bargain."

I had never been so mad at Sox management that I'd written a letter of complaint until after the 1978 season. I wrote Lou Gorman. I wrote a very respectful, three or four-page letter, making some suggestions.

Jeff Bagwell was born in Boston on May 27, 1968. In 1994, he was National League MVP. Frank Thomas was born on May 27, 1968. In 1994, he was American League MVP.

Who the heck cares what I think? I'm just a fan. I really wasn't as connected with the team as I am now. He wrote me back the nicest letter, point by point. Now that's a pro. He didn't have to do that.

———JEFFREY LYONS, 59, native New Yorker

There is one thing I did in connection with the Red Sox about five years ago. I don't know why I did it. I'm ashamed of myself. I was stopped at a traffic light in Weston, Massachusetts. This big Lincoln makes a left turn slowly past me. I look up and it's Lou Gorman, the former general manager of the Red Sox, who let <u>Jeff Bagwell</u> get away. Out of where, I don't know, I rolled down the window. I said, "You traded Jeff Bagwell!" And he's looking, thinking, "Well, who is this nut case?"

I'm embarrassed to talk about it. I'm ashamed of myself. But it came from nowhere. On the other hand, it probably came from forty years of frustration. He probably went home to his wife and said, "Some clown just yelled at me about trading Jeff Bagwell!" He was startled, but kept going. I said, "What the heck did I just do?" I wasn't planning on saying anything. It just came out. I'm sure you've had those moments where sometimes you are so tired, you really feel that you're almost beside yourself, literally. That's how I felt. It was almost like saying, "Who was that person that yelled at him?"

———GERRY MURPHY, 67, Wellesley, MA

Mark Starr

In 1978, I was a grown-up, and on assignment for the *Chicago Tribune* in Israel. This was during pre-season. I went to the Wailing Wall, just coincidentally. I'd never seen it. I went there and was watching everyone praying. I am Jewish, but it was the first time I'd ever seen or knew that people wrote prayers and stuck them in the Wall. So, I asked for a Red Sox pennant. I wrote that down and put it in the Wall. This was '78, the Bucky Dent year. That was God's way of saying, "Screw you. That isn't the kind of thing you pray for, so here comes Bucky Dent." Now, note that I asked for a "pennant," because we didn't even think in terms of something loftier.

In those days, Boston had its own culture. It's was a somewhat dour, Puritan, Irish, black-Irish ethic. It wasn't happy—let's put it that way. So that city's culture was pervasive: not happy and bad food. It was a dour black view of life. It wasn't fused with huge optimism.

——MARK STARR, 55, Brookline, MA

In 1995, the Red Sox unexpectedly won an Eastern Division championship. Tim Wakefield had been picked up from the scrap heap that year and won 14 out of 15 games. He really carried the team on his back. Then the Red Sox lost the first two games of the division series in classic Red Sox fashion. The losses in Cleveland were annoying and disappointing. When the team returned to Fenway, they had to sweep the Indians in order to advance to the play-offs. The Indians came up and must have scored 4 or 5 runs off of Wakefield in the first inning. My buddy was at the game and told me that a guy stood up and yelled at Wakefield, "Hey Wake! You won us a division, now get the—off of the mound!" Everyone cracked up.

——SHAUN KELLY, 48, teacher, Greenwich, CT

I've never gone to a spring training game, though I'd like to. I've gone to minor league games a few times. One time, I went to a game in the late 1970s with a minor league umpire I met hitchhiking out West. We went to see the Holyoke Millers. He told me how he had just umpired a game in Arizona, part of the November Fall League. It's a reputable league that's been around a long time. The guy told me he had just called a game with Tommy John on the mound. He said umping a pitcher like John is no different than being a fan. If the guy is on target, pitching a great game, you, as the umpire, become stimulated. He said that when a game gets very important, very intense, that umpires very, very rarely make the wrong call because the intensity raises the umpire's instincts to higher a level, his perceptions, his eyesight, everything. I found that very interesting.

I also asked him about the phantom tag that you see all the time, when the guy really doesn't touch second base and throws to first. He said they do it because if they made the second baseman always step on the bag, there would be too many injuries. So the unwritten rule with the umpiring, which he said they teach in umpiring school, is if the ball is there ahead of the guy, then he's out. It makes perfect sense.

He also said that when the runner is headed for the plate, you can see plain as day that the guy's foot got in there before the catcher's mitt got down on the guy's leg. So, technically, on a still frame, you can clearly see the guy is safe. But they always call him out. He said that's the unwritten rule. If the ball is waiting for you, you don't call the guy safe. That's just the way it is. I don't know that I have ever seen it. Since he said that, I've noticed it. They don't call the runner safe. If he's seven steps from home plate, and the catcher is just waiting for him, it doesn't matter how he slides. If the ball is waiting for him, he's out.

———**MIKE DONOVAN**, 47, Brookline, MA

HUB FANS BID KID ADIEU

Dick Flavin

From left to right: Johnny Pesky, Dick Flavin, and Dom DiMaggio on the day they leave for their Florida trip, October, 2001.

Baseball is a lifetime experience. It is something that stays with you all the days of your life. When you start following these "larger than life" heroes who are so far beyond anything that you can really imagine, you pick up this love for this game. I just don't know what it is about the game that makes it so wonderful. As much as both sides try to screw it up, they can't. It stays with you all the days of your life. I'm going to die with it. Whether the Red Sox have fulfilled my ambitions is beside the point. I've gotten a hell of a ride out of it. I don't know how it would be if the Red Sox were to finally win—then there wouldn't be any of that poetic moaning.

In the fourth grade in Marymount School in Quincy, Massachusetts, I became the only boy in my class who had to wear glasses. At that point, 1947, Dom DiMaggio was the only position player in Major League baseball who wore glasses. Dom was not only a starter, he was an All-Star every year so he became my role model, my hero.

The night I met him, I was at a function at the New England Aquarium, which was brand new at that time, about 1973. He popped out of a group of people and grabbed my hand and introduced himself. I was thunderstruck. I couldn't even go to sleep that night thinking, "Oh, my gosh, if my father only knew that Dom DiMaggio actually introduced himself to me...." I remember staying up that night and writing him a long, three-page letter telling him how much he had meant to me in my boyhood.

The second time I met him, my wife and I were out having dinner, and we were having a drink in the lounge waiting for our table. The waitress brought over a couple of glasses of wine for us and said a man over in the corner had sent over the drinks. It was Dom and his wife giving me a little wave. As the years passed, Dom used to run a wonderful charity golf tournament, and I would go down and emcee it every year, and I've become like a member of the family.

From a kid's perspective—and I'm still a kid when I'm around these guys—I look at Dom sometimes, and I see his arm thrown up across the back of a chair, and I say, "That's his throwing arm…. That's his glove hand." When he was still playing golf, he would lean over a putt to measure the putt, and I would think "that's the way he used to lean over when he was playing ball—when he was in the outfield."

He played not facing home plate. He played center field facing the left-field line. Nobody ever told him to do it, but he figured that he would just have a better break on a ball, figured if you have a better chance of getting around on the ball as a hitter facing the ball side-ways, you can see it better, he figured he could do that in the outfield better. As a result, he was never frozen on a line drive. You know how, outfielders in particular, when that ball is hit right at them, it will be over their head, and he was never, never frozen on a line drive. To this day, he has the record for most put-outs per game over a career and most chances accepted per game throughout a career, playing in by-far the smallest outfield in the League in those days. Dom played by far the shallowest outfield because he could get back on the ball so well. He was half turned around.

If you look up, there are only three American Leaguers who have had more than five hundred putouts in a season. Dom was the only one who did it before the schedule was expanded. Nobody will ever do it now, because all these center fields are so small in all these new ballparks. It'll never be done again.

Dom is not only still my favorite player after all these years, but he's my favorite person. Most of our childhood heroes turn out to have feet of clay. Here's a man who is still my hero, and I'm in my sixties now. I think it's an injustice that he's not in the Hall of Fame. The reason he isn't is that he was Joe's little brother, and he played next to Ted. Who in the hell wouldn't be overshadowed by that? These guys are right up there with Babe Ruth in terms of being icons who have stayed in peoples' consciousness all these years.

In fall of 2001, I was having dinner with Dom and his wife, Emily. They were getting ready to head down to Florida. Dom said, during the course of dinner, "Well, I don't want to fly with all the problems at airports." This was right after 9/11. He said, "I'm going to drive down." Emily said, "You can't drive down by yourself. You're eighty-four years old." I said, "Well, maybe I'll drive down with you." He said, "Oh, that's a great idea. We'll call Johnny Pesky and visit Ted Williams. They just brought Ted back home from being in the hospital for eight or nine months." We left on Saturday, October 20, from Dom's house in Marion, Massachusetts and drove down in his big Jaguar to Philadelphia for the Philadelphia Athletics Historical Society annual meeting. Then we made it down to Roanoke on Sunday night and on Monday night we pulled into Hernando, Florida and were at Ted's daughter's house on Tuesday morning. We didn't go down I-95. It was Dom's idea to take the inland route on I-81 down through the Blue Ridge Mountains. Dom has made this trip often to spend the winters in Florida, and he thinks it's a much prettier drive at that time of year. It was gorgeous.

I did a lot of listening as Dom and Pesky were talking about the old days. We never even turned on the radio, the conversation was so good. At some points, we would just sing. Dom has a wonderful baritone voice, and he knows all the operatic arias. He was singing the operatic arias, and I was singing Irish songs.

On the way down there, we didn't state it, but everyone knew that this would be the last time we would see Ted. There was no real discussion of it. When we finally did walk in the door, it was very emotional. Dom had flown all the way up to San Diego to see Ted when he was in the earlier part of his recovery and was still essentially in a coma. He spent two days with Ted but never got any recognition from him. So when we walked in, poor Ted was there in a wheelchair, spindly looking, and wasn't even aware that we had come in the door. Dom was trying to run to him on his eighty-four year old legs, and was calling out to him, "Teddy, Teddy, it's Dommie. It's Dommie." Ted lifted up his head as Dom got close to him, and he reached out his arms to hug him and his face lit up, "Hello, Dommie." The tears started coming. It was a very, very emotional thing—what those guys have for each other. It was just extraordinary, and they nurtured it all those years from the time that they were little more than boys when they first came up as strapping young guys, athletes, and now here they're old men in their eighties, and one of them is just about at the check-out counter. It was really something to see. The whole visit was a wonderful tonic, not only to Ted, but for the other fellas as well. I would say that Ted maybe weighed a hundred and sixty pounds, if that. His legs were like spindles. We put as happy a face on as we could when we came back and told people about it, but it was obvious—he was a complete invalid.

They kept talking about Bobby Doerr. They kept saying, "Oh, what a shame that Bobby can't be here." Of course, Bobby's wife, Monica, is not well at all. She has had cerebral palsy for years and years. She has had a couple of strokes now on top of that so he really can't travel anymore. He nurses her, and he is kind of a saintly figure. They were trying to watch their language in front of Bobby when they were together. Even in his best day, Ted would have a hard time watching his language. It's funny, you know, he gets into that kind of talk, and then everyone else gets into it. Dom and Johnny are not great swearers and all that, but when you're around Ted, it becomes a communicable disease. Ted was very chatty, very excited and his recall of the old days was just extraordinary.

The last night we were with Ted, Dom said, "Ted, I want to sing a song for you." So he sang this aria, and then he translated it for him. It was about two guys who were best friends and one guy had a hot-looking girl friend. The other friend wanted to take a shot at the guy's girlfriend and was trying to figure out how he was going to do it. Ted got a tremendous kick out of that.

So I said, "Heck, I can't just have you just singing Italian songs, so I'm gonna sing you an Irish song." So I sang, "I'll Take You Home Again, Kathleen." Ted was applauding, poor old guy, he was in bad shape. Then we finished up our little concert by singing "Me and My Shadow," like Ted Lewis used to do.

When I was much younger and broke, I would recite "Casey at the Bat" in various Boston bars in exchange for liquid fortification against the unknown. On the long drive to Florida, I paraphrased the poem just for Ted…**TEDDY AT THE BAT**

Adapted by Dick Flavin
(With apologies to Ernest Lawrence Thayer)

The outlook wasn't brilliant for the Red Sox nine that day,
The score stood four to two with but one inning left to play
So when Stephens died at first and Tebbetts did the same
A pallor wreathed the features of the patrons of the game.

A straggling few got up to go, leaving there the rest
With the hope that springs eternal within the human breast.
They thought if only Teddy could get a whack at that—
They'd put even money now with Teddy at the bat.

But Dom preceded Teddy and Pesky was on deck.
The first of them was in a slump. The other was a wreck.
So on that stricken multitude a deathlike silence sat,
For there seemed but little chance of Teddy's getting to the bat.

But Dom let drive a single, to the wonderment, of all,
And Pesky, of all people, tore the cover off the ball.
When the dust had lifted, and they saw what had occurred,
There was Johnny safe on second and Dominic on third.

Then from that gladdened multitude went up a joyous yell,
It rumbled in the mountains and rattled in the dell.
It struck upon the hillside and rebounded on the flat,
For Teddy, Teddy Ballgame, was advancing to the bat.

There was ease in Teddy's manner as he stepped into his place,
There was pride in Teddy's bearing and a smile on Teddy's face
And when, responding to the cheers he lightly doffed his hat,
(I'm making that part up)
No stranger in the crowd could doubt 'twas Teddy at the bat.

Ten thousand eyes were on him as he wiped his hands with dirt,
Five thousand tongues applauded as he wiped them on his shirt.
Then when the writhing pitcher ground the ball into his hip,
Defiance gleamed in Teddy's eyes, a sneer curled Teddy's lip.

And now the leather covered sphere came hurtling through the air
And Teddy stood a-watching it in haughty grandeur there.
Close by the sturdy batsman the ball unheeded sped.
"That ain't my style," said Teddy. "Strike one!" the umpire said.

From the benches black with people went up a muffled roar,
Like the beating of the storm waves on the stem and distant shore.
"Kill him! Kill the umpire!" someone shouted on the stand,
And it's likely they'd have killed him had not Teddy raised his hand.

With a smile of Christian charity great Teddy's visage shown.
He stilled the rising tumult and bade the game go on.
He signaled the pitcher, and once more the spheroid flew.
But Teddy still ignored it, and the umpire said, "Strike two!"

"Fraud!" cried the maddened thousands, and the echo answered "fraud."
But one scornful look from Teddy and the audience was awed.
They saw his face grow stern and cold, they saw his muscles strain,
And they knew that Teddy wouldn't let that ball go by again.

The sneer is gone from Teddy's lip; his teeth are clenched in hate.
He pounds with cruel vengeance his bat upon the plate.
And now the pitcher holds the ball, and now he lets it go,
And now the air is shattered by the force of Teddy's blow.

Oh, somewhere in this land of ours the sun is shining bright,
The band is playing somewhere, and somewhere hearts are light,
And somewhere men are laughing, and somewhere children shout.
And they're going wild at Fenway Park 'cause Teddy hit one out!

I recited the poem to Ted with Dom and Johnny there. It is totally impossible to describe what it was like in that room that day. At the end, the four of us smiled and then hugged, with tears streaming down our faces. We all knew that would be our last hug ever. We all knew that we're each going to die sometime—the only questions are "When?" and "In what order?".

But for one shining moment, four "sunshine boys" had an unforgettable experience.

And now we are three.

TO BE CONTINUED!

We hope you have enjoyed the first annual *For Red Sox Fans Only*. You can be in next year's edition, if you have a neat story. You can email it to info@theprintedpage.com (put "Red SoxFan" in the Subject line) or call the author directly at 602-738-5889.

For information on ordering more copies of *For Red Sox Fans Only* as well as any of the author's other best-selling books, go to www.fandemonium.net.

Sample Excerpts From This Book

I want my ashes to be put in the dumpster in the bleachers with all the other garbage the cleaning crew filters on the day I die. It would be a fitting end to my love of the Red Sox. But I'll never feel like my time has been wasted, because it is about the process, not about the product. It's about the love of the game. You just think about the crowd and sharing times with people you love....Whether we ever win doesn't matter because I'm going to follow the Red Sox until I die.

——SHAUN KELLY, Wellesley, MA

My wife, Linda, is a huge Red Sox fan. She's a big believer in the Curse of the Bambino mythology. A couple of years ago, she set up a Babe Ruth shrine in our kitchen. It consisted of a photograph of Babe as a pitcher in a Red Sox uniform. Underneath, she set a little candle and every Friday she would light the candle. Every Friday, she would also go buy the Babe a cigar. These weren't cheap cigars either. After about six months, I told her that the man had been dead for over half a century, and I really didn't feel like spending five bucks a week on cigars for him anymore....

——MARK JURKOWITZ, Boston, Yankee Fan

Any big game feels like history the minute you walk up. You feel the buzz, you feel the energy—everything is different. I sat in the bleachers all my life. We "know" when the bat hits the ball. You listen and you know what's going to happen ahead of time. Your heart is ahead of even seeing the end of the play. There's something about the smell of the park, the ambiance of it. It makes it feel like home.

——DALE SCOTT, Raymond, NH

A lot of my love for the Red Sox—and I get emotional when I think about it—is that I love Fenway Park. I think it is one of the most beautiful places in the world. When you walk up, it's so dirty and so old, but so pure...the way it looks, the way it smells, the way it feels.

——ROBERTA MOCKENSTURM, Clearwater, FL

Rico Petrocelli we loved. We used to see Rico in church. My sister and I would try to cut in front of people in communion line so we could stand near Rico. We got in big trouble for that....I used to pray that I could meet Yaz and marry him. I did not do that in church, just in bed at night.

——**LAUREN DOMBROWSKI**, Lynnfield, MA

Every year I bring my oldest boys with me and a couple of friends and we go on a road trip to a different ballpark. We were at Fenway for the first time. They have these old urinals there that are just troughs. I turned around and there was my seven-year-old son trying to wash his hands in it. He had never seen one before. "Wow, look at this big sink!" he said. I said, "Sean, don't." Too late! That's my Fenway memory.

——**PATRICK HOGAN**, Brooklyn, NY, Yankee fan

...Somehow, my dad arranged for me to shake hands with Ted Williams. I had poison ivy at that time. Ted Williams' huge paw was around my hand. He was not wearing a tie. He wore a checkered sports jacket with flyaway collar. He was like John Wayne....On the way back in the car, I became very anxious and concerned that I may have given Ted Williams poison ivy. I had a lot of respect for Ted Williams. I said, "What if he gets poison ivy and can't hold a bat? Can they trace it back to me?" I knew I was in BIG TROUBLE....

——**JIM COPACINO**, Torrington, CT

...Bucky Dent. By then, I'm 28 years old and had gone through my share of heartbreak with females. But you don't know what heartbreak is until you are sitting in my living room with friends watching that game unfold...

——**ANDY CORNBLATT**, Washington, DC